INFORMATION SYSTEMS MANAGEMENT, CONTROL AND AUDIT

Ian A. Gilhooley, ISP

The Institute of Internal Auditors
Altamonte Springs, Florida

NOTE: Much of this book is based on an early draft of The IIA's *Model Curriculum for Information Systems Auditors*. While the *Model Curriculum* in its final form may differ structurally from earlier drafts, *Information Systems Management, Control and Audit* is contextually consistent with it.

ISBN 0-89413-236-9
Library of Congress Catalog Card Number 91-70740
90173 6/91
First Printing

To
Carol, Richard and Karen
for their patience and understanding
during the preparation of this book.

Foreword

In a technologically advancing world where computer systems of all kinds propagate, a comprehensive approach to information systems auditing is essential to the general practice of internal auditing.

In answer to this demand, The Institute of Internal Auditors developed the *Model Curriculum for Information Systems Auditors*, which "defines the knowledge and skills needed by auditors to be proficient in the Information Age of the 90s."

Information Systems Management, Control and Audit mirrors the Model Curriculum's content, providing the base levels of knowledge and skills required to audit within the various structures of information processing systems.

The approach found in this reference book is designed to help internal auditors submit relevant and accurate reports to management on the results of individual audits, and issue overall reports that indicate whether the internal control and operation within Management Information Systems (MIS) are satisfactory.

When used as a textbook, *Information Systems Management, Control and Audit* provides a solid base of knowledge for the student's future understanding of, and work within, the MIS auditing arena.

Ian Gilhooley is a knowledgeable information systems practitioner with a solid background in information systems auditing. His many years of experience in this area make this project an especially cogent one for anyone who is, or will be, involved in information systems auditing.

A. J. Hans Spoel, CIA
1990-91 IIA Chairman of the Board
Paris, 1991

Acknowledgments

I would first of all like to thank Elaine McIntosh of The IIA for extending the invitation to write this book. Hope Smarrito of The IIA also deserves special recognition for her support and encouragement as the book was being written. Hope was the project administrator charged with responsibility for the administrative details which necessarily go along with writing a book such as this.

There are other people at The IIA with whom I have worked over the years and who have been influential in expanding my knowledge of internal auditing. I would like to extend special thanks to Charlie LeGrand, Frank Allen, and John Dattola

I would certainly be remiss if I did not mention Candy Murray of The IIA who handled the publication details for the book. I have worked with Candy on a number of projects and she has always been cheerful, optimistic and resourceful, regardless of the pressures of the moment. This project was no different.

Most successful authors rely on their editors to fine-tune and polish their manuscripts. In this case, I am indebted to Lee Ann Campbell, IIA Editor. Her task was a formidable one and her efforts are very much appreciated.

When a book like this is written, it must be reviewed by a wide variety of people. I would especially like to thank Jose Hoss from BP Canada and Barbara Davison from the Security Benefits Group of Companies for their contribution to the final product. Special thanks to Jerry Lee, Norwest Audit Services Inc., who not only reviewed the book but also is the architect of the *Model Curriculum* upon which the book is based. I know that there were a number of other "behind the scenes" reviewers whose names I am not aware of. My thanks also to these individuals. This book is much improved as a result of the reviewers' input.

Ray Chiu of BC Gas in Vancouver deserves special thanks for his invaluable assistance in writing Chapters 13 and 14. Not only did Ray critique the original version of the articles but he provided some of the text and directed me to a number of publications which were useful in providing additional background material for some of the sections. The chapters are considerably more accurate and useful because of Ray's input.

Terry Barry and Kim Horan Kelly at Auerbach Publishers lent considerable assistance in the preparation of the manuscript by providing reprint permission for work that had previously appeared in a number of Auerbach publications.

The authors of the original text on *Computer Control and Audit*, William Mair, Donald Wood and Keagle Davis deserve a great deal of credit for writing the first comprehensive, practical guide to information systems auditing. A number of their concepts and ideas have been incorporated into this text.

Finally, I would like to thank "PJ" Corum who is responsible for my involvement in the field of internal auditing. Without "PJ" this book would never have been written. Not only did "PJ" hire me into internal auditing all of 14 years ago, he also encouraged me to write my first articles which led to a fairly constant stream of published material over the years. Thanks 'PJ."

Ian A. Gilhooley, ISP

About the Author

Ian A. Gilhooley, ISP, is Director of GNA Consulting Group, Ltd., a Vancouver-based management consulting firm. Gilhooley has more than 20 years' information systems experience and, prior to forming GNA, was the Vice President and Director of Client Services, which included information systems, for a major securities firm based in Western Canada. Gilhooley spent three years in information systems auditing with the Canadian Chartered Banks and specializes in information systems management and control.

He authored The IIA's drive-time cassette *Developing and Improving Information Systems Audit Capabilities* and was a featured speaker at The IIA's 1990 Advanced Technology Forum. Gilhooley also wrote the proceedings from the previous IIA Forum on "Emerging Technologies and Auditing" and is presently working with The IIA on a number of vital information systems projects.

Contents

The Institute of Internal Auditors

The Institute of Internal Auditors

Figures and Tables

Tables

1
INTRODUCTION

The use of computers in the guise of various forms of information systems is assuming increasing importance in many of today's organizations. We are no longer restricted to operational, transaction-driven systems which rely on cost savings for their justification. Today's systems provide information which will determine the future strategic direction of the organization, generate revenue for the organization, or provide a competitive advantage. Every facet of the information systems arena is undergoing significant change. While always an area that provides a considerable challenge to the internal auditor, information systems has added a new dimension to the necessity and complexity of providing management with adequate assurances that everything is under control.

WHAT THIS BOOK IS ABOUT

Information Systems Management, Control and Audit identifies the knowledge and skills that are required to audit within the various structures of information processing systems and shows how to develop a comprehensive audit approach. When this approach is used, the internal auditor is able to issue relevant and accurate reports to management on the results of individual audits. This approach also allows the auditor to issue an overall report at the end of the fiscal year that indicates whether the internal control and operation within the MIS function are satisfactory across the entire spectrum of MIS activity.

Information processing control and security systems are a large, complex, diverse and, in many areas, highly technical group of structures. When combined, they form the preventive, detective and corrective control framework for data and its processes.

Information control and security experts have typically addressed this control framework from a systems perspective rather than from the traditional internal control perspective. The assumption was that all internal auditors understood the implications of the particular strengths and weaknesses of the control structure within a specific piece of hardware/software (e.g., what an authorized program library facility means to application systems integrity, and how easy or difficult it is to circumvent the controls provided by this facility). However, the reality of the situation is that many auditors do not understand the basic structure and interrelationships which exist in a computer environment. This lack of basic understanding has resulted in many attempts to perform "checklist audits" on complex imbedded system control structures without the knowledge or skills that are necessary to translate identified voids into system weaknesses, risk levels and cost effective risk reduction recommendations.

Thus, the audit risk of improper due diligence because of the unintentional oversight of significant weaknesses or through the inability to recognize the unreliable nature of an imbedded control is a problem of increasing magnitude as computer systems become an integral part of all business functions.

RELATIONSHIP TO THE MODEL CURRICULUM

In 1990, The Institute of Internal Auditors designed a Model Curriculum to "define the *knowledge* and *skills* that are required by internal auditors to be proficient in the Information Age of the 1990s." The Model Curriculum is organized into 13 building blocks, each of which represents a significant aspect of computer technology as it has progressed over the last 35 years or so. Following is a discussion of the building blocks and the reasons for including them in the Model Curriculum.

Information Systems Organization and Administration

The organization and administration of any internal control system starts at the top. This is particularly true for information processing systems because the coordination between the users and the technicians is so crucial to the long-term success of the systems' strategy. Policies, standards and procedures need to be in place for short-range and long-range planning as well as effective and efficient ongoing operations of the systems. The foundation of the internal control and data security program starts in the high-level organization/administration structure which sets the tone for the entire information processing control and security environment.

Information Systems Security

Information, regardless of its source, is a valuable asset to the enterprise. The accuracy and confidentiality of this information is essential to the business. Accordingly, the information must be protected from abuses such as inadvertent or intentional misuse, disclosure and fraudulent activity.

In terms of information systems, the software and the data processed by the software must be secure and must allow access on a "need to know" and a "need to do" basis.

System Development

Before a new system is developed or purchased, there must be a clear understanding of the specific needs that are being addressed. Alternatives should be reviewed by the user and the system analysts to ensure that the best solution is selected. The system should be developed in such a way that it can be easily modified and maintained by someone other than the original developer. Adequate attention must be given to the establishment of security and controls during the design phase to ensure that the system will have integrity once it is installed. Finally, the completed system should be subject to rigorous testing to provide assurance that the results produced are valid and reliable.

System Maintenance and Change Control

Systems must continue to be adapted to meet changing business requirements and circumstances. Modified programs should be subject to many of the same controls as newly developed systems. Most important among these is the requirement that there be thorough testing of the modified system. In addition, accurate records should be maintained that describe the change, the reasons for making the change, and the person responsible for making the change.

Information Systems Problem Management
A key attribute of a well controlled data processing organization is the ability to deliver consistent, high quality, and prompt service. Problems in data processing are a normal part of the business. Often, the difference in the level of performance between data processing installations lies in the ability to manage problems. Successful installations have the proper processes in place to ensure high quality operations by not repeating previous mistakes, by fixing problems based on business priorities, and by detecting problems before they escalate into major issues.

Information Systems Contingency Planning
Every information systems department needs to develop and maintain a disaster recovery plan for all information systems that are critical to the ongoing operation of the business. The objective of the plan is to provide a continuity of business processes in the event that a disaster befalls the primary information systems processing environments. The plan must provide for business continuation which will meet the ethical and legal obligations to the owners, customers, suppliers and employees of the business.

Information Processing Operations
The correct operation of the hardware and software systems is an important element in the control process for large and small system installations. The computer operations control structures must ensure the validity of the input, accuracy of the processing, and the completeness and timeliness of the output. In addition, the computer operations group is the custodian for a large percentage of the organization's electronic data and is, therefore, responsible for the safety and integrity of these data.

Application Systems
The primary mission of any information systems organization is to run the application systems for the users. Application system integrity is crucial to the success or failure of the business. There needs to

be a set of controls in place to ensure that the system processes and logic perform according to the specifications each time the system is run.

Systems Software/Environmental Control Programs

Every computer system incorporates one or more operating systems along with various utility or service programs. These systems and programs are essential to the proper and continuous operation of application systems. Proper management of the system software function significantly improves performance. Sound control structures, in concert with effective program security administration, reduce business risks.

Data Management

In order to more efficiently utilize data on a company-wide shared basis, the management and cataloging of data has become an important science in information processing. The efficient, economical and correct use of data in the information age is a critical element in the efficient conduct of the business.

Data Base Management/Data Dictionary

Vendors are supplying users with data base management systems which allow multiple users to share common data. These types of software products are being utilized in systems that range in size from large mainframes to PC-based systems. The security, control and auditability of the data base is to a large extent dependent on the imbedded control structure supplied with the system. In turn, the reliability of the total control structure is in direct relationship to the quality of the controls administration and the appropriate utilization of the security and control features supplied by the vendor.

Telecommunication Networks

Thanks to telecommunication networking technology, organizations have the ability to utilize computer data at any location, whether they are located right next to the computer installation or many miles away. The important thing to remember is that the data must remain safe from unauthorized viewing, modification, delays, duplication theft or destruction while within the network. Because more and more businesses are relying heavily on continuous network availability, the prevention of network failure and the assurance of rapid recovery have become key issues in telecommunication network design and operation.

Artificial Intelligence/Expert Systems

To provide more efficient and consistent decision making, many businesses are installing a new generation of systems that simulate the human thought processes as defined through the examination and analysis of a group of subject experts. Managing and monitoring these new generation systems takes on an added dimension of complexity because the systems have no fixed logic and, therefore, no right or wrong answer. The challenge is to build validation/testing methods that confine the system results to certain limits. This ensures that unreasonable results will be precluded from propagation throughout the organization.

End-User Computing

End-user computing is not specifically addressed within the context of the Model Curriculum on the assumption that the control principles specified in the 13 building block areas apply to all forms of computing, whether performed on a centralized basis by an information systems department or on a departmental basis by an end user.

However, readers who wish to view end-user computing as a separate control issue can refer to Appendix C which deals with the subject in greater detail.

ORGANIZATION OF THE BOOK

Exposures and their causes and controls are explored in Chapter 2. Chapter 3 looks at how the internal audit department should be organized to deal with information systems and explains how to plan effective audit coverage given the usual situation of limited audit resources. The following chapters deal with each of the building block elements contained within the Model Curriculum. Each of these chapters is designed to provide a complete, stand-alone description of the subject area. The first section of each chapter describes the control perspective for including the chapter topic as one of the basic building block elements of information systems. This section also describes the relevance of this subject area to the skill requirements of the Level 1 and Level 2 auditor. The causes of exposure are described, as are the more common types of control which act upon these causes of exposure. The types of exposure which may occur as a result of a deficiency or breakdown in the control structure are also discussed. Finally, the audits to be performed are described in terms of relevant objectives and frequency.

Following the chapters on the building block elements of the Model Curriculum, there is a chapter on pulling together the results of the various audits that have been conducted and determining an overall assessment of the adequacy of the information services function within the organization.

WHO SHOULD READ THIS BOOK

Information Systems Management, Control and Audit will be of particular interest to those who are involved in the design development and review of controls within a computer environment. This audience includes not only the internal audit community but also the managers and professional staff members from information systems departments. Senior and executive managers will find the chapters on "Exposures, Causes of Exposure and Controls," "Information Systems and Organization," "Artificial Intelligence" and "Assessing the Overall Performance of the Information Systems Department" to be of particular interest.

Within the audit community the book addresses the needs of the Level 1 and Level 2 auditor, defined by the Model Curriculum as follows:

Level 1   Requires a conceptual and definitional knowledge of aspects of information systems auditing. The Level 1 auditor should be able to execute any audit program related to information systems, recognize control weaknesses and assess the materiality of these control weaknesses back to the scope and objectives of the audit.

Level 2   Fully conversant with the conceptual and definitional knowledge of all aspects of information systems auditing. Has the knowledge and practical experience (i.e., skill) to set the scope and objectives for individual audits, prepare the audit programs, lead the audit and approve the overall results emanating from the audit.

The Level 2 auditor will be able to relate symptoms back to the originating cause and to determine if the scope of the audit needs to be expanded to encompass the originating cause of the problem(s). This level is inclusive of any requirements of the Level 1 auditor. It is expected that an auditor who is proficient at Level 2 will have at least two years of practical audit experience.

The needs of the Level 3 auditor (i.e., someone who is fully conversant with specific hardware and software products) are not addressed in this book because the range of products to be covered is too broad for a single text.

The Institute of Internal Auditors

AUTHOR'S PHILOSOPHY

The efficient and effective management of information systems within an organization requires the successful interaction of a number of different departments, namely the information systems department, the end-user departments and the audit department. Each of these departments has their own focus and priorities, not to mention their own unique nomenclature. The common denominator between these various groups is the business issues that need to be addressed at the corporate level.

Rather than focusing on control and audit as an end unto themselves, what I have tried to do is focus on the business issues that are at risk when dealing with information systems and relate the role of control and audit in the overall management of information systems within the organization.

The Institute of Internal Auditors

2
EXPOSURES, CAUSES OF EXPOSURE AND CONTROLS

Every organization should identify those events and circumstances whose occurrence could result in a loss to the organization. These events and circumstances are usually referred to as causes of exposure. Exposures are quantified as the cost of a cause of exposure multiplied by the probability of its occurrence. Controls are those acts which the organization implements to minimize the exposures. Therefore, before any controls are put in place, it is important to know what cause of exposure is being addressed, what is the likelihood of its occurrence and, consequently, what is the organization's financial exposure. There is a particularly relevant maxim which applies to this situation — "the cost of a control should not exceed the exposure it was designed to prevent, detect and/or correct."

CATEGORIES OF CONTROLS

In addition to knowing the cause of exposure that a particular control is intended to act upon, it is also useful to know the type of role the control is intended to perform. There are basically four categories of control:

Deterrent — These controls are designed to deter people (primarily employees, but can include others) from undesirable corporate behavior. Examples of this type of control include written policies on software copyright protection and a stated policy that software hackers will be prosecuted to the full extent of the law.

Preventive — These controls prevent the cause of exposure from occurring at all or, at the very least, minimize the possibility. For example, data base access control software prevents unauthorized access to data.

The Institute of Internal Auditors

Detective — When a cause of exposure has occurred, detective controls report its existence in an effort to minimize the extent of the damage. Certain fire precautions (such as heat detectors) fall into this category.

Corrective — These controls are necessary to recover from a loss situation. For example, without corrective controls an organization risks going out of business due to its inability to recover essential information after a catastrophe.

THE SYSTEM OF INTERNAL CONTROL

A system of internal controls within an organization comprises the policies, procedures and practices that are intended to ensure that management's objectives are met. The policies, practices and procedures will vary from organization to organization depending on:

- The type of business or industry the organization belongs to.

- The organization's management style.

- The culture of the organization.

However, the purpose of the system of internal control does not change between organizations. The combination of the four categories of control as previously described must, on a cumulative basis, provide assurance that management's objectives can be met.

THE IMPACT OF INFORMATION SYSTEMS ON INTERNAL CONTROL

Information systems have not altered the underlying principles of sound internal control but they have altered the means by which the constituent parts of the system of internal control are constructed. For example:

- Many of the controls which were previously performed by supervisors or managers are now embedded in the application logic of an information system (for example, in a banking operation, whether to allow an overdraft based on the presence of an authorized credit limit). With the presence of manual intervention the "common sense" control is always a consideration. A computerized system will respond exactly to what has been programmed with no regard to what makes "sense" in the real world.

- Physical audit trails (i.e., evidence that various controls are in place and working) have been replaced in many instances by electronic audit trails.

- Computer systems have traditionally been built to improve operational efficiency at the clerical level. This will continue to be the case. However, we are now seeing strategic systems, decision support systems and other forms of advanced computer systems that endeavor to improve operational efficiency at the managerial or executive level.

- Managerial policies, statutory regulations, etc., are now contained within the systems being built and can no longer be "seen" to be carried out.

DEFINING MANAGEMENT'S OBJECTIVES

Management's objectives can be described in several ways. From a business perspective the ultimate objectives are profitability, continuity of business, protection of assets, competitiveness, productivity and management effectiveness. Many organizations are looking to automation and technology in the form of information systems to play an increasingly important role in meeting management's objectives. It is useful to examine the impact that information systems can have on each of these business objectives.

Profitability — Information systems affect profitability in a number of ways. They may be used to reduce costs, improve productivity, or as a vehicle for generating revenue. It may be that certain systems are necessary just to stay in a particular business. For example, many financial institutions are having to invest in new systems to produce consolidated, comprehensive statements for their clients simply because the competition is doing the same thing. To be left behind in customer service is viewed, quite correctly, as a major competitive disadvantage.

We have mentioned the positive side of information systems in the profitability equation. There is also the cost side of this equation. The investment in information systems is a significant issue for most organizations. Depending on the types of systems in place there may be hardware costs (purchase and maintenance), software development costs, communication costs, and workstation and terminal costs. The costs can include both one-time capital costs and ongoing operating costs.

Continuity of Business — Many organizations have come to the point of relying on their information systems to continue as an ongoing, viable entity. In the event of a system failure, these organizations would effectively cease to do business. Clearly, a contingency plan to deal with the various possible levels of system interruption is necessary.

Protection of Assets — Computer hardware and communications equipment are major physical assets of the organization and need to be safeguarded against damage or destruction. Computer application systems are also major assets of the organization because they consumed significant resources when they were being developed. Lastly, the data of the organization that is held on computer readable media is now considered to be a major corporate resource that warrants significant measures to protect its integrity.

Competitiveness — As mentioned previously, it is often necessary to develop complex new systems just to stay competitive, let alone gain any competitive advantage. However, there have been quite a number of well documented examples of ways in which certain organizations have been able to use information systems and technology to develop a competitive advantage either through the provision of new services (for instance, the Merrill Lynch CMA account), streamlining and improving the execution of basic services (such as Avis Rent-a-Car) or taking the service directly to the end user (as in the case of American Hospital Supplies' placement of terminals for direct ordering by the customer). The emergence of decision support systems tied into the corporate data base adds many possibilities for the use of management information in the development of strategic systems. This in turn will help in the formulation of a competitive posture for the organization.

Productivity — Increased productivity is one of the more alluring aspects of information systems. It is also one of the most elusive. Efforts at increasing productivity are aimed at every part of the organization that comes into contact with information systems, from the system developer's use of CASE (Computer Aided Software Engineering) tools to office automation to end-user computing. It is widely recognized that information systems can result in productivity gains. The trick is to discover how this can be done within the context of one's own organization.

Management Effectiveness — The traditional approach to building information systems was to build transaction processing systems for use by predominantly non-managerial staff. With the emergence of expert systems and other forms of decision support systems, management is now in a position to make fundamental business decisions based upon the output from information systems. It is obvious that the integrity of these systems is of fundamental importance to the organization.

We have just presented management's objectives from a business perspective and described the impact of information systems on each of these objectives. From an audit perspective, it is customary to describe management's objectives in relation to internal control in somewhat different language:

- Provide reasonable assurance that assets are safeguarded, information (financial and other) is timely and reliable, and errors and irregularities are discovered and corrected promptly.

- Promote operational efficiency.

- Encourage compliance with managerial policies and procedures as well as governing laws, regulations and sound fiduciary principles.

- Provide sufficient information for management to evaluate the rate and level of achievement within each division of the organization.

Regardless of the language being used, it is apparent that information systems have a major impact on the system of internal control within any organization that is more than just a casual user of technology. Therefore, it is important to find some way of bringing together the various definitions of meeting management's objectives in order to align the focus and priorities of the parties involved in the management and use of information systems within an organization (i.e., the information systems department, the end-user departments and the audit function). It is especially important to the auditor for this common nomenclature to be in place. Bridging the gap between the somewhat sterile, controls-focused wording of an audit report and the day-to-day operating concerns of the auditee has frequently been a problem in the past.

TYPES OF EXPOSURE

Earlier in this chapter, definitions were given for controls and exposures and their causes. Controls act upon causes of exposure. Exposures are the impact, in financial terms, of the occurrence of an exposure multiplied by the probability of the cause of exposure actually happening. In order to arrive at a common definition of the exposures which are to be avoided or minimized through the use of controls it is useful to further classify exposures into types. In the original text on *Computer Control and Audit* the authors provided nine types of exposure which were essentially definitions, in business terms, of the impact of an occurrence of a cause of exposure.[1] We will continue to use these definitions as a framework for bringing together the seemingly different points of view and semantics of the users, information systems professionals and auditors.

The types of exposure described in the original text are still valid today and are listed below along with a brief description of each:

Erroneous record keeping is the recording of financial transactions that are contrary to established accounting policies. The errors may involve the time of recognition, value or classification.

Unacceptable accounting is the establishment or implementation of accounting policies which are not generally accepted or are inappropriate for the circumstances. This could also lead to further exposures such as statutory sanctions.

Business interruptions may include anything from a temporary suspension of operations to a permanent termination of the enterprise. At the extreme, this also affects the accounting principle regarding a "going concern."

Erroneous management decisions are objectionable in themselves but may also lead to other exposures. Such decisions may arise due to misleading information, a lack of information, or errors in judgment.

Fraud and embezzlement may be perpetrated at different levels — against management or by management. Direct misappropriation of funds is only one ramification of fraud. Deliberately misinforming management or investors is also fraudulent, even when done to keep one's job.

Statutory sanctions refer to any of the penalties which may be brought by judicial or regulatory authorities who have jurisdiction over an organization's operations.

---

[1] Mair, William C., Wood, Donald R., and Davis, Keagle W. *Computer Control and Audit*, (Altamonte Springs, FL: The Institute of Internal Auditors, 1978).

Excessive costs include any expense of the business which could be readily avoided. A related exposure is also a loss of revenues to which the organization is fairly entitled.

Loss or destruction of assets refers to the unintentional loss of physical assets, monies, claims to monies or information assets.

Competitive disadvantage relates to the inability of an organization to effectively remain abreast of the demands of the marketplace or to respond effectively to competitive challenges.

Obviously these types of exposure are not all mutually exclusive. However, they do include most of the adverse effects that a business may encounter.

THE SCOPE OF INFORMATION SYSTEM CONTROLS

It is clear that information systems have not changed the purpose of a system of internal control nor have they changed the types of exposure that an organization making use of information systems faces (although the occurrence and magnitude of the exposure may change — sometimes significantly). What *has* changed are the nature, location and types of control which need to be applied.

Controls within the entire scope of information systems can be broadly divided to correspond to the building block structure used in the Model Curriculum. Figure 2.1 shows a pictorial representation of this structure. Notice that at the center of the structure is the corporate data repository. In essence, the scope of information systems controls needs to be broad and deep enough to ensure that the integrity of the corporate data repository is preserved. Integrity implies timeliness, relevance, accuracy, completeness, availability (to those who are authorized), and security from unintentional additions, deletions or amendments, whether authorized or not.

Most of the major building blocks of information systems consist of a number of subtopics. Each subtopic needs to be addressed before an opinion can be expressed on the overall adequacy of control within the major topic area. The control issues relating to these subtopics will be addressed in detail in the chapters dealing with each of the building block structures (Chapters 4 through 16).

The scope of information controls can also be thought of as divided into those that specifically apply to an individual application system and those that apply at a generic or environmental level (i.e., to all application systems) running within that environment. In the early days of information systems there was only one environment — the one provided by the corporate data center. Even where an organization was decentralized, the operating environments tended to be homogeneous. This is not the case today. With the advent of end-user computing in all of its various guises there may be many operating environments within an organization. However, the scope of information system controls as just described broadly applies in varying degrees to all operating environments. When each of these environments is dealt with in detail in later chapters the distinctions between the control requirements will become clear.

Figure 2.1 — The Scope of Information System Controls

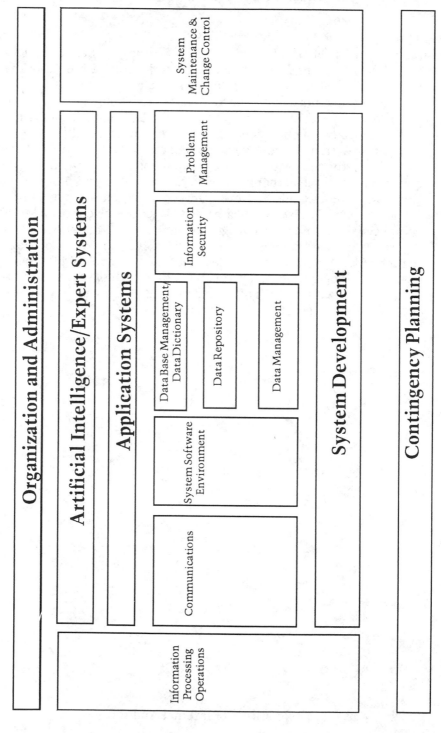

3
THE AUDIT FUNCTION

OVERVIEW

The audit function within an organization is part of the management control structure. The key role played by the auditor is that of an independent observer and reviewer of the internal control system within the organization. There are two distinct aspects of the audit function:

- The Internal Audit Function.

- The External Audit Function.

The objective of the internal audit function is to report to management on the adequacy of controls and the quality of ongoing operations within the organization as they relate to the achievement of the corporate objectives that are established from time to time by management. Within the context of information systems it is the control over the input, processing and output of data that is of paramount importance. Data must be accurately, economically and securely input, processed efficiently and securely, and output in the form of information that meets the needs and expectations of the users of such information.

Therefore, the internal auditor is concerned with all aspects of information systems (or the entire 13 building blocks as defined by the Model Curriculum) and all types of exposure as previously defined.

The external auditor, on the other hand, tends to be primarily concerned with internal control deficiencies that could result in erroneous record keeping or unacceptable accounting practices. External auditors are employed by public accounting firms which are engaged by the board of directors and the shareholders of an organization for the express purpose of rendering an opinion on the fairness and reliability of the financial statements.

The requirement for the internal and external audit functions to work closely together has always existed. However, the growing emergence of information systems as a factor in the production of financial statements has made this requirement even more important. Records that were once kept in file cabinets are now maintained on computer-readable media (perhaps distributed across different nodes within a distributed network of computers). Many generally accepted accounting principles are now embedded in the logic of computer programs. In the past, an external auditor could readily attest to the presence of internal control by checking the physical separation of duties, the levels of supervision and authorization, and so forth.

Today, the auditor must look to the information systems department to determine whether compensating controls have been put in place and whether or not these controls are effective and are being adhered to. However, because of the growing complexity of today's information systems environment and the relative uniqueness of each organization's computer installation, the external auditor cannot realistically assess internal control relative to information systems without spending much more time with each client than is currently being practiced. Not only is this impractical from the external auditor's viewpoint, but it is probably unacceptable to the organization because of increased external auditor fees.

Therefore, many organizations have increased their investment in an internal information systems audit function, either as a separate unit within the internal audit department (typically referred to as the "EDP Audit" group) or as an integral part of existing internal audit functions. As we just discussed, the internal (EDP) auditor's area of responsibility is broader than that of the external auditor; it should, in fact, overlap the external auditor's responsibilities. Part of the internal auditor's function is to communicate with the external auditor to decide to what extent reliance can be placed on the existing system of internal control.

ORGANIZING THE INTERNAL AUDIT DEPARTMENT

For many years there has been considerable debate over whether or not information systems requires a specialized audit function that is separate from the standard financial and operational audit functions which have traditionally formed the basis of the internal audit department. In the formative years of introducing the concepts of auditability and control to the area of electronic data processing (EDP), many internal audit departments created distinct groups to deal with EDP auditing.

Given the pervasiveness of information systems in today's business environment, it is the position of the author that all internal auditors need to know the basic elements of auditing information systems. It is simply not possible to audit "around the computer" and provide management with any meaningful assurances about the adequacy of internal control in any financial or operational entity within an organization. Information systems have become completely integrated with the business functions of many organizations, to the point where it is impossible to think of those functions without taking for granted the support offered by an information system. So too must the internal audit department factor in the presence of an information system when auditing individual business units.

In the Model Curriculum for Information Systems Auditing, The Institute of Internal Auditors has defined three levels of internal auditor:

Level 1   Requires a conceptual and definitional knowledge of the various aspects of information systems auditing. It is expected that it would take about two years of training to become fully conversant with the practical application of this knowledge. It is expected that future internal auditors will receive much of this knowledge in colleges and universities.

The Level 1 auditor should be able to execute any audit program that is related to information systems, recognize control weaknesses, and assess the materiality of these control weaknesses back to the scope and objectives of the audit.

Level 2   Fully conversant with the conceptual and definitional knowledge of aspects of information systems auditing. Has the knowledge and practical experience (or skill) to set the scope and objectives for individual audits, prepare the audit programs, lead the audit and approve the overall results.

The Level 2 auditor will be able to relate symptoms back to the originating cause and determine whether the scope of the audit needs to be expanded to encompass the original cause of the problem(s). This level is inclusive of any requirements of the Level 1 auditor. It is expected that an auditor who is proficient at Level 2 will have at least two years of practical audit experience.

Level 3   Fully conversant with specific vendor hardware and software products. The Level 3 auditor should be able to formulate an audit program with appropriate testing mechanisms, execute the audit program, recognize control weaknesses, assess the materiality of these weaknesses, and relate them back to the scope and objectives of the audit.

Ideally, the Level 3 auditor will be fully qualified at Level 2. However, this may not always be the case. For example, in terms of overall audit knowledge and experience, the Level 3 auditor may be operating primarily at Level 1. The depth of technical knowledge may come from a systems background and the auditor may be seriously challenged to perform at Level 2 for many areas of technical (or non-computer) audit responsibility.

It is clear that Level 1 and Level 2 auditors are performing traditional auditing roles and are expected to factor into this traditional role the fact that part of the overall process being audited happens to run on a computer. However, it is also recognized that there will continue to be certain aspects of information systems which require specialized expertise to audit. The Level 3 auditor classification has been defined to address this need. However, the responsibility of Level 3 is very specifically defined and will form a small part of the overall responsibility of the internal audit department. The vast majority of the work in the information systems area will be performed by Level 1 and Level 2 auditors who will also be responsible for other (or non-computer) financial and operational audits. The technical, infrastructural components of the information systems environment will be dealt with by the Level 3 auditors whose work will, in turn, be relied upon by the Level 1 and Level 2 auditors when dealing with mainstream audits.

STAFFING THE INTERNAL AUDIT DEPARTMENT

External auditors are, typically, qualified accountants; either Certified Public Accountants (CPAs) in the United States or Chartered Accountants (CA) in Canada. Internal auditors, however, can be drawn from a variety of backgrounds. Thus, the management of an organization has several alternatives when staffing an internal audit department that is capable of conducting information systems audits.

Training and education are key elements to consider when establishing an information systems auditing capability within the internal audit department. The Institute of Internal Auditors (IIA) introduced the Certified Internal Auditor (CIA) designation as a means of recognizing a desirable level of professional competence. To achieve and maintain the CIA designation, an individual must pass the certified internal auditor examination and have 24 months of internal audit experience or the equivalent. This experience must be attested to by an appropriate member within the individual's organization. In order to maintain a current continuing professional development (CPD) listing, a certified internal auditor must annually report progress toward completing 100 hours of activity in each three-year rolling period.

Part of the CIA examination deals with information systems auditing. The development of the Model Curriculum for information systems auditing is a major step in positioning The IIA to deal with the educational needs of the internal auditor going forward into the 1990s.

The EDP Auditors Association also has a certification program which results in the Certified Information Systems Auditor (CISA) designation.

Clearly, individuals who possess either the CIA or CISA designation have demonstrated competence in the area of information systems auditing and are ideal candidates for the internal audit department.

A frequent alternative to hiring CIA and/or CISA graduates is to staff the internal audit function solely with professional accountants who have the same designation and background as the external auditors. One advantage to this alternative is that CPAs and CAs are professionally trained auditors. Also, the fact that they have similar backgrounds should aid in internal/external auditor communications.

However, professional accountants may lack the information systems skills and experience required to gain adequate insight into the workings of computerized information systems. In addition, they sometimes experience difficulty with the nomenclature and semantics which seems indigenous to the information systems field. A lack of information systems experience can lead to credibility problems within the information systems department (i.e., with the primary auditee). Many information systems professionals only respond to specific questions from the auditor because of the concern that volunteering information will simply result in a parroting back of this information as an audit point to be addressed. Information systems is a specialized field; to work successfully in this field, one must have knowledge and practical experience.

A second alternative is to staff the information systems audit function solely with information systems personnel. However, they typically lack the formal training in accounting and auditing disciplines that is essential for ensuring a thorough, meaningful audit.

In addition to their lack of auditing and accounting training, information systems personnel often have other more subtle shortcomings. They are often more interested in the technical aspects of the system rather than in whether or not the system is fully compatible with the needs of the users or that sufficient controls and audit trails have been built into the system. Yet, as information systems auditors, they are required to ensure that users are receiving what they need from systems and that the systems have adequate controls. Such people may find it difficult to become sensitive to users' needs overnight or to evaluate the system's level of control rather than its technical advantages.

A third alternative is to draw from the ranks of both accounting and information systems, when staffing levels can afford such a combination. Furthermore, if staffing levels permit, someone with a user department background within the organization can be added to the information systems audit staff. With the practical experience of individuals from the mainstream of the business, it is possible to review systems in relation to the business environment in which they must operate.

Given the focus of the training for the CIA and CISA designations, it is clearly desirable to staff the information systems audit function with individuals who have these designations. If this is not feasible, it is probably better to train the professional accountant in the fundamentals of information systems rather than to train information systems people in auditing fundamentals. This is especially true when an organization relies on its internal audit function to minimize external audit fees.

DEVELOPING AN AUDIT PLAN

As described in Chapter 2, the scope of information systems within an organization can be broad. It is unlikely that the internal audit department has the resources to conduct an audit of every facet of information systems on an annual basis. In fact, it is unlikely that this type of "complete" audit coverage would be cost effective to the organization. What the internal audit department requires is an approach to the prioritization, scheduling and staffing of a sufficient number of audits to deal with the principal issues of concern to the organization as they relate to information systems.

The Institute of Internal Auditors

Figure 3.1 provides a useful matrix in determining audit priorities. The horizontal axis (the columns) contains the 13 "Elements of Information Systems" which map to the building blocks as defined in the Model Curriculum. The vertical axis (the rows) contains the "Types of Exposure" as defined in *Computer Control and Audit* and described in Chapter 2.[1] The horizontal columns for Applications and Artificial Intelligence/Expert Systems represent multiple items (or one item for each major application system of artificial intelligence/expert system).

There are a number of different ways in which the cells within the matrix can be completed. The intention is to get a comparative weighting into each of the cells. One approach is to estimate the exposure for each cell. As previously defined, exposure is the monetary impact of the occurrence of a cause of exposure multiplied by the probability of the cause of exposure actually happening. A commonly used algorithm to calculate the exposure is as follows:

$$e = \frac{10^{(p+c-3)}}{3}$$

where: c is a weighting factor based on the cost to the organization should the cause of exposure occur.

p is a weighting factor based on the probability that the event will occur within particular time frames.

e is the exposure in monetary terms.

Suggested weightings in keeping with this exponential form of equation are given in Table 3.1. The problem with this approach is that the exposure calculated tends to be very inexact because of the subjective nature of the weightings given to the probabilities and costs of occurrence. However, the approach still offers the chance to structure the thinking that goes into building an information systems audit plan. By thinking through the financial exposures within each of the elements of information systems it is possible to structure the audit

[1] Mair, William C., Wood, Donald R., Davis, Keagle W. *Computer Control & Audit* (Altamonte Springs, FL: The Institute of Internal Auditors, 1978).

plan to the organization's specific needs in a rational, defensible manner and not according to the latest magazine article on computer fraud.

The Analytical Hierarchy Process (AHP)

Another potential alternative (or perhaps supplemental) approach to assigning comparative values to the cells within the prioritization matrix is to use a relatively new mathematical technique called Analytical Hierarchy Process (AHP). AHP, developed by Thomas L. Saaty, uses a comparison technique to evaluate the relative merits of various quantitative and qualitative criteria.[2] Taking each of the rows in turn, the column entries are compared against each other to determine which is more important. For example, in the case of erroneous record keeping, which is more important: "information systems organization and administration" or "information systems security;" "information systems security" or "system development?"

All column entries within a row are compared to each other and are given a numerical ranking. Saaty's scale for making the comparisons between items and for assigning numerical values based on preferences for one item over another is as follows:

Equal	Moderate	Strong	Very Strong	Extreme
1	3	5	7	9

Once all of the items within one row have been compared, the next row can be compared. When all of the rows have been compared, the column entries are compared. For example, what is more important: "erroneous record keeping" or "unacceptable accounting;" "unacceptable accounting" or "business interruption?" Using matrix algebra it is possible to ensure internal consistency within and between the decisions being made and to determine the relative weights between the elements of information systems. Finally, using the calculated weights it is possible to decide how the audits should be prioritized.

---

[2] Saaty, Thomas L., *The Analytical Hierarchy Process* (New York: McGraw-Hill: 1980).

The reader may be inclined to think that there is too much work in this approach to warrant its use. If the work had to be calculated by hand, this would be true. However, there are a number of PC-based software packages that assist in laying out the structure of the problem and that contain all of the mathematics required to arrive at a final answer. Two such packages are Expert Choice (EC) from Decision Support Software and Fuzzy Choice from General Decision Support Systems Inc. Additional material on the Analytical Hierarchy Process can be found in *Quantitative Methods for Business*, 4th Ed., by Anderson, Sweeney, and Williams, West Publishing Company, St. Paul, Minnesota, 1989.

Audit Scope and Objectives

The audit scope and objectives must be clearly stated during the planning stage. The audit scope indicates which aspects of the information systems element need examination and which do not. For example, a data security audit can range in complexity from a review of the manual and administrative controls in the data center to an all encompassing review of data security that includes the adequacy and use of the data security software package, the impact of time sharing, and the integrity of the Data Base Management System (DBMS) in use within the organization.

The audit objectives include identifying potential system exposures and should be stated in measurable criteria that, at the completion of the audit, can be answered with a "yes" or a "no." Chapters 4 through 16 discuss possible audit objectives when dealing with each of the building block elements of information systems.

The scope and objectives set during the planning stage are subjective and, as such, are subject to change during the actual audit.

Staffing

Once the audit scope and objectives have been determined, the appropriate number of audit days to complete the audit and the time frame for the audit must be estimated. These staffing plans ensure that adequate staff (in numbers and experience) are initially assigned to the audit. The right combination of Level 1, 2 and 3 auditors is the key to a successfully executed audit plan. However, as in the case of the audit scope and objectives, the staffing plan may be subject to change once the audit is underway.

THE AUDIT PROCESS

Audit Objectives. Although the audit objectives are tentatively established during the audit planning cycle, they should be reviewed and refined, if necessary, at the start of the actual audit. A statement of objectives should be written in this audit step.

The Audit Preview. The audit preview provides general information about the system or operation being audited. This high-level information is used to define the scope and purpose of the system and is obtained from preliminary reviews and discussions.

Preliminary reviews involve gathering information from sources other than the potential auditee. These sources include reference work, previous audit reports, correspondence from internal auditors and overall audit planning material. Preliminary discussions are conducted with user and information systems management to obtain an overview of the system or operational objectives, general system interfaces, primary and secondary users, degree of user satisfaction, current and planned changes to the system or operation and system controlled assets and resources. These discussions should be documented in a memo that states the intent of the audit and notifies all user and information systems personnel of the start and potential impact of the audit.

Detailed Information Gathering. After developing a general understanding of the system or operation and having refined the audit scope, the auditor must gain a detailed knowledge of the system. Detailed information gathering includes defining all data processed by the system, the rules and procedures for processing data and the controls for ensuring that all processing is complete, accurate, secure and timely. This information must then be documented.

The auditor should obtain the required information from available corporate documentation. The purpose of this audit phase is to document how the system or operation is supposed to work. If the documentation is insufficient, the auditor can instead make assumptions on the basis of good business practices and evaluate these assumptions when the audit program is executed.

By gathering detailed information, the auditor is able to identify the primary system controls and any apparent control weaknesses to evaluate the overall level of system or operational control.

The "Control Evaluation Table" introduced in *Computer Control and Audit* provides an excellent framework for defining the controls being relied upon to prevent, detect and/or minimize the occurrence of a cause of exposure within any area of information systems.[3] The detailed information gathering phase of the audit is the ideal point at which to originate or update the control evaluation table for the area to be audited.

The control evaluation table depicts the *expected* relationship between the causes of exposure relevant to the area being audited, the controls which have been put in place to counteract these causes of exposure, and the degree of certainty that the exposure will occur if the control system is inherently inadequate or does not perform as expected. Figure 3.2 shows the format of the control evaluation table. Notice that the table is in four parts:

- Causes of exposure along the horizontal axis.

- Controls along the upper part of the vertical axis.

- An evaluation of the *design* of the overall (the sum of the individual controls) control structure dealing with a specific cause of exposure. This evaluation will be verified later through execution of the audit program.

- Taking up the lower part of the vertical axis is the degree of certainty of occurrence of an exposure should the control structure be inherently inadequate or fail to perform as designed.

Through the detailed information gathering step the causes of exposure should be identified first. Controls acting on each of the identified causes of exposure should then be identified along with the

---

[3] Mair, William C., Wood, Donald R., Davis, Keagle W. *Computer Control & Audit* (Altamonte Springs, FL: The Institute of Internal Auditors, 1978).

certainty of occurrence of an exposure should the control system fail for any reason. An evaluation should then be made on the adequacy of the cumulative effect of the controls which are intended to be in place. This evaluation must be verified through the testing procedures that are built into the audit program.

When the causes of exposure are not identified first, there is a risk of evaluating controls and exposures in a vacuum with the potential of overlooking the need for certain controls or having certain controls in place which are, in fact, superfluous to the business of the organization.

The Audit Program Design. Once the auditor has determined the primary controls and possible exposures, an audit program should be tailored to outline control verification and the quantification of any control exposures. Verification procedures can usually be classified into two categories:

- Compliance Procedures — designed to test compliance with defined controls.

- Substantive Procedures — designed to verify the accuracy of reported information.

When designing the audit program, the auditor must consider the testing technique to be used to verify a particular control including the use of the computer as an audit tool. Both compliance and substantive testing should be defined to ensure that the appropriate controls are established and in use.

In determining the extent of apparent control weaknesses the audit program should account for any compensating controls. Testing of these controls should be particularly stringent.

Audit Program Implementation. Each test in the audit program must be performed and its results documented. For each cause of exposure, the control evaluation table must be updated to reflect the adequacy of the control structure as it exists in practice. This evaluation of the control structure may differ from the evaluation that is performed during the detailed information phase of the audit. Material discrepancies are indicative of a breakdown in the intended control structure. This situation typically requires immediate management attention.

The Institute of Internal Auditors

As the auditee is directly involved in this phase of the audit, audit commencement procedures, which define the protocols to be observed between auditor and auditee, should be established. In addition, standards for the completion of workpapers need to be defined. The primary purpose of the audit workpapers is to document and support the audit evaluation and conclusions. The workpapers also support understanding of the system or operation. The standards governing the preparation of workpapers facilitate a review of the audit work by audit management and external auditors.

Audit Reporting. The audit department is a management support function and, as such, must report its findings to the auditee for possible corrective action and to senior management for information purposes.

Audit report formats should be standardized and targeted to a specific audience. An effective reporting method is a multi-level report that ranges from a management summary to an in-depth account that is given to the auditee. The audit scope and objectives along with a general description of the work performed should be stated in each report level.

Audit Follow-up: A typical audit report describes the control deficiencies, identifies the attendant exposures to the organization, and recommends corrective measures. Once an audit report is issued, the auditor must prepare a procedure for ensuring that control deficiencies are resolved. This procedure must be approved by senior management and communicated to all other organizational managers for the auditor to obtain the cooperation necessary for the follow-up procedure to work effectively.

The follow-up procedure should give the auditee a predetermined time (typically 30 days) in which to reply to the audit report. For each control deficiency this reply should specify the corrective action to be taken and the time frame for its completion. The auditee should be required to report monthly on the progress of correcting any outstanding deficiencies. The auditor can then retest the applicable controls to ensure that the deficiencies are remedied.

Workpapers

The primary purpose of audit workpapers is to document and support the audit evaluation, the strengths and weaknesses, and the conclusions and recommendations. Audit workpapers should follow the same hierarchical relationship as the audit, moving from the identification of scope and objectives to the audit program to the descriptions and results of the compliance and substantive tests performed.

SUMMARY

The audit function is part of the management control structure. There are two distinct aspects of the audit function (internal and external) each with its own distinct focus. The organization of the internal audit function should integrate information systems auditing into the mainstream of the audit process as much as possible. The education and training programs offered by The IIA and EDPAA are helping considerably in this regard.

In developing an audit plan, there should be a rational strategy for prioritizing the audits to be performed. Calculating potential exposures by element is one approach. Analytical Hierarchy Process is an alternative or supplemental approach. The approach to individual audits follows a set pattern. The control evaluation table offers a logical and systematic means of determining the overall adequacy of the system of control, both in terms of design and in practice, for a particular building block element within information systems. Audit workpapers should be structured to indicate the work that was done to evaluate the system of control under review.

Figure 3.1 — Audit Prioritization Matrix

Elements of Information Systems ⟶ / Types of Exposure ⟱	Info. Sys. Org. & Admin.	Info. Sys. Security	System Development	System Maintenance and Change Control	Information Systems Problem Management	Information Systems Contingency Planning	Information Processing Operations
Erroneous Record Keeping							
Unacceptable Accounting							
Business Interruption							
Erroneous Management Decisions							
Fraud and Embezzlement							
Statutory Sanctions							
Excessive Costs							
Loss or Destruction of Assets							
Competitive Disadvantage							

Figure 3.1 — Audit Prioritization Matrix (cont.)

Elements of Information Systems ⇨ / ⇨ Types of Exposure	Application Systems	Systems Software Control Programs	Data Management	DBMS/Data Dictionary	Telecommunications Network	Artificial Intelligence/ Expert Systems
Erroneous Record Keeping						
Unacceptable Accounting						
Business Interruption						
Erroneous Management Decisions						
Fraud and Embezzlement						
Statutory Sanctions						
Excessive Costs						
Loss or Destruction of Assets						
Competitive Disadvantage						

Figure 3.2 — Control Evaluation Table

CONTROLS ⇩	Cause of exposure	CAUSES OF EXPOSURE
		KEY TO RELIANCE ON CONTROL
		3 - High reliance ⇦
		2 - Moderate reliance ⇦
		1 - Control has only a ⇦ peripheral effect on the cause of exposure ⇦
		Blank - No significant impact ⇦
Overall control rating - design		**KEY TO OVERALL CONTROL RATING** ⇦
Overall control rating - tested		3 - Strong control 2 - Moderate but adequate ⇦ control
		⇦ Inadequate control
		EXPOSURES
KEY TO DEGREE OF CERTAINTY OF OCCURRENCE IN THE EVENT OF AN INADEQUATE CONTROL STRUCTURE ⇨		Erroneous record keeping
⇨		Unacceptable accounting
⇨		Business interruption
⇨		Erroneous management decisions
3 - Virtually certain ⇨		Fraud and embezzlement
2 - Probable ⇨		Statutory sanctions
1 - Possible but unlikely ⇨		Excessive costs
Blank - Very unlikely ⇨		Loss or destruction of assets
⇨		Competitive disadvantage

Table 3.1 — Weightings to Calculate Exposures

Probability	p	Value	c
Never	0	$0	0
Every 300 years	1	$10	1
Every 30 years	2	$100	2
Every 3 years	3	$1K	3
Every 100 days	4	$10K	4
Every 10 days	5	$100K	5
Once per day	6	$1M	6
10 times per day	7	$10M	7

4
INFORMATION SYSTEMS ORGANIZATION AND ADMINISTRATION

INTRODUCTION

This is the first of 13 chapters that deal with the building block elements of information systems as defined in The IIA's Model Curriculum.

Each of these chapters is organized in a similar manner. The first section of each chapter describes the control perspective for including the chapter topic as one of the basic building block elements of information systems. This section also describes the relevance of the subject area to the skill set and knowledge requirements of the Level 1 and Level 2 auditor. The causes of exposure are described, as are the more common types of control which act upon these causes of exposure. The types of exposure which may occur as a result of a deficiency or breakdown in the control structure are also discussed. Finally, the audits to be performed are described in terms of relevant objectives and frequency.

CONTROL PERSPECTIVE

The overall strength of any internal control system starts with the actions and attitudes of senior management. These actions and attitudes are viewed through the organization and administration of the various divisions and departments within the organization. Policies, standards and procedures need to be in place to provide for short-range and long-range planning and the effective and efficient ongoing operation of the division or department. This is also true for the information systems department.

The foundation of the internal control and data security program starts in the high-level organization/administration structure which, in turn, sets the tone for the entire information systems control and security environment.

SCOPE OF INFORMATION SYSTEMS ORGANIZATION AND ADMINISTRATION

Information systems organization and administration includes the following subtopics in its scope of activities:

1. Executive administration

2. Information systems budgeting and finance

3. Information systems cost recovery charge-backs

4. Information systems human resources policies

5. Long-range information systems planning

Executive Administration

Sometime during the 1990s, it is entirely conceivable that the information system department will be considered to be part of the corporate organization rather than separated from the mainstream goals, objectives and activities of the rest of the organization. This is particularly true given the changing nature of the use and importance of information systems within many organizations.

The organizational entity which will bring about this corporate integration is that of the Chief Information Officer (CIO). The original view of this function was that the CIO would be a senior executive who was comfortable with and knowledgeable about both the business and the technical milieu of the organization. This person would also be the executive charged with managing the information systems department. However, there is another emerging view of what the CIO function should be. Some say that the CIO "office" should be a corporate planning and monitoring function without the line responsibilities of managing the information systems department. The qualifications for the individual remain the same, but the mandate is very much focused on strategic planning rather than on day-to-day operations.

Whichever view of the CIO function finally prevails there can be little doubt that, in the future, the effectiveness of the executive administration within the information systems function is going to be measured in business terms (i.e., information systems as an investment with an expected return to the organization) rather than in technical terms.

Part of the auditor's mandate is to measure operational effectiveness. A large part of the operational effectiveness for information systems is derived from the vision adopted by the executive in charge of the department. The attitudes and actions of the individual departments within the information systems department toward the issues of control and security will be determined in large part by the explicit and implicit initiatives and actions of this executive.

Information Systems Budgeting and Finance

In many organizations, the information systems department controls a significant portion of the annual operating budget and, often, an even larger portion of the annual capital budget. Where this situation exists, there is a need for stringent financial control over the expenditures controlled by the information systems department.

The budgeting process, expenditures made throughout the year, fixed asset inventory evaluation and associated depreciation (hardware, software and communications equipment) should all be the subject of audit review throughout the year.

Information Systems Cost Recovery Charge-backs

Many organizations are trying to measure the payback associated with the use of information systems. Part of this measurement system is a cost recovery charge-back algorithm which attributes the costs of computer activity to the end user or the initiator of the activity. This computer activity can be related to the development and/or maintenance of computer systems as well as to the operation of the system in a production environment. The level of sophistication of the algorithm can range from a broad allocation system based on such things as head count or budget size of the department to a complete activity capture process which identifies the specific recipient of the benefit derived from the activity.

From an audit perspective, a cost recovery charge-back system can have a major impact on the cost accounting system within an organization and can also influence corporate behavior in its use of information systems. Therefore, the auditor is concerned with the accuracy of the data-gathering techniques that are used and with the analysis and reporting mechanisms used to allocate costs.

Information Systems Human Resources Policies

Adequate hiring, termination, salary administration, training and employee development programs need to be in place within the information systems department. It is commonly anticipated that the current shortage of qualified information systems professionals will continue to be a major problem for most organizations well into the future. The productivity gains from well qualified and trained staff members are considerable. Given that the pressure to produce quality, relevant information systems is more keenly felt than ever, the ability to attract and retain high quality information systems staff is a critical success factor for most organizations. It is essential that effective human resources policies and procedures are in place for the information systems department.

Of particular interest to the auditor, outside of the financial controls associated with the audit of the payroll system, is the entire area of employee education as it relates to the need for security and control. An education program on security and control is intended to familiarize and sensitize employees to the need for security and control. It is also intended to explain the safeguards (or controls) which are currently employed, what the safeguards are intended to protect against (the causes of exposure), how these safeguards work, and the expected results of utilizing each safeguard. The education program should be designed to bring about a general attitude of security awareness on the part of the employees.

Long-range Information Systems Planning

Long-range information systems planning is achieved through the formulation of an information strategy. An information strategy is a plan to meet the organization's information needs over three to five years through the development of computer systems and related services (such as automation and technology). Calling this plan an information strategy rather than a systems development plan is not an arbitrary choice of words. The term *systems development* focuses on the processes to be computerized rather than on the business needs that must be satisfied. The information strategy includes the traditional systems development plan in its primary processes section but also defines the environmental issues that must be addressed in support of the primary processes. The aim of the information strategy is to apply technology to the business — not the reverse, which is where other information systems plans have failed. The information strategy, therefore, deals with all aspects of information systems from the point of view of providing a long-term integrated business environment for the development, maintenance and operation of information systems.

If the information strategy is not consistent with the goals and objectives of the organization, there is little chance that the organization will realize the strategic, competitive and productivity gains which should accrue as a return on the investment in information systems.

LEVEL 1 AUDITOR — SKILL AND KNOWLEDGE OBJECTIVES

Overall Objective

Know the management issues that are associated with information systems organization and administration and the structure of the various audits required to attest to the overall adequacy of control in this area.

Executive Administration

Know the objectives behind each of the constituent elements of executive administration as it relates to information systems. Be able to assess whether or not these objectives are being met based upon the execution of an audit program that is designed to probe into these areas.

Information Systems Budgeting and Finance

Be able to execute a financial audit program.

IS Cost Recovery Charge-backs

Know the principles behind information systems cost recovery charge-backs. Be able to execute an audit program to attest to the accuracy of the data collected and the billing algorithm used.

Information Systems Human resource Policies

Be able to execute an audit program to assess the adequacy of the information systems human resources policies and to assess the degree of compliance with these policies.

Long-range Information Systems Planning

Know the component parts of a long-range information systems plan and the methodology used to arrive at the plan. Be able to attest to the adequacy of compliance to the process.

LEVEL 2 AUDITOR — SKILL AND KNOWLEDGE OBJECTIVES

Overall Objectives

Be able to structure audits that assess the adequacy of control within the entire scope of information systems organization and planning.

Be able to interpret the results of individual audits and present an overall opinion on the adequacy of the management process within the information systems department.

Executive Administration

Have sufficient knowledge and experience to be able to make an overall assessment of how well the executive administration is being handled within the organization. A "value for money" assessment is required.

Be able to prepare an executive an audit program which will deal with each area of executive administration in sufficient detail (including substantive and compliance testing) to allow individual and overall assessments to be made.

Information Systems Budgeting and Finance

Be able to design and execute a financial audit program.

Information Systems Cost Recovery Charge-backs

Be able to understand the various alternative methods of information systems cost recovery charge-backs and the current industry trends in this area. Be able to relate this understanding to the situation within their own organization.

Be able to understand the scope and the technical aspects of the data collection and billing mechanisms related to information systems cost recovery charge-backs. Be able to structure an audit program to properly attest to the accuracy and integrity of these processes.

Information Systems Human Resource Policies

Be able to define the measurement criteria against which the information systems human resources policies should be assessed.

Be able to relate any weaknesses in compliance with the stated policies to the other control issues within information systems.

Long-range Information Systems Planning

Be able to relate long-range information systems plans to the corporate business objectives and corporate culture. Be able to attest to the adequacy of the plan in support of these objectives and culture.

CAUSES OF EXPOSURE

The causes of exposure in the area of information systems organization and administration are as follows:

- Ineffectiveness.
- Inefficiency.
- Competition.
- Cost overruns.
- Inadequate resources.
- Inadequate information.

Ineffectiveness

Management effectiveness means doing the "right" things — targeting the right markets, producing the right products and positioning in the right strategic niche.

Within the context of information systems, effectiveness means building the systems that are right for the organization and investing in the technology that will produce the desired result, whether that result is internally or externally focused (e.g., greater productivity of internal staff or a competitive advantage in the marketplace).

Education and training are also key elements in being effective. There is no point in having the latest technology if the organization does not have the skills to take advantage of the situation.

Ineffectiveness is, of course, the flip side of being effective. There are many examples in corporate history of organizations which became complacent in their current operations to the point where they did not see the need for change. It was only a matter of time before the business results reflected the lack of effectiveness in the management of those organizations. Similarly, a lack of timely investment in keeping existing systems up-to-date with changing business needs and appropriate new technology will, at some point, result in systems that consume a disproportionately large amount of corporate resources to maintain or replace.

For the information systems department to be successful they must have a clear sense of their own identity in the eyes of their existing and potential client bases (e.g., the traditional user base of other line departments, and future users such as in the case of executive information systems). They must also be sure the services that are provided continue to meet the expectations of this client base. Once this proper positioning has been established, the services need to be provided in the most cost-effective, expeditious and consistent manner possible.

Inefficiency

Efficient management means doing things correctly. Once the effectiveness issue has been addressed, it is up to management to "do the right things correctly." Efficiency in information systems is the use of technology for efficient development, maintenance and operation of computer systems. Efficiency also means distributing or centralizing control over computer resources depending upon the approach which best suits the needs of the organization. The structure and use of end-user computing is a major issue in this area.

Inefficiency in the management of the information systems resource within an organization will manifest itself in many different ways. It may be that the organization cannot respond to new business opportunities because of the inability to develop new systems or amend existing ones in a time frame that is consistent with the demands of the marketplace. Projects may overrun budget from a cost and/or time standpoint. Poorly trained and poorly motivated personnel also contribute to inefficiency within the information systems function.

Productivity gains are available through the judicious use of technology particularly as adopted by Computer Assisted Software Engineering (CASE) tools and techniques. However, inefficiency can result from not using CASE tools and techniques or from misusing them.

Measurement tools are available to help in the assessment of the efficient management of information systems resources, such as function point analysis; mean time between failure for hardware, software and communications; response time statistics; up-time statistics; and number of education days per information systems professional. Key performance indicators (KPIs) are most often used to measure management's effectiveness, and are discussed in a later section of this chapter.

Competition

Competition is a corporate problem rather than a cause of exposure that is specific to information systems. It is often necessary to develop complex new information systems just to stay competitive, let alone gain any competitive advantage. However, there have been quite a number of well-documented examples of ways in which certain organizations have been able to use information systems and technology to develop a competitive advantage either through the provision of new services (for instance, the Merrill Lynch CMA account), streamlining and improving the execution of basic services (Avis Rent-a-Car) or taking the service directly to the end user (American Hospital Supplies' placement of terminals for direct ordering by the customer). The emergence of decision support systems tied into the corporate data base adds many possibilities for the development of strategic systems which, in turn, will help in the formulation of a competitive posture for the organization. Therefore, information systems can often provide the vehicle to sustain a particular position in the marketplace, to carve out a new niche in the marketplace or to provide market intelligence which will allow a timely response to what may be developing in the marketplace.

Cost Overruns

Cost overruns are of particular concern in the area of new system development. There have been many well-publicized instances of systems which have required much more than their original budget to complete. Many times the business case used to justify the development in the first place is invalidated by the large increase in cost to actually build the system.

Information systems need to be seen as an investment in an asset which will deliver a return to the organization. As with any investment, the expenditure of funds must be controlled and the return from the investment must be measured and reported.

Inadequate Resources

Resources in information systems fall into the categories of people, facilities, computers and tools. A deficiency in any of these resource categories will have a detrimental effect on the ability to manage the overall information systems resource.

There should be the right number and type of information systems professionals within the information systems department; there must be sufficient office facilities to support these individuals; there should be sufficient availability of and access to computers required to get the job done; and the tools that allow individuals to do their jobs effectively and efficiently should be in place.

Lack of Information

The lack of information is a corporate cause of exposure as much as it is an information systems cause of exposure. However, whereas the stated intent of information systems is to provide information to those that need it, there has been a tendency for information systems to be something similar to the shoemaker's children. The information systems department has typically spent little time investing in the types of information systems which have become a staple of good management in other divisions and departments within the organization.

There is a clear need for a management information system for the information systems function within an organization. This management information system should provide information on the internal operation of the department as well as intelligence on what the organization needs overall from its information systems function. An adequate flow of information is required for the information systems department to meet the needs of the organization. This means being adaptable to the changing environment of the organization's business, incorporating innovative features, and providing the organization with the ability to maintain its competitive posture in the marketplace.

CONTROLS

Applicable controls intended to prevent, detect and/or correct the causes of exposure just described as relevant to the area of information systems organization and control are as follows:

- Long-range planning.
- Separation of duties.
- Human resources policies and procedures.
- Project management system.

- Key performance indicators.
- Education and training.

Long-range Planning

As previously discussed, long-range planning should take the form of a defined information strategy developed by and for the information systems department in support of the corporate strategic objectives. As will be apparent from its content, the information strategy document is a key control covering all causes of exposure in the area of information systems organization and administration.

Figure 4.1 shows the three components of the information strategy: strategic objectives, primary processes and support processes.

The primary and support processes constitute the tactical plan for a defined period (usually one year) which are intended to contribute to the achievement of the strategic objectives. The strategic objectives are a subset of the corporate strategic objectives.

Strategic Objectives

The strategic objectives section of the information strategy should state the primary focus of information systems for the three to five years covered by the strategy. As stressed throughout this chapter, these objectives must be consistent with the corporate strategic objectives.

Primary Processes

The primary processes section defines the products and services that are to be delivered to accomplish the strategic objectives. This section is typically equated with the traditional systems development plan. Development and implementation time frames, along with a cost/benefit analysis, should exist for each product or service. The time frame and cost/benefit figures may only be rough estimates because the detailed work needed to produce accurate figures may not be scheduled until sometime in the future. Nevertheless, the information strategy should provide management with as accurate an estimate as possible.

The corporate philosophy that is to be used when building computer systems should also be referenced in the section on primary processes:

- Are systems to be purchased whenever possible even though there may have to be compromises in functionality?

- Is custom software considered essential for competitive advantage?

- What is the role of end-user computing in the "big picture" of system development?

- Should strategic alliances with other organizations be considered when developing systems?

These and other questions of a strategic nature should be addressed in this section of the information strategy.

Support Processes

The support processes define the environmental issues that need to be addressed in support of the primary processes. The main areas to be covered in this section are:

- Hardware.
- Communications and networks.
- Personnel.
- Education and training.
- Organizational structure.
- Security and control.

Hardware — The information strategy document should list what kinds of hardware will be needed to run the systems developed as primary processes and should include cost estimates. This is a traditional capacity plan. However, there are a number of other issues that should be considered in this section:

- Is the system to be centralized or decentralized?

- Will the concept of departmental versus enterprise mainframes be used?

- What is the standard configuration for user work stations?

- Are facilities management or service bureaus a viable approach to hardware processing?

Communications and Networks — The anticipated configuration of the network, including the communication devices and protocols and the estimated costs of its implementation, should be included in the plan.

The combination of voice and data communications should be considered in the formulation of the strategy. New technological developments in the communications field should also be considered (such as Local Area Networks — LANs and Integrated Services Digital Network — ISDN).

The corporate stand on centralized/decentralized processing also has implications in this section because it greatly influences the traffic pattern (both voice and data) that will travel over the network.

Personnel — If personnel with specialized technical skills must be recruited to develop and maintain primary processes, recruitment plans should be described, including the number and types of personnel as well as salary costs.

Education and Training — The users of the new systems will require education and training. A plan to perform these tasks should be outlined, and should include their associated costs. There may also be a need to educate the system development staff on new tools and techniques to be incorporated into the development environment to improve productivity.

Organizational Structure — The information systems department may require major organizational changes to effectively develop and support new systems. The department may need to establish data administration and data base administration functions if they do not already exist. To support end-user computing, the organization may need to create an information center or microcomputer consulting service.

Security and Control — The information strategy document is not complete without a section on the way security and control requirements change as a result of the new systems. On-line, real-time systems, the corporate data base, end-user computing, and the sheer power of new technology must all be considered from a security and control standpoint. Various additional measures may need to be implemented (such as a data security package, a data security officer, or a disaster recovery plan) if the systems to be developed extend corporate exposure beyond what the current system of security and control can handle.

Cost/Benefit Analysis

In addition the information strategy should include a summary of all costs and benefits of the primary and support processes for the period covered by the strategic plan.

Separation of Duties

Separation of duties is a traditional organizational control designed to ensure that one person cannot initiate, authorize and record a transaction and have sole control over the output from that transaction. The separation of duties is a control that will be seen in many of the building block elements of information systems and is most commonly associated with the protection of assets. In the case of information systems organization and administration, the separation of duties deals with the organizational issues that are involved in being effective and efficient as well as, to some extent, dealing with highlighting whether or not there are adequate human resources to get the job done.

Before the advent of information systems, the separation of duties was effectively implemented by placing specific responsibilities in distinct departments within the organization. In this way, it was intended that no one person could control all aspects of any part of the business. The introduction of information systems saw the emergence of a new department that was responsible for many of the functions that were previously performed by the various user departments. It is interesting to note that end-user computing has had the effect of returning much of this previously relinquished control back to the user department.

To preserve the principles of separation of duties within the information systems department, it is usual practice to have the department split in broad terms between departments responsible for production (i.e., computer operations and communications) and those responsible for system development and maintenance. The principle behind splitting the department this way is to prevent any one person from having both the knowledge and the opportunity to manipulate a production system in an unauthorized manner.

Also contributing to the proper division of duties in a traditional information systems environment is the user who performs checks and balances on the work performed by the department at both the production and development levels.

The underlying rationale for the separation of duties is the protection of corporate assets. Within the context of information systems processing, these assets consist of hardware, software and data. In the traditional information systems environment, the separation of duties across these three asset areas is typically implemented as follows:

Hardware — The purchase of hardware should be controlled through the corporate budgetary and purchasing process. Given the high dollar value of most hardware purchases in this type of environment, it would be very unusual to find the information systems manager authorizing and issuing checks for hardware. Although the manager approves the invoice, the actual issuance of the check should be controlled through the financial controls governing accounts payable. Recording for inventory and depreciation purposes would also be done at this time. Through this procedure, the organization is assured of proper inventory processing and financial recording of purchased hardware.

Software — Software is developed by the system development group, approved by the user and migrated into the production environment by a change control group in computer operations. Once in production, software can only be changed upon approval by the user followed by proper testing and sign-off by the user and computer operations.

Data — Production data is owned by the users and is maintained under the custodianship of computer operations. Development staff should have very restricted access to production data.

Figure 4.2 shows an information systems department organization chart that conforms to the objectives of separation of duties.

We have just been discussing the separation of duties in a traditional information systems environment. There is a clear contrast with the controls which have been put into place in this environment and the situation which all too often exists in an end-user computing environment. In an end-user situation, it is not unusual for the user to perform the analysis, development and operation for a particular system as well as being in sole possession of the output from that system. Does this situation violate the principles of separation of duties? Definitely. Is this a material violation? That depends on what business purpose the system is serving. The real problem is that this last question is rarely asked and acted upon where the answer is in the affirmative.

In addition to the problems just described, there is also the situation where the user is frequently given the authority to purchase hardware. This is justified on the basis that the per unit cost of microcomputers/workstations is not very high. There are several problems associated with this approach, especially in larger organizations. For example, there may be little consistency or compatibility between hardware units; single unit prices may be paid when substantial discounts are available; fixed asset records may not be properly maintained; and users may not know how to obtain maintenance and repair services. The subject of control over end-user computing will be addressed in more detail in Appendix 3.

Human Resources Policies and Procedures

In large organizations, the information systems department often has its own human resources group that is responsible for hiring, firing, rewarding and disciplining employees. In other organizations the information systems department follows the policies and procedures laid down for the rest of the organization. In the latter case there is usually a corporate human resources function serving the entire organization.

Regardless of the organization of the human resources function, there is a need to have formalized policies and procedures governing the management of personnel within the information systems department. In the discussions of assets managed by the information systems department, data is very topical and the hardware, software and communications used in providing information to the users are clearly important. However, the most important asset managed by the information systems department is its people. Without a system development and maintenance staff, computer operators, technical support staff and so forth, there will be no information for the users and the data held for the organization will have no integrity.

With the current and projected ongoing shortage of qualified information systems professionals, it is important that an organization have the facilities in place to attract and retain qualified personnel. Hiring policies must be established for an approved head count. The skills of the individuals required within the department need to be explicitly laid out. Plans to either hire new staff or retrain existing staff need to be in place to ensure that the required skill sets are available. When new staff members are to be hired there needs to be a formal screening and interview process along with full reference checks from previous employers or educators. Performance monitoring, reporting and feedback mechanisms need to be in place to communicate to the employees whether or not their performance is measuring up to expectations. Poor performance should be documented and explicit remedial action plans should be put in place to correct the problem. Salary reviews and benefit packages need to be reviewed regularly to ensure that they remain competitive with the information systems industry and with general practice within the organization's industry.

The causes of exposure that are addressed by human resource policies and procedures include ineffectiveness to the extent that the policies and procedures may be rewarding the wrong type of corporate behavior or stifling desired corporate behavior; inefficiency to the extent that it takes too long to put the right resources in place to get the job done; competition in that other organizations may hire away valuable staff members; and inadequate resources to the extent that the wrong people may be hired or kept on staff.

Project Management System

The essence of an effective project management system is to be able to track tasks at a detailed level, record and report on the time actually spent on each task versus the budget estimates for the same tasks and be able to take corrective action on a timely basis whenever necessary.

Budget figures for information systems projects are notoriously inaccurate and most frequently are set far too low. However, the decision to proceed with a project, to forecast revenues or to make commitments to the user groups is very often made on the basis of these budgeted figures. Therefore, it is necessary that any decisions made be tempered in the light of actual experience even if this means cancelling a project which is subsequently seen to have an unfavorable cost/benefit ratio. The standard time frame for this type of review should be monthly.

An adequate reporting mechanism is essential to effect budgetary control. A project can be thought of as having three distinct phases:

- A planning phase where the tasks to be performed are identified and estimated.
- An execution phase where the tasks are worked on and the actual time spent on each task is recorded along with a status report on the progress.
- A control phase where budget and actual numbers are compared and action is taken accordingly.

The planning phase of project management should produce a budget that is based on the activities to be completed and the associated number of days involved. The execution phase of a project should produce an information base that parallels the budgeted figures. However, if the information base is not organized to allow reporting along the same lines as the production of the budgeted figures, it will not be possible to *analyze* any discrepancies. This may seem obvious. However, it is not uncommon to find that the information base is constructed along quite different lines from the budgeted information. Whereas the budget information is tied to discrete tasks, the execution information base may be tied to the achievement of individual team members. Where more than one team member is working on a task, the project team tends to measure success by individual accomplishment rather than by the overall completion of the task. The execution information base is constructed accordingly, resulting in the "95 percent completion syndrome," (the task is reported as 95 percent complete as though this were an acceptable condition). As the project proceeds, more and more tasks fall into the 95 percent complete bracket. The unexpected and substantial overruns at the end of many projects are a result of having to go back and complete these unfinished tasks.

Possible solutions to this problem include:

1) The creation of a Project Control Office. The Project Control Office is an independent group that has the power to establish and enforce input reporting standards for both budgeted and actual information. The group also produces output reports that accurately reflect the status of the project at a stated time.

2) The creation and enforcement of individual timesheet reporting related to task completion. Figure 4.3 shows a fairly standard weekly timesheet for gathering information on time spent by project for each individual. However, this timesheet is a two-sided form with the reverse side (Figure 4.4) tying the timesheet information to the budget task lists.

3)   The maintenance of a three-month resource development schedule (see Figure 4.5) showing the anticipated time each individual is expected to spend on each active project over this period.   It should then be possible to tie these resource estimates back to the task lists.

4)   Production by the Project Control Office of a "Project Cost Summary" as shown in Figure 4.6. This summary shows the cost and time status for each authorized project on a budgeted versus revised basis. The revised figures are calculated from actual costs and time incurred.

The composition of this summary is as follows:

• **Original Implementation Date** — taken from the task sheets which were prepared during the planning phase.

• **Revised Implementation Date** — calculated from the timely completion or otherwise of the scheduled (or budgeted) tasks.

• **Original Completion Cost ($)** — taken from the task sheets which were prepared during the planning phase.

• **Resource Estimate Cost for the Period** — shows the amount of manpower (in monetary terms) budgeted to be spent in the last review period which is typically the month just ended.

• **Actual Cost for the Period** — shows the amount of manpower (in monetary terms) which was actually expended in the last review period.

• **Cost to Date** — shows the accumulation of actual costs for the project to the end of the last review period.

• **Override/Underride** — is an analysis (in monetary terms) of the impact of any improvement or slippage in the completion of scheduled tasks.

- **Revised Completion Cost** — is a recalculation on a month-to-month basis of the estimated completion cost. This takes into account the override/underride figures calculated on a monthly basis since the start of the project.

5)   Production by the Project Control Office of a "Monthly Time Analysis" as shown in Figure 4.7. The purpose of this analysis is to show, on a monthly basis, the actual time spent by each individual on particular projects versus the time estimated to be spent. The actual figures in this analysis are taken from the timesheets (Figure 4.3). The estimated figures come from the Resource Deployment Schedule (Figure 4.5) for the corresponding time frame. The information provided through this analysis can be used to determine whether any improvement or slippage in the task schedule is due to manpower allocation or some other reason (maybe the task is more time consuming and/or complex than originally estimated).

There are a number of software packages that automate the reporting mechanism just described.

The causes of exposure that are addressed by a project management system include cost overruns; inadequate information to the extent that the project management system is a key component of the management information system within the information systems department; and ineffectiveness to the extent that the actual cost of a project may end up costing more than any benefit to be derived.

Key Performance Indicators

Key performance indicators (KPIs) are the measurements used to determine whether or not the information systems department is doing a good job. Without some formal method of measurement, the evaluation of the information systems function within an organization is subjective at best. Nolan Norton & Company (now part of KPMG Peat Marwick) have been pioneers in the area of key performance indicators and coined the phrase "if you can measure it, you can manage it." The first decision to be made is what constitutes the key performance indicators for the information systems function. Once agreement has been reached on "what" is to be measured, the question is "how" are each of the performance indicators to be measured. The method of data capture, interpretation and reporting are key to the success of a management program using key performance indicators.

Each of the major areas within the information systems department should have its own key performance indicators. In addition, there may be a number of indicators that are common to all areas (for example, adherence to the financial operating and capital budget). Collectively, these indicators tell the tale of how well the information systems department is fulfilling its overall corporate mandate. Although each organization will have some unique requirements in terms of what it wants to measure and report on, there are a number of standard measurements which should be in place:

- **A method of measuring development activity and productivity.** Function point analysis as developed by Alan Albrecht of IBM is one approach of measuring this type of activity, including maintenance activity. Function point analysis is an empirical method of measurement based on what the functions developed within a system are "worth" to the users of the system. Based on the value of the function points assigned it is possible, through experience, to estimate what the develop time should be. The total number of function points earned by the information systems department can then be used as a basic measure of productivity. Increasing the number of function points earned per person means greater productivity is being achieved by the department.

- Another approach that has been used to measure development productivity is the number of lines of code per individual. This has always been an inexact measure and is gradually being replaced by function point analysis.

- Measuring the level of maintenance required on a new program code is a valuable method of determining the attention to detail given to a new system development and to system maintenance. All too often someone rushes a new system into production only to find that a disproportionate amount of maintenance work is required to keep the system up and running. Similarly, when maintenance is performed on an existing system, the quality is often not at an acceptable level. This means that further maintenance is required to fix the problem properly. Key performance indicators should capture both of these situations.

- **A method of measuring operational performance.** In this area, the timely delivery of reports to users is a valuable statistic. The average response time and the average availability time (or "up-time") for on-line systems is also important. Mean time between the failure of equipment is another key measurement in this area.

- The number of reports that are distributed, the number of lines printed, the number of on-line transactions processed and the volume of data stored and maintained may also be included in the measurement process.

- **A method of measuring financial performance.** Adherence to budget on an absolute basis and on a project basis are valid measures of financial performance. Expenditures on mainte-nance versus new development, preventative maintenance expenditures on equipment and the ratio of administrative (staff) costs to production (line) costs also provide useful infor-mation on performance.

- **As a measurement of human resource management.** Turnover ratios, average tenure with the organization, the number of training days per employee, and the dollar amount spent on training per employee are all worthwhile indicators of the adequacy of attention given to the management of human resources within the information systems department.

As a control, key performance indicators act on all the causes of exposure by providing information that will allow the detection of an actual or potential occurrence of any one of them. More specifically, key performance indicators detect actual or potential inefficiency by providing information on how well the work of the department is being done; competition to the extent that industry standards exist for the metrics captured so that comparisons in performance between organizations can be made; cost overruns by the financial information provided; and inadequate resources to the extent that deficiencies shown by the information provided lead to the conclusion that additional or different resources are required.

Education and Training

The world of information systems is changing at a fast pace. In order to keep up with the rate of change, education and training programs are required for all information systems staff members. A record indicating all training courses that have been attended should be maintained for each information systems employee. There should also be a proactive training program in place for each individual which shows the education and training budget for the information systems department. This education and training program should be in place for all employees within the department, from the CIO down to the most junior computer operator. Without a proactive plan, it is too easy to keep postponing education and training because of the occurrence of other priorities. Eventually the lack of education and training will cause the occurrence of other crises as a result of the staff not being able to perform at the level required for the work to be done. The training and education should be at both the technical and business levels corresponding to what is needed by the organization.

Education and training act on practically all causes of exposure related to information systems organization and administration. Without knowing the business needs of the organization, it is unlikely that the information strategy, which forms the basis for the work of the department, will correspond to the corporate business plan. Where there is a discrepancy between the two plans, the information systems department is not being totally effective. Inefficiency is almost certain to occur when the staff members are not fully trained in new tools and techniques. Competition from other organizations for valuable staff resources is often made on the basis of offering superior training programs and educational opportunities. Cost overruns will result from inefficiencies due to a lack of training. Inadequate human resources for the job at hand are an inevitable consequence of a lack of training and education.

TYPES OF EXPOSURE

Listed below are the types of exposure which can occur as a result of the inadequacy or failure of the system of control:

- Erroneous management decisions.
- Excessive costs.
- Loss or destruction of assets.
- Competitive disadvantage.

Erroneous Management Decisions

Almost by definition, ineffectiveness means erroneous management decisions. Ineffectiveness means doing the wrong things. Within the context of information systems this means building the wrong systems or not investing in new tools and techniques which will allow the systems to be developed sooner.

Excessive Costs

Excessive costs are a direct result of cost overruns and inefficiency. Inadequate resources and inadequate information also contribute to excessive costs.

Loss or Destruction of Assets

The assets we are talking about here are the human assets (or the staff members of the information systems department). Competition from other organizations for these assets, inadequate human resource policies and procedures and a lack of education and training all contribute to a loss in asset value.

Competitive Disadvantage

All of the causes of exposure that are listed as being applicable to information systems organization and administration will result in competitive disadvantage. Information systems provide a vehicle for being competitive. However, to do so requires the function to be effective, efficient, to control costs, employ adequate resources and generate adequate management information.

CONTROL EVALUATION TABLE

The Control Evaluation Table for information systems organization and administration is illustrated in Figure 4.8. The evaluation numbers shown are subjective and need to be adjusted based upon the conditions that exist in individual organizations. Note that, in practice, the completion of the Control Evaluation Table is in two parts:

- During detailed information gathering where the key to reliance on individual controls and the "overall control rating (design)" are determined (based on the review of available documentation and the results of personal interviews).

- During the execution of the audit program where, as a result of various audit tests, the strength of individual controls is fully assessed and the "overall control rating (tested)" is determined.

The Institute of Internal Auditors

AUDIT APPROACH

The objectives of auditing the information systems organization and administration are to ensure that the information systems department functions efficiently according to corporate goals and that it segregates incompatible staff functions by providing an appropriate separation of duties.

A review of the department's organization chart and job descriptions will help determine if proper separation of duties is in place. The conclusion arrived at from this review can be further verified from audits in each of the specific information systems areas.

In terms of whether or not the information systems department is functioning according to corporate goals, the auditor should review the information strategy against the template that is provided earlier in this chapter. Once the auditor is satisfied with the format of the information strategy the content needs to be compared to the corporate strategic business plan. Ideally, the information strategy is an integral part of the corporate strategy but this is often not the case. Once the auditor is satisfied that the information strategy properly reflects the corporate strategy then each of the individual audits of the various areas within information systems can be conducted within a known framework.

What happens if the organization does not have an information strategy in place? This is a question frequently asked by auditors when the subject of auditing to an information strategy is brought up. If there is no information strategy in place the auditor should take the time to create one. This is not to say that the auditor has the time to put together an information strategy to the level of detail that one would like to see. However, what is being suggested is that a broad overview of the information strategy should be prepared and then presented to information systems management and corporate management to gain their concurrence that this broad overview is a reasonable basis for future audit work. An important reason to create this information strategy is to develop an understanding of what the corporate philosophies are with respect to information systems. For example, the following questions are really corporate issues. There is no generic "right" answer but each organization will have an answer that is "right" for it. Without having thought out each of these issues ahead of time and arriving at a satisfactory conclusion, there is a real danger that when questions related to these issues come up on a day-to-day basis, they will be answered inconsistently which will ultimately lead to inefficiency and indecisiveness within the organization.

- Should systems be purchased whenever possible even though there may have to be compromises in functionality?

- Is custom software considered essential for competitive advantage?

- What is the role of end-user computing in the "big picture" of system development?

- Should strategic alliances with other organizations be considered when developing systems?

- Should the system be centralized or decentralized?

- Will the concept of departmental versus enterprise mainframes be used?

- What should the standard configuration for user workstations be?

- Are facilities management or service bureau operations a viable and/or acceptable alternative for computer processing?

Audit Frequency

The information strategy, organization chart and job descriptions should be reviewed at the start of each fiscal year and whenever a substantial change occurs.

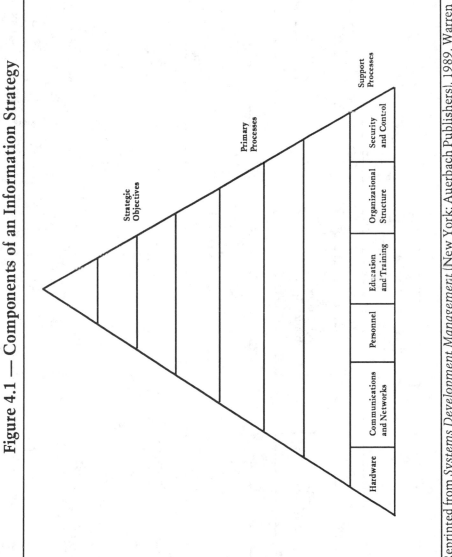

Figure 4.1 — Components of an Information Strategy

Strategic
Objectives

Primary
Processes

Support
Processes

Hardware

Communications
and Networks

Personnel

Education
and Training

Organizational
Structure

Security
and Control

Figure 4.2 — Organization Chart of an Information Systems Department

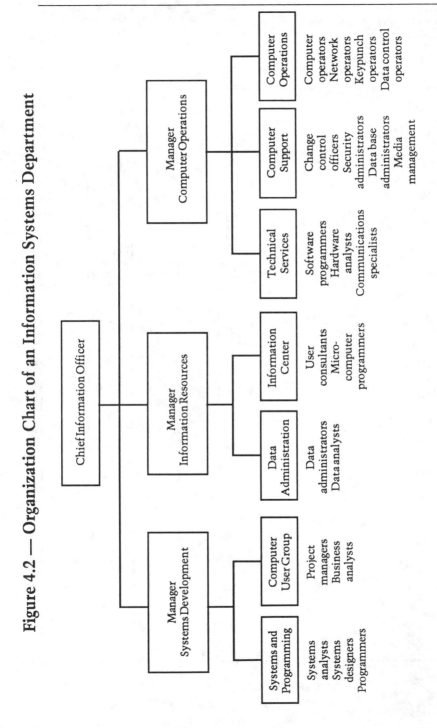

Reprinted from *Systems Development Management* (New York: Auerbach Publishers), 1988, Warren Gorham & Lamont Inc. Used with permission.

Figure 4.3 — Sample Weekly Time Sheet

Weekly Time Report		Page _____ of _____							
		Week Ending (Sun):							
Department		Name							
Project No.	Project Name	Mon	Tue	Wed	Thu	Fri	Sat	Sun	Total
	Subtotal								

Other Time

Code	Type								
	Education								
	Administration								
	Holiday								
	Excused Absence								
	Vacation								
	Sickness								
	Available Time								
	Audit								
	Subtotal								
Minimum Time to be Accounted for (hrs): Day: 7 Week: 35	Total Hours								

Figure 4.4 — Sample Deliverable Report

1. Estimated Deliverables for This Week: Estimated
Worker-days

_____

_____

_____

2. Actual Deliverables This Week: Actual
Worker-days

_____

_____

_____

3. Explanation of Differences Between Estimated and Actual Deliverables: (When an estimated deliverable has not been produced, an estimate of the additional worker-days required and the rescheduled date for completion of these deliverables should be included.)

_____

_____

_____

4. Anticipated Problems in Meeting Future Deliverables:

_____

_____

_____

Reprinted from *Systems Development Management* (New York: Auerbach Publishers), 1988, Warren Gorham & Lamont Inc. Used with permission.

Figure 4.5 — Three-Month Resource Deployment Schedule

Projects \ Project Members	Project A	Project B							Monthly Total by Person	
J. Smith									Month 1	
									Month 2	
									Month 3	
A.N. Other									Month 1	
									Month 2	
									Month 3	
Monthly Total by Project									Month 1	
									Month 2	
									Month 3	

Reprinted from *Systems Development Management* (New York: Auerbach Publishers), 1988, Warren Gorham & Lamont Inc. Used with permission.

Figure 4.6 — Project Cost Summary Form

PROJECT COST SUMMARY — PERIOD ENDING mm/dd/yy

Project	Original Implementation Date	Revised Implementation Date	Original Total Cost	Estimated Cost for the Period	Actual Cost for the Period	Cost to Date	Deviations	Revised Total Cost

Total Expenditures

Reprinted from *Systems Development Management* (New York: Auerbach Publishers), 1988, Warren Gorham & Lamont Inc. Used with permission.

Figure 4.7 — Monthly Time Analysis Form

Projects / Project Members	Project A	Project B							Monthly Total by Person	
J. Smith A									Actual Time	
J. Smith E									Estimated Time	
A.N. Other A										
A.N. Other E										
Monthly Total A									Actual Time	
Monthly Total E									Estimated Time	

Reprinted from *Systems Development Management* (New York: Auerbach Publishers), 1988, Warren Gorham & Lamont Inc. Used with permission.

Figure 4.8 — Control Evaluation Table
Information Systems Organization and Administration

CAUSES OF EXPOSURE

CONTROLS	Ineffectiveness	Inefficiency	Competition	Cost Overruns	Inadequate Resources	Inadequate Information
Long-range Planning	3	1	2	1	2	2
Separation of Duties	2	2			1	
Human Resources Policies and Procedures	2	1	2		3	
Project Management System	1	3		3		2
Key Performance Indicators	2	3	2	3	2	2
Education and Training		3	2	2	3	
Overall Control Rating - Design						
Overall Control Rating - Tested						

KEY TO RELIANCE ON CONTROL
3 - High reliance
2 - Moderate reliance
1 - Control has only a peripheral effect on the cause of exposure
Blank - No significant impact

KEY TO OVERALL CONTROL RATING
3 - Strong control
2 - Moderate but adequate control
1 - Inadequate control

EXPOSURES

EXPOSURES	Ineffectiveness	Inefficiency	Competition	Cost Overruns	Inadequate Resources	Inadequate Information
Erroneous Record Keeping	3	3				
Unacceptable Accounting	2	2				
Business Interruption	3		3			
Erroneous Management Decisions						3
Fraud and Embezzlement						
Statutory Sanctions						
Excessive Costs				3	2	2
Loss or Destruction of Assets					2	2
Competitive Disadvantage	3		3	2		2

KEY TO DEGREE OF CERTAINTY OF OCCURRENCE IN THE EVENT OF AN INADEQUATE CONTROL STRUCTURE
3 - Virtually certain
2 - Probable
1 - Possible but unlikely
Blank - Very unlikely

5
INFORMATION SYSTEMS SECURITY

INTRODUCTION

Information systems security can be defined as the standards and procedures that protect data against unauthorized disclosure, modification or destruction, whether accidental or intentional.

Within a computer environment, it is convenient to categorize data into three types:

Business data — comprises all the computer held information maintained by the various application systems and supported by the data base management system, where installed.

System data — comprises the vendor supplied operating system, utility programs (sorts, merges, copies), compilers, and the application systems developed or purchased to process raw business data into information to meet the business requirements of the organization.

Administrative data — is maintained by the data center in support of the various levels of computer processing. Password data sets, data dictionaries and data base definition tables fall into the category of administrative data.

Information systems security covers all three categories of data and there are clear interrelationships between each of the categories (administrative data defines the business data a user can access; the method of access is by using system data in the form of an application system).

It is difficult to deal with information systems security in isolation as many of the controls related to this subject area will be found embedded in the data base management system, in the telecommunications monitor, in individual application systems, in change control procedures and in the computer operations procedures. Although briefly described in this chapter each of these topics will be addressed in detail in subsequent chapters. This chapter concentrates on the organizational and procedural aspects of information systems security.

The first section of this chapter describes the control perspective for including information systems security as one of the basic building block elements of information systems. This section also describes the relevance of this subject area to the skill set and knowledge requirements of the Level 1 and Level 2 auditor. Causes of exposure are described, as are the more common types of control which act upon these causes of exposure. The types of exposure which may occur as a result of a deficiency or breakdown in the control structure are also discussed. Finally, the audits to be performed are described in terms of relevant objectives and frequency.

CONTROL PERSPECTIVE

Recently, much has been said and written about data as a corporate resource and the need for its proper management. Although data has always been a corporate resource, until recently it has been largely untapped. A resource is something that can be drawn upon to provide a desired product or service. Management has begun to realize the importance of having the right information at the right time in order to run the business efficiently and effectively. The accuracy, completeness, and timeliness of the information is therefore a major competitive issue. Accordingly, the information must be protected from abuses such as inadvertent or intentional misuse, disclosure, fraud and error.

SCOPE OF INFORMATION SYSTEMS SECURITY

Information systems security includes the following subtopics in its scope of activities:

- Physical security.
- Logical security.
- Administration.
- Ownership.
- Custody
- Accountability.
- Distribution.
- Table maintenance.
- Access levels.

Physical Security

Physical security is concerned with safeguarding the hardware used during the processing of data and the media on which the data reside. Physical security includes protection against fire, flood, explosion and malicious destruction. Physical security measures cover a broad spectrum of control objectives.   These control objectives can be grouped into four classifications:

- Temporary, partial loss (such as the loss of a disk drive).
- Temporary, total loss (a power failure).
- Permanent, partial loss (the accidental or intentional destruction of a data file).
- Permanent, total loss (the loss of the data center due to fire).

In terms of this chapter, the focus will be on temporary, partial and total losses affecting data held on computer readable media.

Physical security measures tend to be the most visible within the organization, and there may be a tendency to concentrate on the more glamorous (and expensive) of these measures to the exclusion of less ostentatious but equally effective ones. It should also be recognized that physical control is only the outer layer of control in the context of information systems security. For example, the installation of closed circuit television and complex mantraps will be meaningless if proper control is not maintained over the creation of backup files or if the administrative procedures for the handling and distribution of sensitive reports are inadequate.

A balanced approach to the introduction of physical security measures will ensure that the overall budget for information systems security is applied for maximum coverage. A threat analysis should be conducted which:

- Evaluates the physical threats to the organization's computing sites (ranging from the corporate data center to departmental machines to end-user workstation/PCs).

- Determines the probability of occurrence for each threat (or cause of exposure).

- Estimates the potential loss to which the organization is exposed in the event of an occurrence of one of the causes of exposure previously identified.

- Determines the annual loss expectancy by combining the estimates of the value of potential loss and probability of loss. A possible formula for this calculation was presented in Chapter 3.

When the threat analysis has been completed, management will have a clearer picture of the significant threats and will be able to assess the relevancy of various security measures in relation to their cost and their effect on the significant threats.

Prior to the advent of end-user computing, physical security measures were concentrated around the corporate data center. This situation has changed considerably with the increasing power, capability and functionality of the desktop workstation/PC. The emergence of cooperative processing where the system logic is contained both in the mainframe and at the workstation/PC level (transparent to the user) can only add to the need for physical measures at the end-user level.

Logical Security

Logical security refers to the software or hardware-wired controls built into the system to prevent or detect unauthorized entry into the system or unauthorized access to system, business or administrative data. Logical control ranges from the use of passwords to control access to the system, to cryptography techniques which ensure that sensitive data are only available in clear text mode to authorized systems that process those data.

Logical security tends to be a two-stage approach. First is the identification stage where potential users of the system identify themselves to the system. The user identification can be considered as non-secure information. The second stage is the authentication stage where the users must verify that they are who they say they are. The authentication method must be through a means which can accurately verify the true identity of the person who is trying to gain access to the system. The most common form of authentication method is the use of passwords. Passwords have proved to be an unreliable form of authentication control unless supported by strong compensating controls in the form of management directives on the procedures for keeping passwords confidential and for changing passwords at regular intervals. However, there have been a number of recent developments in the area of biometric technology such as fingerprint scanning, speech recognition, retina scanning and signature verification that show promise in this area of personnel authentication. The use of "smart card" technology will also help in authenticating the identification of an individual.

Administration

To be effective, logical security relies on the integrity of administrative data and surrounding administrative procedures. The identification record(s) held for each user of the system provides a blueprint of the level of access and functionality allowed to that user. Ensuring the accuracy and validity of the contents of these records is fundamental to the ability of the logical security methods and procedures to function as intended.

The primary organizational function having responsibility for the integrity of administrative data and the surrounding administrative procedures is typically that of the data security officer. When this function does not exist within an organization, there may be an administrative function set up within the information systems department or within individual user departments to perform the responsibility of setting users up on the system and specifying the level of access and functionality each user is permitted. The proper separation of duties is a key consideration in deciding who should perform these administrative functions and set up the administrative data records. It is essential that the individual who is responsible for establishing the administrative data records does not have the ability to also benefit from using critical access levels and functions within the system.

Two other organizational functions that have administrative responsibilities for information system security should be mentioned at this time. The data administrator and data base administrator have critical administrative roles over the use of business data. In a data base environment, the intention is to separate data from its uses. This is an extension of the idea of focusing on the data rather than on the individual processes that use any particular item of data. Data independence has always been considered to be a major selling point by data base vendors but, in reality, the data structures in many data base management systems were somewhat inflexible. However, emerging relational data base systems show great promise in making data independence a reality. What this means is that the definition of data is no longer embedded in individual systems. It is maintained in tables which describe to the data base management system how the data is to be interpreted and presented to individual systems. The data administrator is responsible for the preparation of the corporate data model and the logical view of data. It is the data administrator who allows application systems to have access to individual data elements. The data base administrator is a technical function with responsibility for the physical storage of data and for making this data readily available to those who are authorized to use it.

Change control procedures that deal with system data can also be classified as administrative procedures within the framework of information systems security. Change control procedures are discussed in detail in Chapter 7.

The data security officer (in whatever corporate guise the position comes in), data administrator and data base administrator are collectively responsible for ensuring that the administration of the information system security program is effective and that access to corporate data is approved and appropriate for the circumstances.

Ownership

The owner of a data element is responsible for the accuracy and timeliness of that data element. This implies that the owner has update (read and write) authority for this data element. With the advent of normalized relational data bases, the idea of building a corporate data base to communicate the data elements being maintained, and the use of a data dictionary to provide data about data (or meta data), it should be possible to keep only one version of a data element to be shared across all application systems. This is in sharp contrast to the situation of a few years ago when data elements were embedded in individual application systems resulting in the same data element being held multiple times with no link to ensure consistency between the values in each application system.

Where the data element is held once in the corporate data base, it should be possible to attach ownership. With ownership comes the responsibility of deciding on the level of access that is available to other users. In a perfect world, other users of this data element should only have read access. This would ensure that only one copy of any data element was maintained and that the content of the element was completely current. Unfortunately, this is frequently not the case. There are many data elements that are used extensively by many departments within an organization (for instance, a client's name and address). It is not always apparent which department owns the data element. It may be that one department is responsible for the initial loading of the element while another department is responsible for updating the element and yet another department has responsibility for deleting the element. When there is a dispute over data ownership, the data administrator should act as the arbitrator.

Custody

Physical possession of the data elements on computer readable media (or custody) needs to considered separately from the ownership issue. Whereas the ownership issue deals with the content of the data element, the custody issue is concerned with the physical preservation of the data element; the value of the content is of no consequence. Custody means protecting the data from unauthorized access, disclosure, modification or destruction, whether accidental or intentional. The level of custodial control over data varies in organizations from the installation and use of a complete data protection packages (ACF2, RACF) to no formal protection at all. The latter situation is surprisingly common and is becoming even more of a problem because of the growing use of end-user computing and distributed processing.

The custodian of most of the corporate data base will be computer operations. With the trend toward distributed data bases, there may also be a custodial function in the end-user departments.

Accountability

As just discussed, there are various organizational units and functions that are responsible for the overall quality of information systems security within an organization. The question remaining is whether these organizational units and functions are responsible for the overall quality of information systems security.

Accountability stems from an understanding that the results achieved are going to be used in the measurement of performance and the issuance of rewards. The organization needs to take the ""big picture" view of information systems security and ensure that the responsibility and accountability is assigned to the proper individuals and departments for each of the elements of information systems security (physical, logical, administration, ownership and custody). Job descriptions, key performance indicators and the reward system all need to reflect the fact that information systems security is a key accountability. The CIO has the responsibility for putting this "big picture" perspective in place within the information systems department and for relaying the message to other executives within the organization who may also have some level of accountability in this area because of end-user computing or departmental computing.

Distribution

Information should be distributed to the location where it is to be used. The form of distribution may be from a central location, either through the means of on-line access or via printed reports. Alternatively, the data elements themselves may be distributed to departmental machines or workstations/PCs for immediate use by a local user. The emergence of cooperative processing takes this latter approach one step further in that the information presented to the user may be made up of data that is stored locally combined with data sent down a communications line from a central computer.

In addition to the technological implication of distributing information, there is also the administrative side that deals with the policies and procedures surrounding who should have access to what information. In many cases, organizations have concentrated their security efforts on protecting data resident on computer readable media and have ignored what happens to the information once it is printed and ready for distribution. Distribution lists, filing and disposal procedures should be in place for reports produced from individual application systems. In the case of data that is distributed to remote locations, policies and procedures should be put into place to ensure the currency and relevancy of this data.

Table Maintenance

Many of the parameters and options used to maintain information systems security are held in tables. These tables should be updated periodically to reflect current requirements. The content of these tables is crucial to the overall integrity of information systems security and must be protected against unauthorized access and/or manipulation.

Access Levels

Access levels are intended to provide a level of security based on the following criteria:

- Access authorization is user based.

- Access by the user is limited to information that is required on a need-to-know basis as defined within the organization.

- All attempts at unauthorized access are detected, rejected and reported.

The growing awareness of the need for comprehensive treatment of information systems security has led to the introduction of several access control software packages designed around these access control objectives. The classification of users by access level and the classification of data according to their relative need for security are two important administrative functions which must be put in place in concert with the implementation of an access control software package.

Another major issue concerning access level is the question of read versus write access to data. As discussed in the section on ownership, this can be a complicated issue particularly when more than one department maintains a single data element. However, these access levels need to be determined and input to the access control software package.

LEVEL 1 AUDITOR — SKILL AND KNOWLEDGE OBJECTIVES

Overall Objective

Know the control objectives for information systems security, the different levels of control which can be used and the audit processes used to attest to the adequacy of these controls.

Physical Security

Know the physical controls which can be expected in an information security system and be able to execute an audit program to assess the adequacy of controls in this area.

Logical Security

Know the underlying principles behind the need for logical security and be able to identify the various levels of logical security that are necessary for overall protection.

Administration

Know the administrative responsibilities that are associated with the custody and ownership of the various aspects of information systems security. Be able to execute an audit program to attest to the adequacy of the administrative controls on place within the organization.

Ownership

Know the concept of data ownership (including those of limited right of ownership) and be able to audit the criteria used to determine ownership and the privileges that accompany ownership (rcad, write, update).

Custody

Know the organizational functions charged with custodial responsibility for information systems security and the objectives that are to be achieved by these organizational functions. Be able to perform an audit of these organizational functions to ensure that the custodial aspects of information systems security are being complied with.

Accountability

Know the division of accountabilities relating to information systems security and be able to perform an organizational audit to attest to the fact that *all* accountability has been correctly assigned.

Distribution

Know the need for organizational policies and procedures regarding distribution of information. Be able to audit the policies and procedures in place for adequacy against accepted standards and for compliance.

Table Maintenance

Know which of the information systems security measures are controlled by parameters and options contained in tables. Be able to execute an audit program that is designed to attest to the adequacy of the parameters and options selected and to the control over access to changing these tables.

Access Levels

Know the philosophy behind the allocation of various access levels related to information systems security. Be able to execute an audit program to attest to the adequacy of the policies and procedures governing the setting of access levels and the adequacy of the administrative procedures surrounding the actual establishment of these access levels.

LEVEL 2 AUDITOR — SKILL AND KNOWLEDGE OBJECTIVES

Overall Objectives

Be able to structure audits of all aspects of information systems security. Demonstrate a solid understanding of the individual components that comprise information systems security and the interactions between these components.

Physical Security

Be able to structure audits to fully assess the adequacy of physical security. Be able to extrapolate the principles of physical security to an end-user computing environment.

Logical Security

Show an understanding of the technology in place within the organization to effect an adequate level of logical security and be able to structure audits to attest to the adequacy of logical control.

Be able to relate any weaknesses identified in the system of internal control to the applications most affected. Be able to provide management with an assessment of the implications of control weaknesses to these applications.

Administration

Understand the inter-relationships and responsibilities between the various organizational functions responsible for information systems security (Data Security Officer, Data Administrator, Data base Administrator, etc.). Be able to put together an audit program that properly attests that the individual workings of each group add up to an adequate level of information systems security.

Ownership

Understand the role played by technology in the enforcement of the rules of ownership. Be able to structure an audit program that attests to the adequacy of the rules and the technology as well as the degree of compliance with the stated intent of the rules of ownership.

Custody

Understand the technology used in the execution of the custodial responsibilities relating to information systems security and be able to design an audit program to properly attest to the adequacy of the technology in the role it is designed to play.

Accountability

Can construct audits which address the accountability issue from a number of different perspectives (such as organizational, technical, administrative). Be able to factor the results from these audits into an overall conclusion on the adequacy of the allocation of accountability.

Distribution

Understand the technology used to control the distribution of information. Be able to factor in objectives dealing with distribution control when conducting audits of this technology.

Table Maintenance

Know where all of the tables are located, what their primary purpose and functions are, and the control implications (at least in broad terms) of each of the parameters and options.

Be able to design an audit program which can attest to the adequacy of the parameters and options selected within a particular table and to the control over access to changing these tables.

Access Levels

Understand the technology that controls access levels. Be able to design an audit program that attests to compliance between policies and procedures and what has been entered into the system through the use of the technology.

CAUSES OF EXPOSURE

The causes of exposure in the area of information systems security are as follows:

- Loss of data.

- Distortion of data.

- Disclosure of data.

- Unavailability of data.

- Outdated information.

- Human error.

Loss of Data

Loss of data ranges from a dropped block of data due to a hardware malfunction all the way to a complete loss of all data due to a catastrophic occurrence at the central data center.

All stored data (business, system and administrative) should be safeguarded until deleted or moved to archival storage.

Distortion of Data

Distortion of data means that the data being maintained is different from the data that was supposed to have been maintained. There could be a number of reasons for the distortion of data. It may be that an incorrect version of the data file was loaded; a data file may have been corrupted by an application system or a hardware failure; or the data may have been deliberately corrupted by someone who was able to gain access to the data base.

Disclosure of Data

As a corporate asset, data should be accorded the same protection as other assets. It is unlikely that an organization would condone the unauthorized use of its assets. Similarly, data must be protected against misuse. It is through unauthorized disclosure that data can be misused.

Data should be available only to those who are authorized to receive and use the data. Once received, the data should not be disclosed to those who do not have a right to it. The inadvertent or deliberate disclosure of data by someone who had a right to the data to someone who was able to use the information to the organization's disadvantage is a common cause of exposure.

Unavailability of Data

Information systems security is concerned with ensuring that data is protected against unauthorized disclosure, modification or destruction, whether accidental or intentional. There is an implied assumption in this concern — that data should be available to those who are authorized to receive it and that this very availability leads to certain causes of exposure which need to be controlled. Not only must the information systems security measures control the availability of data, they must also ensure that the data is available in the first place. Unavailability of data may be as a result of a loss of data for reasons previously defined. It may also be the case that the data exists but has not been set up to be accessed by those who have a legitimate need for access. Unavailability in this situation may simply be the result of having set the wrong access levels for particular individuals.

Alternatively, the problem may be that the data has been classified incorrectly. These problems are usually easily remedied through amendments to the access control software. However, the problem may be the result of a lack of a sufficient access method to the data in question due to poor data design and/or poor information reporting capabilities. In this situation the organization may be severely handicapped in its use of computer-held data.

Outdated Information

If data is worth protecting, it must be current and accurate. The accuracy element has been discussed in the section on the distortion of data. In terms of the information being current there are a number of considerations. Many systems today are on-line, real-time systems. This means that the information must be up-to-date at all times. Part of the security measures which must be put in place for all data are those relating to backup and recovery. Where an on-line transaction does not properly complete or where a systems problem subsequently develops, there should be a roll back and roll forward process which minimizes any lost data. The users of the system must also be made aware of any lost transactions. Many of the controls in this area belong in the data base management system and the application system. However, there are also procedural controls which must be in place to ensure that the correct files are used for recovery and that there are backup files available in the event that live data must be re-created.

Human Error

Training and the existence of adequate, documented procedures are essential in the area of information systems security. As previously discussed, information systems security is a complex area comprising a tapestry of different control considerations. This chapter has been dealing with information systems security in a broad conceptual sense. There are many different detailed facets of the subject area which must be understood and mastered if an organization is to have an effective program of information systems security. Given the complexity and importance of this subject area, human error is a major factor which must be addressed in the control structure.

CONTROLS

Applicable controls intended to prevent, detect and/or correct the causes of exposure just described as relevant to the area of information systems security are as follows:

- Environmental controls.
- Operating controls.
- Organizational controls.
- Education program.
- Access controls.
- Policies and procedures.

Environmental Controls

Environmental controls are designed to act on the physical loss of data. There are a number of environmental "causes" which can result in the physical loss of data. Fire is one of these environmental causes. Fire precautions can be considered in the categories of those that detect the fire's occurrence or the imminence of a fire, and those that endeavor to correct the situation with a minimum of damage. Within each of these categories the controls can be further broken down into those that are people dependent and those that are mechanical.

Preventative Controls

- The materials used in the construction of the data center should have an adequate fire rating.
- The design of the data center should minimize the possibility of fire spreading from one area to another.
- Administrative procedures should be in place to avoid the risk of fire (for example, the storage and disposal of combustible materials).

Detective Controls

- Detective controls should be designed to detect the early signs of a fire (such as excessive heat and smoke), activate the corrective device, and provide an audible danger warning to employees.

- Heat detectors, smoke detectors, and manually activated fire alarms should be placed in strategic areas within the data center.

- Administrative procedures should describe the people-dependent functions to be activated in the event of a fire (such as the identity, role and responsibilities of the fire marshall).

Corrective Controls — Mechanical

- Water is still widely used as an extinguishing agent for fire and can be applied at the scene of the fire by means of a sprinkler system that is activated by the detection controls mentioned before. The advantage of using water in fire fighting is its low cost relative to other means.

- Halon and carbon dioxide are gases used in fire fighting especially where electrical equipment may be involved. The use of carbon dioxide must be carefully controlled and the area evacuated before its use because of its harmful effects on people. Halon, when used in small quantities, does not have this harmful effect on people but is very expensive to use.

Corrective Controls — People Dependent

- Personnel should be trained in what to do in case of fire.

- Fire marshalls should be appointed for each department or functional area and assigned specific responsibilities for their area.

- Emergency exits and all fire fighting equipment should be clearly posted.

- The fire department should be invited to review the fire precautions within the data center. Since the fire department may be called in to fight a fire, it would be advantageous if they were

The Institute of Internal Auditors

familiar with the layout of the data center and knew what fire fighting facilities were readily available.

- After the fire has been brought under control and extinguished, there should be clearly defined procedures for getting the data center back into production status.

In addition to the controls for the prevention, detection and correction of fire, there must also be ancillary controls to recover from the smoke and water damage which accompanies fire damage.

Power Supply

Computer hardware is built to withstand variances in the power supply, but only within certain tolerances depending on the particular piece of hardware. A continuous power supply can be effected by using a bank of batteries designed to smooth out variances in the power supply. When the power supply is completely shut down, the power from the batteries will take over, enabling an orderly shutdown of the equipment or the activation of an alternate power supply such as an oil fired generator. Other less expensive methods for dealing with a sudden surge include voltage regulators. Again, data center management must take into consideration what it is trying to protect and evaluate the exposures before deciding what specific protection is required.

Insurance

Insurance should be considered as a component of an integrated system of security and not as a substitute. Security plans, even good ones, cannot possibly cover every eventuality. Insurance should be taken out as a conscious effort to cover exposures which cannot be totally eliminated by other means and whose cost of occurrence would be too high to absorb. Many types of insurance policies are available, each with its own limitations and endorsements. Generally speaking, the wider the coverage, the greater the cost. Listed below are high-level descriptions of the types of policies that are available:

- Policies to cover physical damage or destruction (through fire, flood or storm) of the hardware and computer readable media (such as tapes and disk).

- Policies to cover the cost of recreating data (as opposed to simply replacing the media on which the data were held) are available at additional cost.   Adequate backup procedures (discussed under "operational controls") including the use of off-site storage, can reduce the need for a policy of this type.

- Policies to cover the loss of business due to an insured peril. An organization may suffer from severe competitive disadvantage if its data center is put out of action for an extended period of time due to fire. Contingency planning can effectively counter this eventuality and may either nullify the need for such a policy or substantially reduce the premiums.

Again, it should be stressed that insurance is only part of the environmental control program. The premiums, and indeed the availability of insurance, will depend on the other components of the program.

Operating Controls

Operating controls include backup and recovery procedures, retention policies and good housekeeping controls.

Back-up and Recovery Procedures

All files should be backed up on a regular basis. Application system design has a partial responsibility in this regard:

- In the case of on-line systems there is a need for a transaction log to be maintained so that in the event of a systems failure there can be a re-creation of all master and transaction files up to the point of a failure in the system, or as close as possible.

The Institute of Internal Auditors

- In the case of long-running batch jobs there needs to be a policy on checkpoint and restart times so that in the event of a systems failure while the job is running, it is not necessary to restart the job from the beginning.

The computer operations staff is also responsible for backing up files on a regular basis. This will enable them to respond in the event of a disaster that is more global than a malfunction within a single application (such as the crash of a disk pack).

Retention Policies

Typically, disk packs are backed up to tape on a daily basis and the tapes are stored off-site in a vault of some type. The tapes are rotated on a cyclical basis depending on the needs of the organization. A monthly basis is not an unusual time frame; the month-end backup tapes are then retained for a period of 12 months.

Also of interest in the area of retention policies is the use of partitioned data sets which tells the operating system which files are to be used for that day's processing. Once again, a cyclical approach is used but in this situation the cycle time is usually one week. The advantage of this type of file retention is that reruns can be executed quickly through the use of parameters to tell the system which version of the file(s) to use.

Good Housekeeping

The reasons for good housekeeping are innumerable and are fairly obvious:

- Large amounts of paper stored in the computer room can create a fire hazard.

- Food and drink should not be allowed in the computer room.

- Operational problems and security exposure can result from the improper filing of tapes and disks. If files are continually misplaced, it may take a long time to realize that a file has actually been lost or stolen.

- Management's tolerance of poor housekeeping practices is not conducive to establishing the level of awareness about information systems security that is desirable among employees in a computer environment.

Organizational Controls

In the case of information systems security, organizational controls are synonymous with adequate separation of duties. Within an organization, there are a number of functions which should be in place to effect adequate organizational control over the processing of data into information. These functions include:

- Data control.
- Production control.
- Computer operations.
- Data administration.
- Data base administration.
- Data security officer.

Data Control

This function is responsible for ensuring that all the data necessary to run the various batch application systems is present and that all output information received from the system is complete and distributed properly. Because the data control group is responsible for gathering the input data for many systems, adequate, up-to-date data control manuals are essential for each system. Each data control manual should state the source of the various forms of input, the media involved, and the time frame in which such input should be available.

Production Control

Production control is responsible for job scheduling, job submission and media management (for instance, allocating disk space, compressing scratched files and deleting unused files). Job scheduling may be done manually or with an automated scheduling package. Effective scheduling is essential if the computer resources are to be used at optimum efficiency.

Computer Operations

This function is responsible for monitoring the execution of the various tasks operating in the computer, providing the resources (tapes, disks, and special stationery) requested by application systems, and correcting any problems during the execution of those systems.

Data Administration

The data administration function links the computer systems and the business functions they are designed to serve. The group responsible for data administration builds and maintains the corporate data model. A properly constructed data model places the systems to be developed into a proper business perspective. This model is also instrumental in the preparation of the information systems department's strategic plan.

Data Base Administration

The data base administration group translates the logical view of the corporate data model (as developed by the data administrator) into a physical form on computer-readable media, which supports the required business functions. The data base administration group is also concerned with the integrity of the data contained in the data base, the performance issues relating to data access, and the various security issues associated with the data base. This includes backup and recovery as well as the technical details for interfacing the DBMS across the various hardware that may exist.

Data Security Officer

The data security officer function is responsible for setting up the access levels that dictate what data an individual should be able to read, write and/or update. The data security officer is also responsible for ensuring that the day-to-day use of data is consistent with the policies and procedures set by the organization. The data security officer may well have had significant input into what these policies and procedures contain. Reports of violations should be routed to the data security officer for follow-up action. The placement of the data security officer function varies between organizations. Where an official position exists, the data security officer usually reports in through the data center manager. However, in many organizations, the data security officer's responsibilities are contained in the job descriptions of various administrative functions within the user departments. Either scenario is acceptable assuming that the policies and procedures to be enforced are clearly defined and the mandate to enforce is clearly stated.

Education Program

The personnel within the information systems department and the various user departments serviced by the computer need to be made aware of what information systems security means to the organization, and that people are perhaps the most important component of any security system.

- Many cases of unauthorized disclosure of information have been caused by the careless actions of authorized recipients of this information.

- Password systems are meaningless unless the employees are made aware of the reasons for maintaining the confidentiality of their password.

The Institute of Internal Auditors

- The most elaborate entry systems are meaningless when employees exercise "common courtesy" and hold the door open for the person following to enter into secured areas.

Employees must learn the requirements of an information security system. They must also understand that disciplinary action will be taken against anyone who violates the organization's policies and procedures. These policies and procedures should be clearly stated in writing and should be readily available to all employees. New employees should be made aware of the organization's requirements and should read the appropriate documentation. Existing employees should be given refresher courses and be kept up-to-date with any enhancements or changes in the security program. One way to ensure that employees are periodically reminded of the information systems security requirements of the organization is to ask them to complete a staff declaration to the effect that they are aware of the security requirements and have no knowledge of any breach in them. The staff declarations could be completed on an annual basis, perhaps on the individual's anniversary of starting work with the organization, or at whatever frequency is deemed necessary.

Access Controls

Access controls can be thought of as having three levels:

- A general access to the system.
- A direct access to specific items of data.
- An access route to specific items of data that are application system controlled.

Passwords are the typical control mechanism used to ensure that a general access to the system is allowed only to those who are authorized. Password validation comes in two parts — an identification phase and an authentication phase. A non-secure user identification is used for the identification phase and a secure password is used for the authentication phase. The general access password simply allows the user into the system. The other two levels of access control determine where the user can go and what the user can access beyond this initial entry point.

The access control software tied to the data base management system is the second level of access control. Each data element is assigned a security level as is each user of the system. The access control software ensures that the security levels are compatible when a request is issued from the user to access particular data elements. This level of access control will be discussed further in Chapter 13.

Within individual application systems, the user is allowed access to approved functions and to approved data elements. What the user can do within these functions and with these data elements is also controlled by the application system. The access control software discussed above determines the access level allowed to the application system.

Policies and Procedures

Information systems security is a complex area and covers a broad scope of activities and responsibilities. As a result, it is usually difficult for an employee who is not specialized in this area to have an intuitive appreciation of what should be done to ensure that data is properly secured against unauthorized modification, destruction or disclosure. It is for this reason that clearly documented policies and procedures must be in place and must be communicated to all employees. It is these policies and procedures which form the cornerstone of the education program previously described.

TYPES OF EXPOSURE

Listed below are the types of exposure which can occur as a result of the inadequacy or failure of the system of control to prevent the occurrence of a cause of exposure in the area of information systems security.

Erroneous Record Keeping

Given that the financial accounting record keeping for many organizations is one of the key business applications run on the computer, any loss of data, distortion of data, outdated information and human error would almost certainly result in erroneous record keeping.

Unacceptable Accounting

The backup transactions to the general accounting records of the organization are frequently held on computer-readable media. The loss or distortion of these records with no ability to recover them could lead to unacceptable accounting in that the auditor would be unable to attest to the accuracy of the general accounting records. A situation where data is unavailable and information is outdated may also result in timing and accrual differences in the financial records.

Business Interruption

For many organizations, particularly in the services sector, the provision of information is the business that they are in. Without complete, accurate and timely information there would inevitably be business interruptions to some extent. These interruptions could range from the inability to respond to a client's request for information to a complete inability to function as an organization (such as a result of losing accounts receivable and/or accounts payable information). The loss of data, distortion of data, unavailability of data, outdated information and human error could all lead to business interruption.

Erroneous Management Decisions

One of the principal causes of erroneous management decisions is inaccurate, incomplete, or out-of-date information. In looking at the causes of exposure in the area of information systems security, the loss of data, distortion of data, unavailability of data and outdated information could all lead to erroneous management decisions.

Fraud

The distortion and disclosure of data could lead to fraud where the perpetrator was able to translate the transgression into personal gain.

Statutory Sanctions

Many organizations have regulatory reporting requirements that must be met. The loss of data, distortion of data, unavailability of data and outdated information could all lead to late filing of the required reports with the attendant risk of statutory sanctions.   Filing incorrect and/or misleading reports due to outdated information or human error could also lead to statutory sanctions.

Excessive Costs/Deficient Revenues

In the area of information systems security, excessive costs may be the result of too much control as opposed to insufficient control. The area of physical controls is one that requires management attention to ensure that the dollars spent are commensurate with the risks involved.   A threat analysis and business case are important in justifying the expenditures in this area.

The loss of accounts payable and/or accounts receivable information could certainly lead to excessive costs (for example, paying accounts payable more than once and having to recover the additional payments) and/or deficient revenues (not being in a position to collect accounts receivable in a timely manner).

Loss or Destruction of Assets

Data is a corporate resource and, as such, is a major asset of the organization.   Any exposure which interferes with the value of corporate data is contributing to the loss or destruction of an asset. The value of information is measured in terms of completeness, accuracy, availability and timeliness.

Competitive Disadvantage

Information is clearly a major competitive tool. Any reduction in the timeliness, availability, completeness or accuracy of information could lead to a competitive disadvantage. Similarly the disclosure of sensitive information to a competitor could also result in competitive disadvantage. For organizations in the service sector, information may be the product that is offered to the client. In a manufacturing organization, information may drive the assembly lines and control the management of inventory. Any reduction in efficiency, either operational or cost, may lead to a competitive disadvantage in the long run.

CONTROL EVALUATION TABLE

The Control Evaluation Table for information systems security is given in Figure 5.1. As is the case with all of the sample control evaluation tables presented in the text, the evaluation numbers are subjective and need to be adjusted based on the conditions which exist in individual organizations. Note that, in practice, the completion of the Control Evaluation Table is in two parts:

- During detailed information gathering where, from the review of available documentation and the results of personal interviews, the key to reliance on individual controls and the "overall control rating (design)" are determined.

- During the execution of the audit program where, as a result of various audit tests, the strength of individuals controls is fully assessed and the "overall control rating (tested)" is determined.

AUDIT APPROACH

Having said that it is difficult to isolate information systems security from the controls that are inherent in the data base management system and within individual application systems, there are three formal audits that can be conducted to determine the adequacy of information systems security as it applies to the overall environment within which data is maintained and offered to the end user. Two of these formal audits (the data center audit and a data security audit) will be discussed in this chapter. The third audit concerns change control procedures and will be the topic of Chapter 7.

Data Center Audit

The data center is the custodian of the organization's data and is responsible for the protection of these data against loss, distortion and destruction. In a batch environment the data center also has the responsibility for the completeness of data submission to individual applications. In an on-line environment, the data center has responsibility for network operations. The on-line responsibilities will be discussed in Chapter 15.

The "data center audit" is typically a compliance audit based on the policies, practices and procedures that are stipulated in the data center manual. This audit is concerned with the control being exercised over the assets of the organization (such as the physical hardware assets and the software data assets) and the management of those assets in the provision of application system services to the organization. The data center audit encompasses the various departments within the computer operations group (technical services, computer support and computer operations — see Figure 4.2 in Chapter 4) along with an assessment of the organizational controls and physical security applicable to the data center.

The objectives of a data center audit include ensuring that:

- Adequate segregation of duties exists within the organizational structure of the data center.

- Physical security measures are adequate and properly utilized to ensure that processing continues.

- The data center provides timely, complete and accurate processing of data.

- The controls over the receipt, processing and dispatch of work provide for secure processing and handling of data.

- Management is provided with sufficient information to manage the data center effectively.

The data center audit is usually conducted annually. The effectiveness and coverage of this audit can be supplemented between audits by additional testing that is carried out when individual applications are being audited.

Data Security Audit

To conduct a data security audit, the auditor needs evidence that an orderly approach has been taken to data security. The approach taken must be flexible enough to allow the organization to adjust to a changing business environment, whether these changes occur at the application system or at the technical environment level.

An orderly approach to data security implies that the organization has assessed what data it needs to protect and has instituted the appropriate controls (both technical and procedural) to address these identified needs. The data security audit is directed primarily at the level and adequacy of the access controls that are present within the system software, any access control software and within the data security administration procedures exercised within the computer operations area.

In the case of system software controls and access software controls, the services of a Level 3 auditor (a technical specialist in these software products) may be required.

A data security audit should be conducted annually or whenever a major change occurs in this area.

Figure 5.1 — Control Evaluation Table
Information Systems Security

CAUSES OF EXPOSURE

CONTROLS	Loss of Data	Distortion of Data	Disclosure of Data	Unavailability of Data	Outdated Information	Human Error
Environmental Controls	3		2	3		
Operating Controls	3		1	2	3	
Organizational Controls	2	2	2		2	2
Education Program	1	1	3			3
Access Controls	3	3	2	1		
Policies and Procedures			2			3
Overall Control Rating - Design						
Overall Control Rating - Tested						

EXPOSURES

	Loss of Data	Distortion of Data	Disclosure of Data	Unavailability of Data	Outdated Information	Human Error
Erroneous Record Keeping	3	3		2	2	3
Unacceptable Accounting	2	2		1	1	1
Business Interruption	3	2	1	3	2	1
Erroneous Management Decisions	2	3	2	2	2	2
Fraud and Embezzlement		3	2			
Statutory Sanctions	1	1		1	1	
Excessive Costs	2	2		1		2
Loss or Destruction of Assets	3	3	1	2		
Competitive Disadvantage	2	2	3	2	2	

KEY TO RELIANCE ON CONTROL
3 - High reliance
2 - Moderate reliance
1 - Control has only a peripheral effect on the cause of exposure
Blank - No significant impact

KEY TO OVERALL CONTROL RATING
3 - Strong control
2 - Moderate but adequate control
1 - Inadequate control

KEY TO DEGREE OF CERTAINTY OF OCCURRENCE IN THE EVENT OF AN INADEQUATE CONTROL STRUCTURE
3 - Virtually certain
2 - Probable
1 - Possible
Blank - Very unlikely

6
SYSTEM DEVELOPMENT

INTRODUCTION

System development has essentially three components: people, plans and processes. To be successful, an organization must find a way of pulling these diverse entities into a cohesive whole so that systems can be developed to meet the needs of the end users, on time and within budget.

When viewed in its traditional role, system development was concerned with operational systems, processing one transaction at a time. The users of the systems were at the clerical, supervisory and middle management level. Recently, however, senior managers and executives have been involved in system development through the potential of building strategic systems for competitive advantage and, perhaps more directly, through the development of Executive Information Systems (EIS) which are a combination of basic office functions, custom developed reports from the corporate data base, and ad hoc enquiry capabilities. The potential benefits of new system development is now apparent at all levels of the organization. What is equally apparent is that the promise of improved efficiency, productivity, competitiveness and profit is not without considerable risk. There have been many stories of system development gone wrong. Careful management and control is absolutely critical in the area of system development.

The first section of this chapter describes the control perspective for including system development as one of the basic building block elements of information systems. This section also describes the relevance of this subject area to the skill set and knowledge requirements of the Level 1 and Level 2 auditor. Causes of exposure are described, as are the more common types of control which act upon these causes of exposure. The types of exposure which may occur as a result of a deficiency or breakdown in the control structure are also discussed. Finally, the audits to be performed are described in terms of relevant objectives and frequency.

CONTROL PERSPECTIVE

New system development requires a considerable investment of scarce corporate resources. Once the system is developed, one can expect it to remain in production for a period of seven to 10 years. During this period the system, as originally developed, will undergo considerable enhancements to its functionality. It will also require ongoing maintenance to correct errors in the original development and in subsequent enhancements. It is estimated that up to 80 percent of most organizations' system development budget goes to maintaining and enhancing existing systems. Generally speaking, the enhancements and maintenance only maintain the status quo in terms of the system's value to the organization. This means that only 20 percent of the budget is available for brand new system development.

This situation seems to imply that the reader should skip this chapter and go straight to the next chapter which deals with "System Maintenance and Change Control." However, the percentage of resources that has to be committed to maintenance is, in itself, a major reason why *more* emphasis needs to placed on system development rather than less emphasis. If new systems can be developed that require less maintenance and/or can be enhanced by the users of the systems rather than by the system development staff, it should be possible to devote a greater percentage of the system development resource to new system development. This is where the potential lies for strategic, competitive systems with all the attendant benefits that these types of systems can provide.

Before a new system is developed or purchased, there must be a clear understanding of the specific needs being addressed by the proposed new system. Alternatives should be reviewed by the user and system analysts to ensure that the best solution is selected. Development should be done with the purpose of producing a system that is easily modified and maintained by someone other than the original developer. Adequate attention must be given to the establishment of security and controls during the design phase to ensure that the system will have integrity once it is installed. Finally, the completed system should be subject to rigorous testing to provide assurance that the results produced are valid and reliable.

SCOPE OF SYSTEM DEVELOPMENT

System development includes the following subtopics in its scope of activities:

- Process.
- Audit Roles.
- Development Phases.
- Management Issues.

Process

Fifteen years ago, the system development process was very informal. There was mounting corporate criticism and dissatisfaction with the seemingly low rate of return on investment produced by the system development function.

- Systems were developed which did not meet the needs of the user.

- Inappropriate systems were developed (the system was not flexible enough to meet the business needs for which it was designed).

- The system went beyond what seemed to be a reasonable budget.

- The system overran its development schedule by a significant period of time.

- Systems were developed without proper management approval.

- Systems were developed which were difficult and costly to maintain.

- Systems were developed which did not fit in with the long-term business, financial and/or computerization plans for the organization.

It was against this background that considerable effort was expended to develop a standard approach to systems development. The thrust of this effort was made by individual organizations and software vendors. The results were systems development methodologies. A systems development methodology is a formalized approach for pulling the three inherent components of systems development (people, plans and processes) together in a logical, structured fashion so that they are transformed into a successfully developed and implemented computer system. Methodologies may be developed internally or may be purchased from a third-party vendor.

Not only must the methodology pull each of these diverse entities into a logical whole but it must also be capable of adjusting to a rapid rate of change in each of the component areas and constituent entities. Failure to do so will render the methodology obsolete or, worse, counterproductive to the end goal of developing the "right" systems on time and within budget.

Although various methodologies differ at the detail level, they are consistent in that they attempt to break down the system development life cycle (SDLC) into manageable phases (and constituent tasks) with appropriate project control and management review functions. This ensures that the development is still on track before proceeding to the next phases of development. See Figure 6.1 for an example of a typical breakdown of a system development life cycle. Each of these phases will be described in greater detail later in this chapter.

A methodology is usually thought of as dealing with a specific project. The methodology pulls together the various components (people, plans and processes) required to bring the project to fruition. However, before we talk about building individual systems there should be an understanding of the corporate framework and the project framework which must be in place to support the many projects which are going on simultaneously. Figure 6.2 shows this integrated framework required to support successful system development.

The corporate framework has three components:

- Organization.
- Strategy.
- Resource management.

Organization

In order for any methodology to work effectively, there must be a corporate commitment to information systems development. This commitment can be demonstrated in several ways and applies to every component within the corporate framework. However, there are a number of key ways organizationally with which to demonstrate this commitment.

1. The chief information officer concept was discussed in an earlier chapter. Whether this function is aligned along traditional lines by having line responsibility for the information systems department or is used more in a strategic planning capacity is not the issue here. What is important is having a senior executive who is responsible for the future use of technology (including new systems) in the attainment of corporate goals and objectives.

2. A computer steering committee comprising senior executives from the primary user departments should be in existence with a mandate to:

   - Approve the allocation of resources for individual systems development on the basis that they are consistent with the information strategy (see next section) and are supported by a solid business case.

   - Monitor the progress of each development project and act as the approval mechanism when projects need to move from one phase to another with a concomitant increase in financial expenditure.

   - Reset priorities when the need arises.

The Institute of Internal Auditors

3. For each system being developed there should be an executive sponsor whose performance is judged in part on whether or not the development succeeds or fails. Ideally the person should be the executive who has overall responsibility for the primary user departments. It has been recognized for some time that the development process requires iterative decision making. There are many variables and almost an equal number of correct answers. What is needed is someone to set policies and then choose alternatives which are consistent with these policies. The executive sponsor should be in a position to make these decisions and to make them stick.

4. There should be a support group for the system developers. The mandate of this support group is to introduce new concepts, tools and techniques into the development process. A key component of this mandate is to incorporate these changes into the development methodology so that the organization continues to have a logical, integrated and standardized approach to system development. A possible approach for organizing this support group is through the use of the development center concept.

Strategy

The intent of computer systems is to play a role in the translation of corporate policy into operational systems. This implies that the computer systems that are developed and operated are consistent with the goals and objectives set by the organization. Traditionally, however, the information systems department has been treated in isolation as far as overall corporate planning is concerned. What is required is a redefinition of the role of information systems within the corporate framework; a redefinition which recognizes the strategic and competitive advantages that well-designed systems can provide. In order to do this effectively, there must be an information strategy. This is a plan that meets the organization's information systems and technology needs for a three- to five-year time frame through the development of computer systems and related services. To be effective, the information strategy must form an integral part of the corporate strategy (see Chapter 4). The information strategy should reflect the corporate culture as much as possible. This includes the use of end-user computing and the question of whether systems should be centralized or decentralized.

Resource Management

Within the corporate framework, the resource that should be considered is data. Generally, an organization's data base remains relatively stable as long as the organization remains in the same line of business. However, the type and volume of information to be determined from these data change over time. Therefore, there is a need in the corporate framework for strong data resource management (DRM) which is the term used to describe the methods of managing the corporate data resource in such a way that it provides the required information in the most effective manner. The three inherent principles of data resource management are as follows:

- Focus on the data. This entails the incorporation of specific data items into a corporate data base which is reflected (typically through an integrated data dictionary) in the computer systems which are developed to convert these data into information.

- Separate the data from its uses. This is an extension of the idea of focusing on the data rather than on individual processes.

- Structure the data for varied access. This allows a variety of computer systems to be developed to access the corporate data base according to their individual needs.

Project Framework

The project framework is created within the corporate framework. This is the physical organization established for each system under development. There are many approaches to describing a project framework. However, although the nomenclature may be different, the functional entities are fairly standard. There should be an executive sponsor with overall responsibility for the project. The executive sponsor solicits and approves the project plan, ensures that the project gets initiated correctly and makes sure that the appropriate resources are committed. During the project, the executive sponsor reviews the status reports and ensures that the commitment of resources and momentum is being maintained. He or she arbitrates when there are disagreements between the project manager and acceptor, and helps resolve problems that cannot be handled effectively at a lower level. At the completion of the project, the executive sponsor reviews the acceptance document and ensures proper acceptance.

The review committee is formed at the discretion of the executive sponsor to provide support and additional input to the project. Typical duties for this committee would be to:

- Ensure that all divisions are meeting their commitments.
- Review key technical decisions.
- Represent respective divisional points of interest in the project.

The project manager has the overall day-to-day responsibility for the project. He or she creates the project plan and the project status reports, prepares a weekly activity planning schedule, directs the technical activities of the development team, and provides the necessary training, technical assistance and other resources required by the team members. The project manager is the key interface between the development activities and the acceptor.

The acceptor is responsible for ensuring that the end product meets the user's needs and can be supported. He or she represents the individuals or groups who could be affected either directly or indirectly by the installation of this system. Acting for these groups, he or she accepts the project specifications, ensures that acceptance tests are run (this person may prepare the test data) and accepts the end product. Once the product has been accepted, the acceptor (not the project manager) is responsible for any product deficiencies.

The acceptor is the prime interface between the project manager and the organization. In this capacity, he or she is responsible for keeping the relevant people informed of the project status, negotiating product changes with the project manager, and representing the interests of the product users and the product support departments.

For large projects, it is advisable to form an acceptance group. This will reduce the acceptor's workload and simplify the transfer of information and decision-making process.

In forming this group, the acceptor must define the principal areas that are affected by the product and obtain a representative from each area. This group would typically include representatives from the end-user department, the maintenance group, operations and marketing. These individuals have veto power and, therefore, must have the authority to fully represent their area.

The Development Process

As explained in Figure 6.1, the development process consists of a series of phases each with its own clearly defined deliverables and management review points. What Figure 6.1 does not describe, however, are the tools and techniques which may be used in each phase of development. These are shown in Figure 6.3.

Structured analysis is used to define and describe the system that best satisfies user requirements, given specified time and budget constraints. Although structured analysis can be implemented in several ways, all versions share important features: the use of models, user involvement and iteration. Structured analysis consists of four primary tools:

- Data flow or activity diagrams.
- Data structure and entity diagrams.
- Transform descriptions or mini-specifications.

Data Flow or Activity Diagrams — These tools enable the analyst to partition the system into components and show the connections or interfaces among the components. Each component can then itself be partitioned, resulting in a collection of diagrams that present the system in a top-down fashion.

Data Structure and Entity Diagrams — These tools are used to describe static relationships among data items and represent the first stage of data base design. All are user oriented and independent of particular data base management systems.

Transform Descriptions or Mini-specifications — Every system activity is described by a lower-level diagram or, for lowest-level activities, by a transform description which states the policy governing the transformation. Several tools are available to express this policy. The tool that is selected depends on the policy itself and the experience of the personnel involved. Recommended tools include decision tables or trees and structured English, which is a version of English with a limited vocabulary and limited ways of expressing logic. The collection of transform descriptions constitutes the system specification.

Because maintenance has been shown to be the costliest part of a system's life, the goal of structured design is to minimize that cost by emphasizing maintainability. The basic premise is that the solution should match the problem; components and connections in the solution that do not have a counterpart in the problem should be kept to a minimum.

Some of the features of structured analysis apply to **structured design**. This technique also uses models for understanding and communicating. Iteration and review are important as well. In addition, structured design includes a collection of evaluative criteria to assist designers and reviewers. It provides strategies for producing rough designs quickly from the results of analysis. The tools used in structured design include the data flow diagram and structure chart.

Several similar objectives initiated the development of **structured programming**. Perhaps the primary goal, however, was to produce a more readable, understandable, and maintainable program code through the use of a limited group of logical constructs. One of the purposes of such programming is to make the program code comprehensible to someone who is unfamiliar with either the program or its creator; because a program is read more often than written, it is more important that it be easy to read than easy to write. Another objective is to produce a code that is easily proved correct.

Automated development encompasses a vast array of tools and techniques, all of which are designed to reduce the manual intensity of the system development process. There are automated tools available for each discrete phase of development.

Computer-aided software engineering (CASE) is the latest concept which attempts to automate the development process. One of the main benefits of CASE concepts is its focus on an open architecture for its constituent products. With this open architecture, it will be possible to move from phase to phase without human reinterpretation of what has been developed to date. The result will be an integrated approach to system development which will allow an error-free code to be developed straight from the analysis phase.

Prototyping is a design technique that recognizes that systems development is an iterative process. Acceptance of the inevitability of change and the need for continual revision in systems development has been slow in coming. Many installations still fail to accept the need for revision. In others, acceptance has been restricted to the development of decision support systems for corporate executives or the development of systems by the end user. Actually, however, all systems development is iterative in nature — or should be.

Prototyping recognizes that system developers cannot always foresee and understand all sides to a problem and that end users cannot always completely communicate their needs. Finally, prototyping recognizes that system developers are constantly looking for ways to improve the system, and the prototyping process makes it easy to incorporate changes.

In the traditional approach to systems development, a great deal of effort was expended to document and then freeze user requirements. To signify that all requirements had been defined, the user was typically presented with the prepared documentation and asked to sign off on the documentation. This indicated that the system documentation was complete and that requirements could be frozen. This approach was always unrealistic and is even more so today, given the rapidly changing business environment.

Prototyping attempts to show the user what is to be developed. The system developer sits at a terminal with a user and designs the screens of information that are meaningful and functional to the user. It is irrelevant that the final disposition of this information may be on paper in the production system. The purpose of the exercise is to extract the required information from the user by allowing the user to view the information in a real context. Designing these screens is an interactive process supported by a screen handler, which is an integral part of the programming language used for prototyping.

The Institute of Internal Auditors

Prototyping has always been an option for systems developers. Until recently, however, the technological tools were simply not available to enable the system developer to design the prototype within a short time frame and a reasonable budget, and as more than just a throwaway commodity. In addition, the available coding structure was not flexible enough to allow the constant and often radical change that is usually necessary to develop an acceptable prototype. The result of this inability to build systems dynamically reinforced a batch mentality in systems developers, even though the systems themselves had progressed from batch to on-line, real-time processing. System requirements were captured at one point in time and were processed under set conditions. Inquiry and updating of stated requirements could be made only at predetermined times and according to rigid rules.

Recently, new interactive development tools have become available to enable on-line design of prototypes. These development tools are generally based on a fourth-generation language (4GL) integrated with a relational data base and data dictionary.

Currently, **purchased software packages** cover a wide variety of business needs. Some packages are generic and multifunctional, allowing the user to program the software to particular needs; a lot of microcomputer software falls into this category. Other packages are application specific; they are designed to solve particular business problems. Examples of this type of software package include payroll, accounts receivable and payable, general ledger and inventory management systems. These packages automate basic business functions that do not vary considerably from one organization to another. The current trend, however, is to provide as much flexibility as possible, even in specific application packages. This is achieved through the provision of multiple parameters that can be set to tailor the software to the best possible fit for each user.

The major advantage of purchased software is rapid implementation. The software is ready, tested and documented. Depending on the extent of modifications that are required to bring the system in-house, an organization should be able to implement a purchased system far more quickly than if it developed the same system in-house. This can help solve the application backlog problem faced by many organizations.

The second major advantage is cost savings combined with a high degree of certainty about the eventual cost of the system. It is doubtful that a system could be developed in-house for less than the cost of an available package. In-house development is also notoriously prone to exceed budget estimates in both time and cost.

The third major advantage is that purchased software has been rigorously tested in production before its implementation at the current customer site. With systems developed in-house, glitches are common when the new system is implemented. With a purchased package, these problems should be minimal. Related to this advantage is that the risks associated with in-house development are minimized.

End-user computing can be defined as computer processing which takes place outside the realm of responsibility that is traditionally associated with the corporate information systems department. However, from a systems development standpoint, end-user computing can play a major role in ensuring the development of the "right" systems at the "right" time . . . IF . . . the end-user computing capacity within the organization is properly integrated into the system development process.

The information systems department and end-user computing must complement each other. Information systems must continue to develop the basic systems (such as data gathering, data management and basic reporting). Users must also be given controlled access, within the end-user computing environment, to the data captured and managed by the basic system. The users can then perform the specialized manipulations and reporting they need. The most common method of integrating basic systems and end-user computing is the establishment of an information center.

The Information Center — Organizationally, the information center is part of the information systems department. Functionally, however, it is a technical support group for the user community; it allows individual users to access their own data in a friendly environment. The information center staff creates this environment by selecting appropriate software tools, ensuring that the appropriate data is accessible, and acting as consultants to the user community when required.

The information center enables users to access their data rapidly and flexibly without submitting requests for development resources to the information systems department.

The information center allows the user to develop and run small systems that are tailor-made for their immediate needs. This leaves the information systems department free to concentrate on the larger, global systems that in turn feed data back through the information center for manipulation by the end user.

The information center encourages all users to adopt a consistent approach to data access and manipulation and decreases the possibility that users will select individual means of obtaining information systems capability (such as purchasing incompatible microcomputers or contracting with outside service bureaus).

Audit Roles

The audit role in system development begins with a review of the system development methodology and supporting corporate, project and development frameworks currently in place. Any weaknesses or omissions should be brought to the attention of management. The auditor should then develop a checklist of audit department activities, requirements and outputs from each development phase. This checklist should be presented to the systems development department so that a protocol can be established. In this way, the auditor is made aware of significant events regarding the development of new application systems. The auditor must also establish criteria for determining which systems under development will be the subject of an audit.

It is now generally recognized that auditors must become involved throughout the development stages of a computerized system so they can attest to the adequacy of control within the completed system. The systems being developed today are too complex to be comprehended within the limited time frame allowed for an operational audit once the system has gone live in a production environment. In addition to an understanding of the system and the controls within the system, two other important advantages imparted by auditor involvement throughout system development are:

- **Audit subsystem** — Participation during system development provides an opportunity for auditors to define their own requirements, which can then be built into the system as an audit subsystem. Through the use of an audit subsystem, it is possible for the auditor to perform a continuous audit of the system; an audit file could be created containing information on exception conditions. This file could be accessed by the auditor at any time, and the authenticity of these items could be verified. It is also possible for the audit subsystem to take on the guise of an expert system. By having the ability to analyze transactions and situations as they arise, the audit subsystem may be able to highlight instances that would, in a conventional test process, consume a large amount of time and resources, assuming that the transaction or situation caught the attention of the auditor in the first place.

- **Timeliness** — When the auditor only reviews a system immediately prior to its implementation into the production environment, or, as is often the case, after it has gone into production, the difficulties and costs associated with correcting control weaknesses within the system are vastly greater than during the early stages of development.

A system development audit is basically a compliance audit based on the development methodology and supporting frameworks currently in force. The audit is designed to ensure management that:

- The system is being developed to meet the defined, approved needs of the user and of the organization.

- The system is being developed on schedule and within the approved budget.

- The system contains sufficient controls over input, processing and output.

The Institute of Internal Auditors

The auditors must retain independence and objectivity during system development and not become so involved in the development process that they begin to have a sense of ownership about the system. Although this independence and objectivity issue should not prevent the auditor from participating in the systems development process, the following steps should be taken to ensure that auditor independence and objectivity are maintained:

- The auditor must remain organizationally independent of the systems development team; the auditor should not be an actual member of the system development team and should not take direction from the project manager.

- The auditor should write reports independently from the project team. The auditor's opinions, recommendations and judgments should not be included in the project team's status report because the one who issues the reports (usually the project manager) has the editorial authority to modify the auditor's statements.

- The auditor should carry out the audit investigations independently of the project team. The project team may be restricted to certain contacts and authority, but the auditor has free access to information and people throughout the organization. The auditor should use this access whenever necessary.

In the traditional approach to systems development, a great deal of effort is expended to document and then freeze user requirements. To signify that all requirements have been defined the user is typically asked to sign-off on the documentation. This provides an audit trail confirming that the systems documentation is complete and that requirements can be frozen. From the auditor's perspective there are a number of attractive features about this type of development methodology:

- The audit community was a powerful voice behind the reasoning for the introduction of a rational approach to system development. This "system to develop systems" was in contrast to the haphazard approach which tended to be adopted in the early days of computer system development where organizations were totally dependent on the quality of their development staff.

- The sequential, methodical approach to system development represented by traditional methodologies allows the consideration of auditability and control issues to be planned at discrete points in the development process. The auditor can, therefore, structure participation in the development process according to when these issues are supposed to be addressed.

- The sign-off process and management approval points built into the traditional methodologies provide an audit trail that the system being developed meets user and operational needs and has the ongoing approval of management from both functional and budgetary points of view.

There is, however, a powerful argument that says that system development is an iterative process and is not purely linear. The technique most commonly used to expand on this idea of iterative development is **prototyping**. Prototyping is a design technique that recognizes that system development is an iterative process. Unfortunately, this is in direct conflict with most development methodologies that operate on the basis that system development is a sequential process and that once a checkpoint has been passed there is no going back. From the auditor's perspective the sequential, milestone approach is ideal because it allows the audit and control process to catch up to the design-and-build process.

Prototyping recognizes that system developers cannot always foresee and understand all aspects of a problem and that end users cannot completely communicate their needs. Finally, prototyping recognizes that system developers are constantly looking for ways to improve the system, and the prototyping process makes it easy to incorporate changes. Prototyping is a potential threat to the way in which it has become customary to audit systems under development. This situation poses real problems to the auditor for a number of reasons:

- The auditor is concerned that prototyping is a return to the "old" days of catch-as-catch-can system development where requirements were not properly thought out and development was conducted on a trial and error basis. There are many organizations still operating under the legacy of this type of poorly controlled system development (for instance, excessive maintenance costs, systems which were scrapped after consuming large dollar budgets, poor credibility and working relationships between user and information systems departments because too many systems did not meet requirements).

- Prototyping, almost by definition, focuses on what the user wants. There can be a tendency in this type of arrangement to ignore the corporate need for systems control (such as backup/ recovery, data security and audit trails). As an iterative process there does not seem to be a point in the prototyping approach at which there is time for reflection on the overall system which would include a review of the systems control structure.

- As an iterative process, when is a prototype complete and when does "real" development work begin? The auditor is concerned that the user will see the results of the prototype and will pressure the developers into building the prototype to a point where it can be put into production without really considering some important factors such as system response time and the effectiveness of system resource usage. More fundamentally, the auditor is concerned that without appropriate checkpoints and management approval to proceed, the system may be built to a level of functionality beyond which the organization was prepared to commit and pay for.

As clearly indicated, prototyping has a potentially major impact on the development methodology. The issue is to ensure that the advantages of prototyping are achieved while still retaining the required level of control.

The first thing to recognize is that prototyping is not suitable for all applications. Batch systems are typically not good candidates for prototyping. Although an on-line systems development project is a candidate for prototyping, some areas of on-line systems may not lend themselves well to prototyping. These areas include interfaces to batch systems, complex calculations and logic processing.

Prototyping should be recognized as being only one part of a productive systems development environment. System developers need to understand that prototyping should be used within the context of a proper development methodology and not as a substitute for an orderly approach to system development. The benefits derived from prototyping depend on how the technique is employed, the technological tools available, and the level of understanding of both the systems personnel and users involved in building the prototype.

Prototyping should reduce the amount of redundant documentation that tends to litter the development of systems using the traditional life cycle methodology. Nevertheless, prototyping cannot replace all types of documentation. Operating documentation dealing with run time instructions to the operators, program documentation for maintenance purposes, user procedures and the business case rationale must all continue to be produced.

Prototyping concentrates on functional capability rather than correctness and completeness of the logic. The testing of a prototype tends to be informal. This mind-set cannot be allowed to carry through to the development of the production version of the system. Proper testing procedures must continue to be in place prior to the system's acceptance into the production environment.

Project planning, tracking, reporting and review (or a complete project management system) continues to be applicable when prototyping is being used as an aid in development. Management sign-off at discrete points in the life cycle is still a requirement.

The auditors' concerns about prototyping are consistent with those that should be uppermost in the minds of system developers. There are limitations to the use of prototyping. However, there is also little doubt that prototyping is a productive, effective means of system development in a large number of situations. The issue is to balance the benefits with the risks and to refine the development methodology to include prototyping as an option while still retaining the essence of good management control over the process.

Development Phases

Figure 6.1 shows the breakdown of the various development phases within a system development life cycle. Tables 6.1 through 6.5 provide self-explanatory examples of the types of tasks that are completed in each of the phases of development. Notice particularly the need for management approval to proceed at the end of each phase. This is an important step given that things change within the life of a system development, particularly in the case of large system developments. Management must be kept abreast of what is happening in system development. Certainly, the interaction with the steering committee should provide much of the required involvement on a regular basis. However, system development is a business investment; new opportunities arise which offer the potential for a greater return on investment. In short, priorities change. It is at the formal review points that management has the opportunity to reappraise the future benefit of the system development in terms of the current climate rather than according to the conditions which existed when the system was last reviewed.

Another noteworthy comment about the task lists is the early inclusion of security and audit considerations and the thought given to the approach to testing the system once it is developed.

Management Issues

There are three levels of management issues:

- Corporate management issues.
- System development line management issues.
- User department management issues.

Corporate Management Issues

The corporate management issues center around the concept of value for money and the ability to maximize the return on investment in system development. As discussed in Chapter 4, the key to the resolution of corporate management issues is the presence of an information strategy. Ideally, the information strategy should be an integral part of the corporate business plan. As such, the information strategy needs to be updated as part of the corporate business planning cycle (usually on an annual basis). The construction and operation of an effective steering committee is also key to the timely and appropriate resolution of corporate management issues.

System Development Line Management Issues

These issues relate to the management of resources (such as people, money, computer time and elapsed time) required for the successful development of a new system. As part of the detailed planning process, the project manager will define which tasks must be completed within each of the phases relevant to the project and will estimate worker days by resource type (the systems analyst, designer, programmer, etc.) for each task to be completed and will indicate a completion date for each task. It is then possible to calculate, from the resource estimates provided, the estimated cost for each project phase and for the project overall. The estimated completion date for the project can be determined by the project manager based upon the completion dates for the various tasks associated with the phases of the project.

The phase of development having the greatest impact on planning is the general design and feasibility phase. It is during this phase that the economics, priority and risk are determined for the system to be developed. Once these factors have been determined and documented in the form of the general design and feasibility report, the steering committee can approve the project as part of the development plan. The major sections of the general design and feasibility report should cover:

- Business or system problems.
- Existing environment.
- Possible system solution (including the purchase of a third-party software package).
- Proposed system solution.
- Cost/benefit analysis.

- Risk analysis (this will help plan the level of future management, steering committee and/or audit participation in future phases of development).

User Department Management Issues

A new system development has tremendous implications for the user department. To be successful there is a requirement for considerable user involvement in the development phases of the project. In addition, the user should be trained on the operation of the new system and must convert from the old system to the new, which is usually a considerable undertaking. Meanwhile, the user must still attend to business as usual. The ideal situation is for the user to use, on a full-time basis, the resources required to build the system and to hire replacement staff to cope with the existing volume of business. This is frequently not a practical approach for either monetary reasons or because of the learning curve associated with someone new coming in to work in the user department. Somehow, however, the user must find a way to be fully involved in the development project.

The introduction of a new system may have a significant impact on an organization quite beyond what was anticipated in the analysis phase of the systems development life cycle. Unless the impact of this implementation is identified and planned for, the effects may extend throughout the organization and be difficult to control because the underlying cause is not understood. An impact analysis (which is conducted after the system is built) assesses how the system will affect the organization after it is implemented. Appendix 2 discusses in detail the benefits and methods of conducting an impact analysis.

LEVEL 1 AUDITOR — SKILL AND KNOWLEDGE OBJECTIVES

Overall Objective

Understand the methodology approach to system development, the techniques and tools associated with system development and the audit approach to be taken when dealing with systems under development.

Process

Know the basic phases and constituent tasks that are inherent in the methodology approach to system development including the principle control review points.

Know the basic framework of controls that have to be built into both on-line and batch systems and the point in the life cycle at which these controls should be addressed. Be able to assess how well a methodology addresses the need for building controls into systems under development.

Know the concepts of structured development and the options that are available to the system developer when building systems (such as the portfolio approach to system development). Be able to assess how well a methodology addresses these issues which relate directly to the effectiveness of the development process.

Know where CASE tools fit into the overall development process and the control implications of using CASE tools.

Audit Roles

Be able to execute any audit program relating to a system under development.

The Institute of Internal Auditors

Development Phases

Be able to operate in an audit capacity throughout all phases of the development life cycle.

Management Issues

Know the philosophies, tools and techniques of systems development project management. Be able to assess the effectiveness of the development process *for a particular system.*

Know the organizational roles and responsibilities associated with system development. Be able to assess the adequacy of these roles and responsibilities *as they apply to individual projects.*

LEVEL 2 AUDITOR — SKILL AND KNOWLEDGE OBJECTIVES

Overall Objectives

Be able to apply the principles of "good" system development to whatever type of system is required within the organization. Provide management with an opinion on the efficiency and effectiveness of the system development function.

Process

Be able to address the control implications of using CASE technology in the development process.

Be able to relate the methodology to the overall business requirements of the organization and thereby assess the overall adequacy of the methodology.

Audit Roles

Be able to plan audits of systems under development including selecting the audits to be performed and setting the scope and objectives for the audits.

Be able to specify audit requirements where a continuous auditing subsystem is to be built as part of the overall system.

Development Phases

Be able to act in the capacity of an end user for the development of an audit subsystem.

Management Issues

Be able to assess and report to management on the *overall* effectiveness of the development process.

Be able to assess and report to management on the *overall* adequacy of the system development organization.

CAUSES OF EXPOSURE

The causes of exposure in the area of system development are as follows:

- Inappropriate systems.

- Late delivery.

- Cost overruns.

- High maintenance.

- Lack of user acceptance.

Inappropriate Systems

Inappropriate systems means that the systems do not reflect the business needs of the organization. It is not enough for systems to meet the defined needs of the user. Systems must go beyond what is required for individual user departments. The principal reason that systems become inappropriate for the organization is that a broad enough view is not taken when the system is first designed. As a generalization, all systems process data into information and most systems maintain data about some facet of the organization's operation. If these data cannot be made available to other processes without extensive modification to the system, then the design of the system is inappropriate for the needs of the organization.

Apart from being inappropriate from a design standpoint, a system can also be inappropriate from a functional standpoint. One of the biggest complaints that the user community has about system development is that the finished product does not meet their stated requirements. The counter argument from the system development staff is that the users do not know what they want until they have seen something. By that time it is too late to adequately respond to their new-found set of requirements. There is some truth in both sets of arguments. Prototyping has been viewed as an effective way of solving this problem. Although it does solve the problem to some extent, in terms of inappropriate systems it may actually exacerbate the problem. An organization may have in mind a bare bones approach to system development (such as the 80/20 rule). The users may want to have the remaining 20 percent functionality without really considering the cost.

Late Delivery

System development is notorious for coming in well beyond the original time estimate. Even when the original time estimate is met, the delivered product may only be a subset of what was originally envisioned. Late delivery is clearly disruptive to the users of the system for a number of reasons. First, there is a sense of expectation developed in the user community toward the introduction of a new system. This sense of expectancy generates considerable adrenalin which, when properly managed, can result in the level of increased effort which is usually required to make a new system a success. When the system does not arrive as planned, this enthusiasm wanes and is very difficult to rekindle when the time actually comes to install the system. Secondly, training and education on the system have to be performed close to when the system goes live but with enough advance warning that the training materials can be prepared, the training facilities organized and the users scheduled to attend the sessions. Late delivery usually means that the training should be conducted again. Notice that we say "should" be done again; in practice it rarely is because of time constraints. The other situation which often happens when the system is late is that the training does not get done at all. Because of the uncertainty surrounding the implementation date and the pressures to actually implement the system, the emphasis on training takes second place to other "priorities."

The cost of late delivery to the organization is that the benefits that were promised with the system will be correspondingly delayed. In extreme cases where the delay is considerable, the loss in benefits may nullify the business case which justified the building of the system in the first place.

Cost Overruns

Cost overruns are usually, but not always, related to late delivery of a system. Cost overruns stem from increased manpower costs to build the system or increased capital costs to support the eventual operation of the system. Increased manpower costs may be from the additional allocation of internal resources to the project or from having to hire external consultants or contractors to finish the project.

An increase in costs may invalidate the business case supporting the development of the system. It is important to try to anticipate an overrun in costs as early as possible in the development cycle so that a reappraisal to the original business case can be made.

High Maintenance

High maintenance stems from poorly designed and/or developed systems. The pressure associated with implementing systems also contributes to high maintenance; corners are cut on testing to maintain the schedule and functions are omitted from the original implementation only to be built at a later stage. Where the system was not designed to be flexible enough to respond to changes in the business environment, maintenance cost will be high because radical surgery has to be performed to the system to meet these changing requirements.

Given that 80 percent or more of the system development budget goes to maintenance, the addition of newly developed, hard to maintain systems simply exacerbates what is already a chronic condition in the system development field.

Lack of User Acceptance

There have been numerous instances when a system has been delivered and not used. There are many reasons for this situation arising, including:

- The inability to properly specify user requirements.

- A lack of user involvement in the development process.

- A simple fear of the unknown on the part of the user community.

For a system to be successfully implemented and used, the user must feel a sense of ownership about the system and believe that the system is being developed to enhance the well being of the user; otherwise, the user may feel threatened by the introduction of the new system.

The amount of user training and education on the new system is also directly proportional to the level of user acceptance. Even with graphical user interfaces (GUI), most systems are not intuitively obvious in terms of what they do and how they do things. Properly constructed training programs which also explain the benefits of using the system are essential to user acceptance.

CONTROLS

Applicable controls that are intended to prevent, detect and/or correct the causes of exposure just described as relevant to the area of system development are as follows:

- Corporate and project framework.
- Development methodology.
- Development standards.
- Project management system.

Corporate and Project Framework

The constituent elements of the corporate and project framework which should surround each system development were described in detail earlier in this chapter. Briefly, the corporate framework ensures that the system being developed is in line with the corporate business strategy; the project framework ensures that the user is properly involved in the development.

Development Methodology

The components of the methodology have also been described in detail earlier in the chapter. The development methodology provides consistency to individual system development and allows for appropriate review points so that management can make informed decisions on the future progression of the system.

The key tasks from a computer control and audit perspective are:

- The addressing of control and audit issues early in the development life cycle.

- The ability of the auditor to specify requirements for an audit subsystem in the same manner as any other user would specify requirements.

- Education and training are dealt with throughout the life cycle and not just as an add-on during the implementation phase.

- The user has sufficient review and sign-off opportunities.

- There are sufficient management review points.

Development Standards

Within the overall standard of a development methodology, several standards should be established to ensure the development of a quality system. The auditor should ensure that standards are established and strictly adhered to for documentation, system and program control, programming, testing and implementation.

Documentation Standards

System and program documentation serves as a means of communication among project team members during systems development. Adequate documentation also facilitates the development effort and provides the information needed for the system to be used effectively. In addition, documentation is essential for program maintenance and modifications and for auditing. The following sections discuss the documents that must be prepared during a development project.

Systems Documentation — These documents include a narrative system description and a flowchart of all input, output, programs and files. The layouts, valid codes, and abbreviations of input forms, output reports, and screen displays also should be listed. The use of structured analysis and design techniques in the development process will greatly facilitate the production of proper systems documentation.

A user manual should be developed to address, at a minimum, the methods for preparing input and correcting errors.

Program Documentation — The function performed by each program should be described briefly in comment statements at the beginning of each source listing. Source listings and programs should be well annotated. A program that is not annotated or does not contain meaningful names for paragraphs and data fields requires a logic flowchart or decision table. In addition, file layouts should be prepared for each file. There are a number of automated documentation systems which are able to take program source code as input and produce "standardized" program documentation.

Operations Documentation — Operations personnel (such as computer and terminal operators) should receive complete instructions for operating the system. Documentation must be kept up-to-date. Access to documentation should be granted on a need-to-know basis only. Production control information (special handling, job stream sequences and dependencies, scheduling considerations, etc.) properly forms part of the operations documentation.

Programming Standards

Programming standards should provide consistency among the work of individual programmers. In addition, they can be used to teach programmers the optimal use of the programming language. General programming standards should define any required structured techniques, the programming language to be used, program or module size (such as the number of statements), the necessary level of source statement comments, and any available optimization tools (or compilers). Standards should specifically address the programming language; for example, in a COBOL environment, the standards should specify field definitions and rules governing subscripting and the use of certain commands. The availability of common routines (such as I/O routines, error routines and data definitions) and the method of invoking these routines should also be included in programming standards.

Testing Standards

A typical program contains many logic paths, each of which must be tested to ensure that the program produces the correct output from the supplied data. Through the development and formulation of standards in advanced programming techniques, application developers have attempted to reduce the complexity and interrelationships of the logic paths within a program. These techniques include modular programming, top-down design, and structured design, analysis and programming. The need to decrease the complexity and interrelationships of the logic paths was recognized primarily because of the inordinate amount of time required to test new systems, the unsatisfactory final results regardless of the amount of testing performed, and the vast resources required to maintain a system once it becomes operational. There are automated tools available which identify each logic path and can generate test data to ensure that each logic path is exercised during a test run. Successful systems development therefore depends on the existence of a comprehensive and effective test plan that rigorously tests all facets of the system. An effective test plan provides reasonable assurance that the system functions in production according to its specifications.

The following levels of testing must be included in this plan.

Module Testing

A program module has its own entry point, return point and specific functions to perform. Typically, a calling module passes certain input (parameters) to another module, which then returns the output derived from the input. Output is usually placed in a parameter field, which is also supplied by the calling module. Module testing is particularly useful in a top-down environment, where each module is tested before it is integrated with the other modules of the total program.

Program Testing

An application system typically consists of an edit, an update and a reporting program. Program testing should be performed by the application development group. It brings together the various modules within a program to ensure that they properly interact with each other.

System Testing

In system testing, each program is linked to the other programs in the application system. Test data is then run through the entire system.

The primary function of system testing is to ensure that each program in the job stream is compatible with the next. Program development and testing are typically performed by developers who have a predetermined concept of the input to and output from the program. When programs are developed by different teams, inconsistencies can arise within the predetermined concepts. To resolve these incompatibilities, the application development group usually must perform some form of system testing.

Acceptance Testing

Two types of acceptance testing should be performed:

- User acceptance testing — Primary and secondary users own the application system and, therefore, are responsible for ensuring that the application functions according to their expectations, not just those of the application developers. For this reason, users should prepare their own test data and run their own tests before signing off an application.

- Operations acceptance testing — To ensure that a new or modified system functions within the production environment without adversely affecting existing applications, operations personnel should conduct testing in a simulated production environment. This testing is not intended to verify the accuracy of the results but to ensure the operational adequacy of the application.

Testing standards should stipulate that the test-plan documentation describes the conditions to be tested, the test transactions and the expected test results. Space should be allotted for insertion of the actual test results, including an acknowledgement of whether the tests were satisfactory. The test plan can also be used to test future system modifications. Testing standards should include procedures for maintaining test-plan currency.

The Institute of Internal Auditors

Implementation Standards

Once developed and tested, a system is ready for implementation in the production environment. Implementation standards ensure that all users of the new system are aware of its implementation date, are trained to handle its demands and use its services, and most important, approve its implementation. This sign-off indicates that the users (including computer operations personnel and auditors) are satisfied that the system has been fully tested and meets the specified and approved functional requirements.

Project Management System

The project team assigned to develop a system has finite manpower resources. Additionally, the various tasks to be completed have various interdependencies with other tasks. In order to properly plan the available manpower resources (after taking into account the tasks to be completed and the order in which they should be completed), it is advisable that formal resource and task management be employed in the form of a project management system. Typical standards in this area include the use of bar charts (also known as Gantt charts) to portray manpower deployment. Critical path networks (CPNs) are regularly used to show the sequence in which tasks are to be completed and consequently the interrelationships and dependencies between individual tasks. A 'critical path' can be identified through the creation of a CPN. The 'critical path' in a CPN is the path in the network of tasks which takes the longest estimated time to complete. Therefore, any delays in the completion of tasks forming part of this critical path will have a detrimental effect on the final completion date of the entire project.

As discussed in Chapter 4, the essence of an effective project management system is to be able to track tasks at a detail level, record and report on the time actually spent on each task versus the budget estimates for the same tasks and be able to take corrective action on a timely basis, whenever necessary. A detailed method of project management tracking is provided in Chapter 4.

TYPES OF EXPOSURE

Listed below are the types of exposure which can occur as a result of the inadequacy or failure of the system of control to prevent the occurrence of a cause of exposure in the area of system development.

Erroneous Record Keeping

A key element of effective systems is to ensure that corporate and user needs are properly incorporated into the system through accurate specification of functional requirements. Given that many organizations maintain their primary records through the use of computer systems there is a strong chance of erroneous record keeping where there there is a disparity between what the users and the organization requires and what is actually defined for development. Inappropriate systems is the catch-all term used to define the cause of exposure relating to inadequacy in the definition of needs to be developed.

User review and sign-off of the functional specification combined with proper testing by the user of the system are key controls to detecting the occurrence of erroneous record keeping.

Unacceptable Accounting

Once again, the inability to properly define the functional requirements for a new system can lead to many downstream problems. Typically, where systems are of an accounting nature, there is a strong reliance by the technical project team on the accounting expertise in the user area. If this expertise is not properly tapped, the accounting principles built into the system by the technical group may be unacceptable from a GAAP point of view.

Adequate user involvement in the definition of the functional specifications combined with proper testing by the user of the system prior to its introduction into production are key controls in detecting the occurrence of unacceptable accounting.

The Institute of Internal Auditors

Business Interruption

The late delivery of a system can certainly cause business interruption. The extent of the interruption can vary widely depending on the type of system and the degree to which the organization is depending on the system being delivered on time. Some systems (such as those that must be ready for the start of a new accounting period or those that must be ready to meet new regulatory requirements) must be delivered on a certain date. In other cases, the organization may have reorganized in anticipation of the new system and will have to revert back to the original way of doing business with the attendant confusion and business interruption that this situation can cause.

The lack of user acceptance of a new system can also cause business interruption to varying degrees. If the users are dissatisfied or uncomfortable with a new system there will inevitably be disruption in the user departments until the problem is resolved.

Erroneous Management Decisions

New systems are often built to enhance management decision making. Inappropriate systems or systems that are delivered late may impair management decision making to the extent that erroneous information is delivered by the system (inappropriate systems) or no information is delivered by the system (late delivery).

Fraud

Fraud is an unlikely result purely from a cause of exposure in system development. It is more likely that fraud is a consequence of poorly designed systems from a controls perspective. There needs to be a breakdown in the control structure during the operation of the system for the perpetrator of a fraud to realize any benefit from a fraudulent action. However, it may be that the program code to support a future fraud is built into the system as it is being developed. Development standards, including structured walkthroughs of the program code, are key elements in preventing this type of "Trojan horse" from being built into the system.

Statutory Sanctions

Many organizations have regulatory reporting requirements that must be met. These reporting requirements are often met through the reports produced by computer systems. When a system that reports directly or provides the information upon which the reporting is to be based is late in being delivered, the organization may be unable to meet its reporting obligations and be subject to statutory sanctions.

Excessive Costs/Deficient Revenues

Cost overruns and/or high maintenance costs contribute to excessive costs. Poorly designed systems may also result in excessive costs because of the operational costs associated with the system.

Competitive Disadvantage

Systems are built to provide competitive advantage or, in some cases, simply to maintain a competitive position. Late delivery of a system or the development of a system which does not meet the needs of the organization (inappropriate systems) could readily result in competitive disadvantage. To be a competitive tool the system must be usable by those for whom the system is intended. Where the system suffers from a lack of user acceptance, a competitive advantage situation may be lost which may in turn actually develop into a competitive disadvantage. With the speed in which things change in today's marketplace, the opportunity for a competitive advantage does not last long.

CONTROL EVALUATION TABLE

The control evaluation table for system development is given in Figure 6.4. The evaluation numbers are subjective and need to be adjusted based upon the conditions that exist in individual organizations. Note that, in practice, the completion of the control evaluation table is in two parts:

- During detailed information gathering where, from the review of available documentation and the results of personal interviews, the key to reliance on individual controls and the "overall control rating (design)" is determined.

- During the execution of the audit program where, as a result of various audit tests, the strength of individual controls is fully assessed and the "overall control rating (tested)" is determined.

AUDIT APPROACH

The audit approach to system development was covered in detail in the section of this chapter dealing with "audit roles." The primary point to remember is that the auditor must remain independent of the system development process but must be involved in all stages of development for those systems that warrant audit attention. The issue of risk management is important to the auditor. Given that there are usually insufficient resources to audit all of the systems under development, the auditor must develop a selection criteria using risk to the organization as the main influence for selection.

Before individual systems are reviewed, the auditor should have conducted a complete review of the methodology in place within the organization along with a review of the adequacy of the corporate and project frameworks.

Figure 6.1 — Typical System Development Life Cycle

Life Cycle Phase	Purpose	Deliverable
Project definition	To document a business or system problem to a level at which management can select a system solution.	Project assignment sheet
General design and feasibility analysis	To prepare a high-level design of a proposed system solution and present reasons for adopting the solution.	General design and feasibility report
Detailed design	To expand the general design of an approved system solution so that programming and procedure writing can begin.	Test strategy, detailed design report
Program and procedure development	To develop and trust all computer programs and manual procedures (i.e., develop the total system)	Program specifications programs, procedures, test results, approved systems implementation
Implementation	To ensure that the system meets operational requirements and is smoothly integrated into the production environment.	Implementation plan

Reprinted from *Systems Development Management* (New York: Auerbach Publishers), 1988, Warren Gorham & Lamont Inc. Used with permission.

Figure 6.2 — Framework for System Development

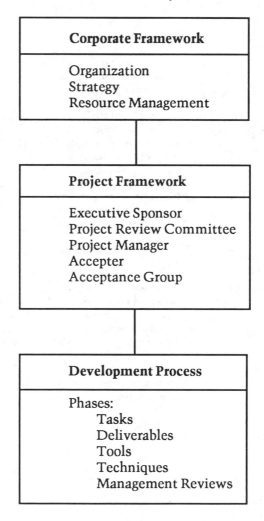

Reprinted from *Systems Development Management* (New York: Auerbach Publishers), 1988, Warren Gorham & Lamont Inc. Used with permission.

Figure 6.3 — The Development Process

Project Definition	General Design and Feasibility Analysis	Detailed Design	Program and Procedure Development	Implementation
	Structured Analysis	Structured Design	Structured Programming	Prototyping
	Automated Development	Automated Development	Automated Development	End-User Computing
	Prototyping	Prototyping	Prototyping	
	Purchased Software			
	Risk Management			

Table 6.1 — Sample Task List for Project Definition

1. Define the project purpose.
2. Define the project objectives.
3. Define the project scope.
4. Define the project phases.
5. Assign a project leader.
6. Define the required tasks for each project phase, including the worker-days and completion date.
7. Determine the estimated completion date and estimated cost of the project.
8. Prepare a project assignment sheet.
9. Obtain management approval to proceed.

Reprinted from *Systems Development Management* (New York: Auerbach Publishers), 1988, Warren Gorham & Lamont Inc. Used with permission.

Table 6.2 — Sample Task List for General Design and Feasibility Analysis

1. Describe the business or system problem.
2. Describe the existing environment.
3. Describe the possible solutions including a possible purchase of existing software.
4. Prototype a possible solution.
5. Recommend a proposed solution.
6. Prepare a data flow diagram of the proposed solution.
7. Determine the educational requirements of users of the proposed system.
8. Estimate the staff needed to meet the educational requirements.
9. Define the legal considerations.
10. Estimate the staff needed to resolve the legal issues.
11. Define the security and audit requirements.
12. Assess the risk associated with this project.
13. Prepare a general design and feasibility report.
14. Estimate the cost and time frame for the next sequential project phases.
15. Prepare an implementation strategy for the proposed solution.
16. Prepare a presentation to management on the proposed solution.
17. Give the presentation to management.
18. Obtain management approval to proceed to the next phase.

Reprinted from *Systems Development Management* (New York: Auerbach Publishers), 1988, Warren Gorham & Lamont Inc. Used with permission.

The Institute of Internal Auditors

Table 6.3 — Sample Task List for Detailed Design

1. Divide the system into subsystems.
2. Enhance the prototype to reflect each subsystem.
3. Prepare data flow diagrams for each subsystem.
4. Define all input by subsystem format and media (i.e., forms, screens and machine-readable data).
5. Detail any input security and audit requirements.
6. Define all manual and computer processing by subsystem (i.e., forms, screens and machine-readable data).
7. Detail any processing security and audit requirements.
8. Define all output by subsystem format and media (i.e., forms, screens, machine-readable data and reports).
9. Detail any output security and audit requirements.
10. Design a test strategy.
11. Detail the requirements for resolving the legal considerations.
12. Prepare a detailed design report.
13. Estimate the cost and time frame of the next sequential project phases.
14. Obtain management approval to proceed.

Reprinted from *Systems Development Management* (New York: Auerbach Publishers), 1988, Warren Gorham & Lamont Inc. Used with permission.

Table 6.4 — Sample Task List for Program and Procedure Development

Program Development
1. Prepare logic flowcharts of the program modules.
2. Prepare a schedule for writing the module specifications.
3. Prepare the module specifications.
4. Prepare a schedule for coding each module.
5. Code each program module.
6. Prepare test specifications and test data for each module.
7. Test each program module.
8. Perform module testing.
9. Integrate the modules and retest.

Procedure Development
1. Prepare a table of contents for the procedures manual.
2. Prepare a schedule for writing each section of the manual.
3. Write the procedures.

Acceptance Test Development
1. Design the operational acceptance testing strategy.
2. Prepare the operational acceptance test data.

Legal Procedures
1. Prepare a schedule showing the various legal procedures to be developed.
2. Write the legal procedures.

Reprinted from *Systems Development Management* (New York: Auerbach Publishers), 1988, Warren Gorham & Lamont Inc. Used with permission.

Table 6.5 — Sample Task List for Implementation

1. Execute the legal agreements.
2. Provide billing information to the appropriate department.
3. Transfer the programs to acceptance testing libraries.
4. Run the operational acceptance test for both the users and computer operations.
5. Design tests to ensure that existing logic has not been adversely affected by system enhancements.
6. Run the tests to verify system logic.
7. Issue system documentation, forms and procedures.
8. Conduct comprehensive user training.
9. Obtain approval to implement the system.
10. Implement the system in the production environment.
11. Prepare and issue a post-implementation review.

Reprinted from *Systems Development Management* (New York: Auerbach Publishers), 1988, Warren Gorham & Lamont Inc. Used with permission.

The Institute of Internal Auditors

Figure 6.4 — Control Evaluation Table
System Development

CAUSES OF EXPOSURE

CONTROLS	Inappropriate Systems	Late Delivery	Cost Overruns	High Maintenance	Lack of User Acceptance
Corporate and Project Framework	3	2		1	2
Development Methodology	3	2	2	2	3
Development Standards	2	2	3	3	2
Project Management Standards	1	3	3		1
Overall Control Rating - Design					
Overall Control Rating - Tested					

KEY TO RELIANCE ON CONTROL

3 - High reliance
2 - Moderate reliance
1 - Control has only a peripheral effect on the cause of exposure
Blank - No significant impact

KEY TO OVERALL CONTROL RATING

3 - Strong control
2 - Moderate but adequate control
1 - Inadequate control

EXPOSURES

EXPOSURES	Inappropriate Systems	Late Delivery	Cost Overruns	High Maintenance	Lack of User Acceptance
Erroneous Record Keeping	3				
Unacceptable Accounting	3				
Business Interruption	2	2			2
Erroneous Management Decisions	2	2			
Fraud and Embezzlement	1				
Statutory Sanctions	1	1			
Excessive Costs	2	2	3	3	2
Loss or Destruction of Assets			2		
Competitive Disadvantage	2	2	2	2	2

KEY TO DEGREE OF CERTAINTY OF OCCURRENCE IN THE EVENT OF AN INADEQUATE CONTROL STRUCTURE

3 - Virtually certain
2 - Probable
1 - Possible
Blank - Very unlikely

7
SYSTEM MAINTENANCE
AND CHANGE CONTROL

INTRODUCTION

With 80 percent of the typical system development budget being devoted to system maintenance, it is clear that the entire issue of change control over systems which are already in the production environment but which require change, is significant to the user, the auditor, information systems management and to senior corporate management.

It is essential that an organization's application systems, when used in production, are authorized, meet the criteria for which they were designed and do not perform any additional (and, in particular, any unauthorized) functions. It is also true to say that the integrity and stability of computer systems are inversely related to the volume, complexity and frequency of change. Therefore, an effective method of system maintenance and change control is essential if an organization is to have a stable and reliable processing environment in which to run its computer systems.

The first section of this chapter describes the control perspective for including software maintenance and change control procedures as one of the main building blocks of information systems. This section also describes the relevance of this subject area to the skill set and knowledge requirements of the Level 1 and Level 2 auditor. Causes of exposure are described, as are the more common types of control which act upon these causes of exposure. The types of exposure which may occur as a result of a deficiency or breakdown in the control structure are then discussed. Finally, the audits to be performed are described in terms of relevant objectives and frequency.

CONTROL PERSPECTIVE

In Chapter 5 there was a discussion on the classification of data within a computer environment. One of the major classes of data was system data which was defined as the vendor supplied software (such as operating systems, utilities, compilers) and the application programs purchased or developed to process raw business data into the type of information required to meet the business needs of the organization.

This chapter addresses the subject of control over application programs: those developed in-house and those purchased from a software vendor. Although the controls that are pertinent to the introduction of new or amended versions of the operating system (utility programs and compilers) are not addressed specifically in this chapter, many of the concepts presented (such as segregation) are relevant.

Systems must continue to be adapted to meet changing business requirements and circumstances. Modified systems should be subject to the same controls as newly developed systems. Most important among these is the requirement that there be thorough testing of the modified system. In addition, accurate records should be maintained that describe the change, the reasons for making the change, the person authorizing the change, and the person responsible for making the change.

There has always been a need to have effective change control procedures in place. However, recent developments in the computer industry have placed even greater emphasis on this need.

Management of Resources — Even with 80 percent of the information system department's budget going into correcting and enhancing existing systems, it is recognized that the average application backlog is in the region of two to three years and growing. Application backlog is the estimated time required to meet the current user demands for computer services. Generally, the application backlog does not include the anticipated future development of major new systems, but does include changes and enhancements to existing systems.

End-user Computing — The explosion of microcomputers in the business world and the emergence of the information center concept are two primary reasons for the end users of computer resources being able to develop systems by themselves without relying on information systems. The impact on controlling change is immense in an end-user computing environment.

When all development and maintenance was the responsibility of one department (such as the information systems department), it was possible to focus attention on this department when dealing with change control. However, in an end-user computing environment, the responsibility for developing and maintaining systems is widely spread throughout the organization. Materiality is now a major component in determining the extent of change control to be applied.

The advantages of microcomputers and the tools associated with the information center are their flexibility and ease of use. A fine line must be drawn between curtailing these advantages in the name of control and losing control of the areas that make use of end-user computing. This fine line is based on materiality.

Computer Systems Reflect Corporate Policy and Procedure — Many organizations have come to rely on their computer systems to the point where they can no longer function without them. Rules which embody the organization's policies and procedures for doing business are contained within computer programs. Any deviations from these policies and procedures could change the nature of the business and result in customer dissatisfaction, competitive disadvantage and erroneous accounting.

Increased Importance of Administrative Data — Previously, program change control procedures concentrated solely on systems data. However, with the continuing move toward data base technology and the concept of data independence, the control of certain elements of administrative data has become as important as controlling the logic instructions contained in the systems data (or in the application programs).

Interpretative Programming Languages — Fourth-generation programming languages are generally interpretative in nature; the source code does not need to be converted to machine code *prior* to execution, rather the conversion takes place *during* execution. From a change control standpoint, interpretative programming languages have good and bad points. On the positive side there is no longer a need to control source and machine code members for a single program and ensure that the machine code version in production truly reflects the authorized version of the source code. However, a substantial benefit of the fourth-generation interpretative language is the power of individual instructions and their flexibility for change. Once again the fine line between productivity and control must be drawn when dealing with the change control aspects of interpretative programming languages.

SCOPE OF SYSTEM MAINTENANCE AND CHANGE CONTROL

System maintenance and change control includes the following subtopics in its scope of activities:

- Objectives.

- Segregation — test versus production.

- Migration procedures.

- Prioritization.

- Stratification/release management.

- Custody.

- Ownership.

- Authority to change.

- Testing.

- Quality control.

- Externally initiated changes.

- Modification of purchased software.

- Optimization/retrofits.

Objectives

The objectives of system maintenance and change control is simply stated as "to ensure that changes are authorized, prioritized, properly tested and migrated into the production environment in a controlled fashion, including having been properly signed off by the owner of the system."

Segregation — Test versus Production

Figure 7.1 gives a simplistic view of the libraries involved in creating an executable program. The sequence of events that lead to this executable program are as follows:

- The programmer writes source statements using a programming language. These source statements, which comprise a module or program, are usually stored magnetically in a source statement library.

- A compiler translates these source statements into a form that the computer understands. This translation involves producing machine-language statements (such as an object code) that correspond to the source statements coded by the programmer.

- The object code is put into a utility program called a Linkage Editor, which creates an executable program from the supplied input components.

In the case of interpretative languages (those languages that do not have to be compiled before execution), the source code statements are input directly to an interpreter which produces the executable code directly, thereby eliminating the compiler step.

A distinction must be made between the environment in which programs are developed (such as the test environment) and the environment in which they are used to process live data (the production environment). Typically, a test environment is not intended to provide a high level of protection to business or system data. Because the source test and executable library members are moved into production after the amended program has been tested (see Figure 7.2), system maintenance and program change control procedures must ensure that only authorized, fully tested changes are moved to the production source and executable libraries.

Migration Procedures

Migration procedures are concerned with the movement from a test environment to the production environment. In basic terms the migration must be approved and performed in a controlled manner. A controlled manner means under the control of the custodian of production libraries and with the proper documentation in place. Controlled manner does not mean under the control of the programmer who is responsible for making the change(s).

However, the actual method of migration can depend very much on the type of change that is being made. A change may either correct an identified problem within the system or may provide an enhancement to the functions of the system. Changes can be initiated for a variety of legitimate reasons, including:

Emergency Changes — An emergency change is required when a system either fails during a production run or produces erroneous results which must be corrected immediately. Due to time constraints it is usually not possible to follow the standard migration procedures when dealing with emergency changes. This is especially true when the change must be made in the middle of the night so that the appropriate users will have the results by the following morning, or in the situation of a material error in an on-line, real-time system.

What is important when dealing with emergency changes is to ensure that an adequate degree of follow-up is in place. It may not be possible to prepare the appropriate documentation before the change is made, but it should be standard policy to prepare this documentation as soon as possible.

One-time Changes — A one-time change may be required to correct an incorrect record which, due to a previous programming error, has been written to a master file or to initialize previously unused fields within a record ready for use by a subsequent change to the system. The point about this type of change is that it may not be necessary for it to migrate into the production environment; the system may be executed from a secure intermediate library on the required date. Alternatively, the change may be coded as a set of data dependent instructions and left, suitably documented, within the production version of the system.

Critical Changes — Critical changes (such as corrections or enhancements) fall into the category of those which, although they do not have to be implemented immediately (for example, an emergency fix), must be implemented by a certain date. Examples of this type of change would be the introduction of government legislation requiring compliance by a certain date or the production or correction of figures prepared at a specific time (such as month end).

These changes should have sufficient lead time to enable the standard migration procedures to be followed.

Non-critical Changes — Non-critical changes (correction or enhancements) fall into the category of those upon which the success or failure of the system does not depend. They can, therefore, be implemented at a time that is convenient to all concerned (the user, the systems development group and the computer operations area). These changes will have sufficient lead time to enable the standard migration procedures to be followed.

Prioritization

Given the volume of changes which regularly occur in any organization, the impact these changes have on the various users and the finite resources available to make the changes, management must have a method of prioritizing the changes, scheduling their implementation and communicating the priority and schedule to all interested parties.

The majority of maintenance changes to a computer system are initiated by the user and given to the information systems department for resolution. In many organizations, an attitude exists among users that they are not getting an adequate level of service from information systems when it comes to system maintenance. The most frequent reason for this feeling of dissatisfaction is that the user has no direct say in how maintenance resources are allocated. The user sees these resources being spent in servicing non-critical change requests while other requests, which have a direct impact on the operational effectiveness of a system, are ignored.

The change review board concept of change management revolves around the creation of an interdepartmental committee (for instance, the change review board) that is responsible for the review and prioritization of all change requests.

The change review board should be made up of representatives from:

- Information systems.
- User sponsors — drawn from each department that is a major user of any system. These users represent the 'owners' of the systems being discussed.
- Computer operations.
- Audit.

The change review board should meet at regular intervals. The period of time between meetings will vary from organization to organization depending on the number and size of systems and the volume of change. Priorities for changes which have arisen since the last meeting will be set at these meetings. Typically, the change will be scheduled for a future release of the system. In special situations it may be necessary to schedule the change outside of a regular release, such as in the case of emergency or time-critical changes.

Stratification/Release Management

Rather than dealing with changes on an individual basis, the recommended approach is to use the *release concept* for change implementation. Using this concept, changes are prioritized and inserted into a future, scheduled release of the system. Whether or not a change can be inserted into the next release will depend on available resources, other changes already assigned to the release and the relative priority of the change in question. Typically, new releases of the system are scheduled at three-month to four-month intervals.

Custody

Custody over the production version of source and object code should belong to the computer operations group in the same way as this group is responsible for all production data. Once a production program has been moved over to the test environment for changes to be made, the development group has custodial responsibility. Clearly, testing of the changed version of the programs is fundamental to a smooth transition back into the production environment. For this reason, operational acceptance testing is a key part of system maintenance and change control procedures.

Ownership

The owner of the system that is being changed is the primary user of that system. The authorization of changes should come from this person. To prevent frivolous changes, the costs of making program changes should be charged back to the owner.

Authority to Change

A key element in system maintenance and change control is the proper documentation of the change, including the documentation of the authority to change. Figure 7.3 presents a sample Program Change Request form. The format of this form will undoubtedly vary from installation to installation. This is intended to serve as an illustration of the type and extent of information required to support making program changes.

A Program Change Request form usually consists of three sections:

1. **The Problem Definition** where someone identifies a problem or a deficiency within the system. This person would complete Section 1 of the Program Change Request form and obtain authorization from the appropriate user manager. It does not really matter where the change originates as long as it is approved by the user.

2. **The System Solution** as prepared by the programming group. When it is necessary to amend or enhance existing systems, a brief description of the various changes should be entered in Section 2 of the Program Change Request form. Expansion of these changes may require additional documentation to be attached to the basic form. The changes that are identified should be approved by a senior member of the programming group.

3. **The Implementation Checklist** (or Section 3 of the form) contains a list of activities which must be completed and approved prior to migrating the amended system into the production environment.

Testing

Before programs are placed into the production environment, they must be tested using data specially suited to the new and/or changed functions. Testing should be conducted at various levels — by the programming team responsible for creating or amending the programs, the user department that will use the output from the programs, and the computer operations area, whose acceptance test will ensure that the programs will run successfully in the production environment.

The computer operation acceptance test is usually conducted using live production data. This does not present additional exposure because this area already has custodial responsibility for these files. The sole purpose of the operations acceptance test is to ensure that the amended version of the program executes successfully in the production environment, not that the changes do what they were intended to do.

However, the user and programmer testing will be carried out in the test environment, where data files are not afforded the protection inherent in a production environment. The transaction data for these tests may be relatively simple to create. In fact, there may not be suitable data available on any live files. There are situations, however, when it may be considered necessary to use live data for user and programmer testing. The advantages of using live data are as follows:

- Expediency. Live files are always available, and there may not be time to create a suitable test file.

- A variety of conditions are likely to be found on a live file.

- Live files are up-to-date. The problem with maintaining a test file is that it is very often not kept current.

The disadvantages of using live data are obvious. The increase in the potential for unauthorized modification, disclosure or destruction of these files is tremendous. Therefore, when it is necessary to use live files in the test environment, consideration should be given to the following:

- A copy of the live file should be used in testing. This procedure eliminates the risk of modification or destruction of a live file; the risk of disclosure remains, however. In the case of very large production data bases, this option may not be appropriate. On-line data can be made non-sensitive by removing critical fields, such as names and addresses, before being used as test data.

- Procedures and standards for copying production files into the test environment should be established and documented, allowing the computer operations area control of the process.

The Institute of Internal Auditors

- Procedures for controlling the output (printed and otherwise) from test runs that use live data should be established.

- Ensure that all copies of live files are scratched from use in the test environment once they have served their purpose.

- Data security measures should be used to control and report on any unauthorized access to production data.

The preceding discussion assumes that production files in the test environment are necessary. Careful planning at the design and development stages of a system can, however, prevent this necessity to a large degree.

A **Regression Testing Facility** requires setting up a master file and a transaction file that contain all known conditions. The contents and purpose of each record in the test are documented. The documentation for the transaction file should also contain a section on the results that are expected after application of the transactions. Tests of the system are run using these files. Whenever the system is changed, the tests can be rerun and the two sets of output compared (such as the output before and after the change was made). Any unexpected discrepancies must be followed up by the person conducting the test. Output results can be compared visually, which can be a long, tedious, error-filled task, or by using an automated file-compare facility. A regression testing facility requires thorough documentation and a high degree of commitment to keep both the documentation and the files in line with the current production environment. This entails updating the test files and documentation whenever a new condition is encountered in production mode.

The **Integrated Test Facility (ITF)** entails the incorporation of certain records into the live master file for testing use. These records can be created, deleted and amended according to the needs of the test. Transactions can be submitted for processing by the system in its production environment without disrupting the run. Care must be taken, however, to ensure that the ITF records are not confused with live data and are not used in reporting the organization's results.

A typical example of an ITF is an on-line banking application where, for each branch serviced by the application, a range of account numbers have been designed as test, or dummy, accounts. These accounts are generally used by trainee tellers when learning the functions of the on-line application. A more sophisticated ITF is a dummy branch (or a dummy bank) in which all the accounts are treated as dummy accounts.

An ITF must be designed into an application as it is being developed. Such a facility allows the creation of dummy records on the production master file; the application processes these records as it would live ones.

The main disadvantage of the ITF concerns the risk of dummy records being treated as part of the live data. When reports are produced, the dummy records must be highlighted as such or be reported separately from live information. It is also essential to exclude any financial data held on dummy records from the organization's totals accumulated by the application programs. Additionally, access to these dummy records must be restricted in order to prevent the loss of any real data resulting from negligence or fraud.

Quality Control

Clearly, with 80 percent of the system development budget going to system maintenance, the quality of this work is of crucial importance to the organization. Systems which are changed and put into production without proper testing will require additional maintenance which, in turn, compounds the problem of having to devote so much of the scarce system development resource to maintenance. There should be some form of quality control mechanism in place to ensure that the investment in system maintenance is productively employed. Statistics on the volume and frequency of changes by module and by program provide an insight into the level of quality of the original system development and subsequent maintenance. When quality can be improved, it is entirely likely that less maintenance will be required in the future.

Externally Initiated Changes

Changes that are externally initiated can occur for a variety of reasons. The requirement to meet regulatory requirements (such as compliance with tax laws) may require changes to existing systems. Automated interfaces to other organizations, or Electronic Data Interchange (EDI), may need to be changed as a result of changes to systems by the organization being interfaced with. Externally initiated changes must usually be completed and implemented by a specific date. There is usually sufficient lead time for these changes to go through regular system maintenance and change control procedures. The one problem that does arise concerns testing. Part of the testing process may require an interface test with the external party that initiated the change. Consideration needs to be given to the turnaround time between sending the test results (or test files) and getting back a response indicating how well the test met the requirements. Sufficient turnaround time needs to be factored into the testing and implementation schedule.

Modification of Purchased Software

Purchased software must be tested and promoted just like in-house developed software. Purchased software will usually be received on a release basis. The users must make themselves aware of the changes that are in the new release and prepare test data accordingly. Once the new release has been properly tested by both the users and computer operations, the system should be migrated into the production environment. For some software packages, the user has the choice of deciding which of the changes in a new release to accept. From experience, it is better to take all the changes. By only taking part of them, error resolution with the vendor becomes very difficult if a problem develops with the installed software.

Although not recommended, there are times when an organization may want to make its own modifications to purchased software. In this situation, the standard system maintenance and change control procedures should be followed. However, it is also important that the organization understands the legal implications of making these changes. Many vendor contracts contain clauses which negate any guarantees or warranties in the event that the system is altered by the purchaser. These clauses can also greatly complicate the integration of future vendor releases.

Optimization/Retrofits

Many organizations are at the stage where their main systems are very difficult to maintain because of poor initial design and many years of patchwork maintenance. Optimization/retrofit provides an opportunity for organizations to revitalize these applications. Through the use of specially designed software, the source code for these systems is analyzed and restructured into structured code which can be readily maintained. Once the code has been restructured, a complete acceptance test is required because it is possible that all of the functionality will have had changes made in terms of how the system is coded. Before being implemented into production, the system can be optimized for production running through the use of an optimizing compiler which provides more efficient executable code than the standard compiler.

Another technique which is gaining prominence in this area is system re-engineering where the existing code is analyzed and the data base structure around which the code is organized is optimized. The purpose of systems re-engineering is to identify the data structures that are inherent within the coding and convert them into a more efficient form, typically using a relational data base.

LEVEL 1 AUDITOR — SKILL AND KNOWLEDGE OBJECTIVES

Overall Objective

Know the control objectives, constituent elements and levels of control which relate to system maintenance and change control. Know the audit processes that are used to attest to the adequacy of control in this area.

Objectives

Know the objectives of a systems maintenance and change control process and be able to relate these objectives to the process which is in place within the organization.

Segregation — Test versus Production

Know the protocols involved in keeping the test environment separate from the production environment and the steps involved in moving between the two environments.

Migration Procedures

Know the protocols involved in migrating software from a test into a production environment, including an understanding of the different types of migration procedure that may be required.

Prioritization

Know the different types of software changes that occur and the relative priority that can be attached to each. Be able to audit the prioritization process.

Stratification/Release Management

Know the concept of release management. Be able to attest to the control over the content of each release and its orderly migration into the production environment.

Custody

Know the concept of custodial responsibility for program and source code libraries. Be able to execute an audit program to attest to the adequacy of control over the custody of these libraries.

Ownership

Know the concept of ownership responsibility for systems maintenance and change control. Be able to differentiate between the controls that are relevant to ownership and those that are relevant to custody.

Authority to Change

Know the different levels at which authority to change is required. Be able to execute an audit program to attest to the adequacy of controls relating to this issue.

Testing

Know the various levels of testing that can be performed and be able to attest to the adequacy of testing where changes have been made to an application system.

Quality Control

Know the concepts of quality control as it relates to systems maintenance and change control.

Externally Initiated Changes

Know the sources that can initiate change. Be able to relate these changes to the prioritization process and to the systems maintenance and change control process overall.

Modification of Purchased Software

Know the steps which should be taken to ensure a controlled introduction of a modified purchased system.

Optimization/Retrofits

Know the rationale and approach behind the concepts of optimization and retrofit of application software.

LEVEL 2 AUDITOR — SKILL AND KNOWLEDGE OBJECTIVES

Overall Objective

Be able to structure individual audits to attest to the adequacy of the constituent elements that comprise the overall system of maintenance and change control.

From the conclusions drawn from the individual audits, be able to draw an overall conclusion on the adequacy of systems maintenance and change control or expand the scope of the individual audits to further investigate areas of potential weakness.

Objectives

Know the technical interaction between the components of a systems maintenance and change control process. Be able to develop an audit program to determine if the objectives of a systems maintenance and change control process are being met.

Segregation — Test versus Production

Know the manual and technological procedures that make up the systems maintenance and change control process. Be able to audit the adequacy of these procedures to properly segregate the test from the production environment.

Migration Procedures

Know the manual and technological procedures that make up the migration procedures. Be able to design audits that attest to the adequacy of these procedures.

Understand the issues of migrating software to distributed locations whether electronically or otherwise.

Be able to factor in an audit of these various procedures when conducting other types of audits.

Prioritization

Know the organizational interactions that take place in the prioritization process and be able to attest to how well this process meets the corporate needs for resource utilization.

Stratification/Release Management

Be familiar with the software that is used to manage the release management software. Be able to prepare an audit program to address the adequacy of the controls provided by this software as well as the adequacy of the administrative procedures surrounding this software.

Custody

Be able to factor in the various environmental issues which have an impact on the custodial responsibility over program and source code libraries. Arrive at an overall conclusion on the adequacy of control in this area.

Ownership

Be able to discern appropriate splits in responsibility for custody versus ownership in situations where the traditional split is not considered appropriate, such as departmental computing and end-user computing.

Authority to Change

At a technical level, understand the technology used to restrict change to authorized personnel only. Be able to schedule reviews of this technology within a number of different audits.

Testing

Be familiar with more advanced forms of testing (regression testing, automatic test data generation, integrated test facility) and be able to attest to the adequacy of the use of these techniques when auditing changes to application systems.

Quality Control

Be able to factor in the results of a quality control audit relating to systems maintenance and change control into the broader picture of an organizational efficiency and effectiveness audit.

Externally Initiated Changes

Be able to structure audits to deal with the situation where the external change is the result of a technical change at the external entity which causes the software interface between the two entities to change.

Modification of Purchased Software

Understand the legal ramifications and future maintainability of in-house modification of purchased software.

Optimization/Retrofits

Understand the technology required to perform the optimization, retrofit process and be able to structure an audit to attest to the adequacy of an application that has been through the optimization/retrofit process.

CAUSES OF EXPOSURE

The causes of exposure in the area of system maintenance and change control are as follows:

- Unauthorized changes.

- Poorly specified changes.

- Poorly documented changes.

- Poorly tested changes.

- Inappropriate changes.

Unauthorized Changes

Unauthorized changes may be made directly by the programmer or they may be the result of a user's change request that is not authorized by management or is not in the best interests of the organization.

The initiation of a change request, the approval and authorization of the change request, and actually making the appropriate changes must be seen as distinct and separate activities with proper authorization procedures in place between each of the activities.

Poorly Specified Changes

Once the need for a change has been identified, it is then necessary to analyze just where the change should be made (which module or program is involved) and what the change should be (what lines of code need to be amended, added or deleted). This analysis should also include a sizing of the change. When this analysis is not properly conducted, the change that is made may not reflect what is required and may, in fact, produce a result which is *not* required. This type of situation leads to further changes being made and compounds the entire problem of system maintenance. Once the necessary changes have been identified it is a good practice to have a second person check the analysis. In some situations, a structured walk-through of the proposed changes may be appropriate.

Poorly Documented Changes

Documentation of system changes should occur at several levels. First of all, the change itself should be documented. As previously discussed, a Program Change Request form should be completed for each change. Part of this form deals with the issue of updated documentation (see Section 3 of Figure 7.3). The documentation to be updated includes the system documentation (both the program listing and the accompanying narrative documentation), the user documentation and the computer operations documentation.

Failure to update documentation simply compounds the problem of trying to maintain systems. As more changes are made to the system the original documentation decreases in value.

Poorly Tested Systems

There are three reasons why changes to existing systems should be tested:

- To ensure that the changes work as they were intended to.

- To ensure that the rest of the system works as it did before the changes were made.

- To ensure that only the intended changes have been implemented. In some situations there may be a number of concurrent changes being made which are intended to be implemented separately. It is important to ensure that these sets of changes are not intermingled, particularly as the level of testing may differ depending on when each set of changes are scheduled to go into production.

It is possible that new test data will be required to test the changes that have been made. In other situations (for instance, when a correction to an existing function is the reason for the change), existing test data may be sufficient. In terms of ensuring that no additional functionality has been inserted, or that the changed code does not produce an adverse "ripple" effect through the rest of the code, the regression testing facility is a useful testing technique.

Inappropriate Changes

Inappropriate changes differ from unauthorized changes in that inappropriate changes are authorized. However, the two types of changes are similar to the extent that neither should be made. Inappropriate changes may be the result of responding to the "squeaky wheel," where particularly vocal users are able to garner a disproportionate level of the available maintenance resource. There may also be situations where a system has reached the end of its productive life and should be either rewritten or re-engineered. Constantly trying to maintain systems beyond their productive life is an inappropriate use of corporate resources. Finally, the question of priorities and timing should be discussed under the topic of inappropriate changes. Changes that "need to be made yesterday" are contrary to an orderly approach to system maintenance and change control. There will certainly be occasions when emergency and time critical changes have to be made. However, these types of changes should be the exception rather than the rule. If an organization finds that many of its change requests fall into the category of emergency or time critical changes, further examination of the appropriateness of these change requests is in order.

CONTROLS

Applicable controls that are intended to prevent, detect and/or correct the causes of exposure as relevant to the area of system maintenance and change control are as follows:

- Library management system.

- Change review board.

- Separation of duties.

- Testing standards.

- Change documentation.

Library Management System

A library management system is an automated method of keeping the production and test libraries separate and distinct. It will also provide access only to those who are authorized to have it. The library management system will keep track of the version numbers of the production system and will maintain an audit trail of the changes that have been applied over the most recent versions of the system. The library management system requires a set of support procedures to be in place. These support procedures provide the framework for requesting moves between library members (for example, from production to test and back to production). The documentation that is produced as a result of these administrative procedures provides an important audit trail when trying to piece together the authorization for particular changes.

Separation of Duties

Adequate separation of duties depends on the division of responsibility for program change activity between the users, the programming group and the computer operations group:

Initiating the Change — The request for a program correction may be initiated by either the programming group or the user group. However, all changes that fall within the category of enhancements should come from the user.

Authorizing the Change — The authorization of a program change, whether to correct or enhance the program, should be under the control of the user. To prevent the authorization of frivolous changes, consideration should be given to charging back to the user the cost of making the change.

Making the Change — The programming group should be responsible for changing the appropriate source statements and compiling the amended version of the program. The computer operations area should have custodial responsibility for the production source statement library. The programming group should request computer operations personnel to move members that must be changed to the appropriate test library.

Testing the Change — The programming group should test the change before passing the amended program to the user and computer operations groups, who should conduct their own tests.

Controlling Migration into the Production Environment — Because the computer operations area has custodial responsibility for all libraries, they should control the movement of new and amended library members (such as source, executable and procedure) from test to production libraries.

In the traditional computer environment (which has been the basis of discussion to this point) there is a clear delineation of responsibility between the users, the programming groups and computer operations. This is not the case in an end-user computing environment where the user may perform many roles (such as user, programmer and operator). However, the basic fundamentals of segregation of duties should still apply in both environments. In other words, one person should not have total control of the system. In a change control environment this means that one person should not be able to initiate and implement a change without the involvement of at least one other person.

What has happened in many departments that perform end-user computing is that one person has become the recognized authority for all systems within that department. The other members of the department effectively hand over all responsibility for computer processing to this one individual. The question that management must ask is "What is the risk to the organization in having one individual in such a position of dominance?" For many reasons, the department (or management) cannot abdicate its responsibility for providing proper control over end-user computing; a major part of this control is control over changes. In an end-user computing environment there should be authorization of changes and there should be an implementation procedure which includes proper testing. The separation of test from production environments should apply to both the traditional computer environment and to the end-user computing environment.

Testing Standards

Testing standards are similar to those that are discussed in Chapter 6 when dealing with new system development. The same levels of testing still apply (module, program, system, user and operations acceptance). Stress and volume testing are usually not required when dealing with changes to existing functionality although either type of test may be required if significant functionality is being added. Regression testing, to ensure that existing functionality is not adversely impacted, should be added to the traditional levels of testing when dealing with system changes.

The idea of release management and testing changes in batches rather than individually also leads to stronger reliance on the test results. The overhead of individual change testing, assuming proper regression testing is in place, is too high to warrant this treatment except in genuine emergency cases.

Change Documentation

In order to provide an effective audit trail it is essential that all changes are supported by relevant documentation. This documentation is likely to take the guise of a Program Change Request form (see Figure 7.3). Retention policies that indicate how long the documentation is to be retained on file need to be in place.

TYPES OF EXPOSURE

Listed below are the types of exposure which can occur as a result of the inadequacy or failure of the system of control to prevent the occurrence of a cause of exposure in the area of system maintenance and change control.

Erroneous Record Keeping

Inadequately specified, unauthorized and/or poorly tested changes can result in erroneous record keeping.

Unacceptable Accounting

The principles of accounting for an organization may be the subject of change requests. Typically, these types of changes require significant levels of enhancement. If the changes are not properly authorized, specified and/or tested, unacceptable accounting may be the result.

Business Interruption

Some changes are required to respond to specific business issues and must be completed by a certain date. Failure to comply with this date may cause business interruption to some degree, depending on the criticality of the change to the organization. The reason for missing the scheduled date may be the lack of resources due to priority being given to other, perhaps less critical, changes.

Erroneous Management Decisions

Changes that are poorly specified may lead to erroneous management decisions on the part of either the user or information systems management. The erroneous decision may involve the change itself or the results produced once the change has been made. For example, if the change is specified as being straightforward and worthwhile, the decision may be made to proceed. However, if the change turns out to be complex and expensive to code and test, the after-the-fact decision may be that the change was not worth making. Similarly, if the change is made and incorrectly specified and/or tested, the results produced by the change may lead management to make erroneous decisions. The approval of inappropriate changes is a form of erroneous decision making.

Fraud and Embezzlement

Unauthorized or poorly tested changes could certainly lead to fraud and embezzlement. Similarly, a tolerance of poorly documented changes could easily mask the addition of codes to facilitate fraud and embezzlement.

Statutory Sanctions

Some changes are required to comply with statutory requirements. If these changes are poorly specified and/or poorly tested, statutory sanctions could result.

Excessive Costs

Excessive costs can result from poorly specified and poorly tested changes given that further work will be required to correct the errors that were made. Poorly documented changes, to the extent that they contribute to the high overhead of system maintenance, also result in excessive costs. Inappropriate changes are clearly excessive in their cost given that such changes should not have been made in the first place.

Competitive Disadvantage

In certain situations, an opportunity arises to change an existing system in such a way as to provide a competitive advantage. In fact, this is the preferred situation rather than having to rely on an entirely new system development initiative. As such, poorly specified changes, poorly documented changes (particularly from a user procedure standpoint) and poorly tested systems can all lead to the inability to realize a competitive advantage and, in some cases, to a competitive disadvantage (such as where the changes were being made to maintain a competitive posture which is subsequently not achieved).

CONTROL EVALUATION TABLE

The Control Evaluation Table for system maintenance and change control is given in Figure 7.4. The evaluation numbers are subjective and should be adjusted based upon the conditions which exist in individual organizations. Note that, in practice, the completion of the Control Evaluation Table is in two parts:

- During detailed information gathering where, from the review of available documentation and the results of personal interviews, the key to reliance on individual controls and the "overall control rating (design)" are determined.

- During the execution of the audit program where, as a result of various audit tests, the strength of individual controls is fully assessed and the "overall control rating (tested)" is determined.

AUDIT APPROACH

With approximately 80 percent of the information systems budget going into correcting and enhancing existing programs, it is obvious that the auditor should plan to spend a large percentage of his or her time dealing with system maintenance and change control. However, because of the rapid rate of change which is taking place almost continuously within the computer environment, there has been some difficulty in providing effective audit coverage in this area.

The following is a list of activities that are designed to improve this coverage and to provide senior management with a meaningful picture of the effectiveness of the change control procedures in place within the organization.

Review and Communication of Existing Procedures — Based on the recommendations and observations made in this chapter, the auditor should review the organization's system maintenance and change control procedures in force at the present time and take note of any weaknesses or omissions. See Figure 7.5 for a validation checklist to be used during this review. The change control procedures that are reviewed should include those (if any) which are formally applied to end-user computing departments.

The auditor conducting the review should discuss his or her concept of change control procedures with the users (especially those with their own computing facilities), programmers and computer operations personnel to determine that all views coincide.

Establishment of a Notification Procedure — The auditor should establish a procedure through which the information systems and end-user departments can notify the audit department when significant changes are going to be made. If a proposed change is extensive, the audit department may want to follow its progression from initiation through to implementation in the same way that new system development is tracked. The audit department must establish criteria for determining which changes should be reviewed individually.

Development of an Audit Program — The auditor should develop an audit program to test compliance with system maintenance and change control procedures and assess the ongoing adequacy of these procedures. This program must track changes through their various stages. Changes should be tracked:

- **As they are being made.** If a change will affect the system of internal control in some way, the auditor should follow the change from initiation to implementation.

- **During the audit of an application system.** When auditing an application system, the auditor can ensure that changes have been handled according to defined procedures and can assess the cumulative effect of these changes on the application's internal control features. If documentation procedures have been followed, the auditor should be able to review a change from initiation to implementation. The auditor should be especially careful to ensure that documentation is on file for emergency and one-time changes.

- **As part of the data center audit**. The auditor should be able to compare the data center environment with the environment that was documented during the last data center audit. By testing for changes to hardware, software and telecommunications equipment, the auditor can assess whether changes are being processed according to procedures.

- **As part of operational or financial audits of end-user departments**. When an end-user department depends on its computing capabilities for daily operations and management, the auditor must assess the integrity of the applications used and the changes made to them.

Figure 7.1 — Creation of an Executable Program

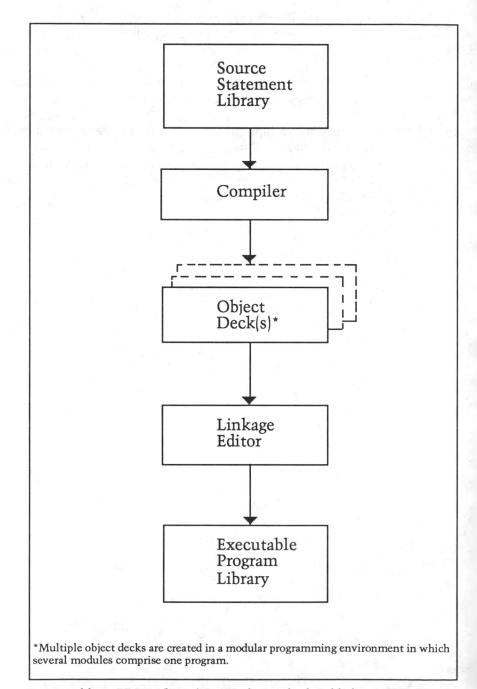

*Multiple object decks are created in a modular programming environment in which several modules comprise one program.

Reprinted from *EDP Auditing* (New York: Auerbach Publishers), 1980, Warren Gorham & Lamont Inc. Used with permission.

Figure 7.2 — Migration into the
Production Environment

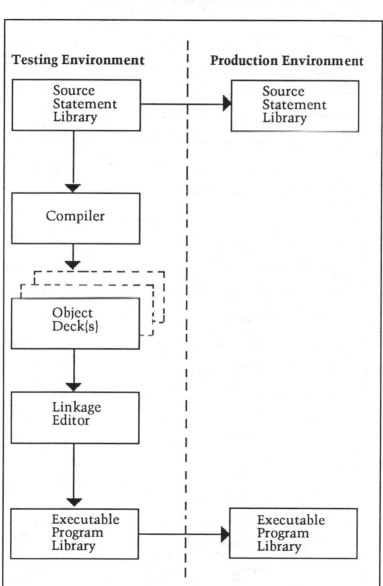

Reprinted from *EDP Auditing* (New York: Auerbach Publishers), 1980, Warren Gorham & Lamont Inc. Used with permission.

Figure 7.3 — Sample Program Change Request Form

PROGRAM CHANGE REQUEST FORM

Section 1: Problem Definition (to be prepared by the initiator)

Originator _____ Department _____

Description of Change(s) _____

_____

_____

Reason for Change(s) _____

_____

_____

Date Required _____

Authorized by _____ Date: _____

_____

_____

Section 2: System Solution (to be prepared by the programming group)

Programs Affected _____

_____

Description of Change(s) _____

_____

_____

_____

Approved by _____ Date: _____

_____

_____

Section 3: Implementation Checklist

Testing	Program Testing Approved	_____	Date	_____
	User Testing Approved	_____	Date	_____
	Acceptance Testing Approved	_____	Date	_____
Documentation	Program Documentation	_____	Date	_____
Updated	User Manual	_____	Date	_____
	Data Control Manual	_____	Date	_____

Date of Implementation _____

Implemented _____

Reprinted from *EDP Auditing* (New York: Auerbach Publishers), 1989, Warren Gorham & Lamont Inc. Used with permission.

Figure 7.4 — Control Evaluation Table
System Maintenance and Change Control

CAUSES OF EXPOSURE

CONTROLS	Unauthorized Changes	Poorly Specified Changes	Poorly Documented Changes	Poorly Tested Changes	Inappropriate Changes
Library Management System	3		2		
Change Review Board	3	2	2	1	3
Separation of Duties	3	2	2	2	2
Testing Standards	1	3	2	3	
Change Documentation	2	2	3	2	
Overall Control Rating - Design					
Overall Control Rating - Tested					

KEY TO RELIANCE ON CONTROL
3 - High reliance
2 - Moderate reliance
1 - Control has only a peripheral effect on the cause of exposure
Blank - No significant impact

KEY TO OVERALL CONTROL RATING
3 - Strong control
2 - Moderate but adequate control
1 - Inadequate control

EXPOSURES

EXPOSURES	Unauthorized Changes	Poorly Specified Changes	Poorly Documented Changes	Poorly Tested Changes	Inappropriate Changes
Erroneous Record Keeping	3	2		2	
Unacceptable Accounting	2	2		1	
Business Interruption	1	1		1	
Erroneous Management Decisions	2	3		2	3
Fraud and Embezzlement	3	1	1	1	
Statutory Sanctions		1		1	
Excessive Costs	2	3	2	3	3
Loss or Destruction of Assets					
Competitive Disadvantage	1	1	1	1	1

KEY TO DEGREE OF CERTAINTY OF OCCURRENCE IN THE EVENT OF AN INADEQUATE CONTROL STRUCTURE
3 - Virtually certain
2 - Probable
1 - Possible
Blank - Very unlikely

Figure 7.5 — Checklist for Change Control Procedures

Item	Response		
	Yes	No	NA
Management Control Are format change control procedures in place? Are service-level agreements in effect? Is there a method of assigning priority to requested changes? Did representatives from the user community, information services, and computer operations help develop the method? Is there a method of dealing with emergency changes? Are changes tested before being implemented into the production environment? Is there a method of scheduling changes for implementation? Is there a method of notifying the user when changes will be implemented? Is there a method of assessing the effect that a change will have on other systems or users? Are changes authorized before being made to production systems? Is computer operations informed of changes to be implemented? Are there adequate management reports of the incidence and types of changes being requested and implemented? **Segregation of Duties** Does a different employee make a change than the one who requests it? If not, is another person involved in the change before it is brought into production? Are changes authorized by someone other than the person requesting them? Is there a clear delineation between the testing and production processing environments? Are there procedures to transfer programs from testing to production? Are there procedures for emergency changes? Is there a procedure to ensure that all changes are properly tested by the user and computer operations before they are transferred into production? **Documentation** Is there a procedure for documenting requests for changes?			

Figure 7.5 — (Continued)

Item	Response		
	Yes	No	NA
Documentation (Cont.) Is there a method of bringing these change requests to the attention of the department (or persons) responsible for making the change? Is there a method of logging all change requests and providing a history of what happens to the request from initiation to final disposition? Does the logging procedure include formal documentation of the system solution? Does the logging procedure record the completion of all activities concerning the introduction of the change into the production environment?			

8
INFORMATION SYSTEMS PROBLEM MANAGEMENT

INTRODUCTION

There has been a consistent shift over the years in terms of the types of systems that are being built and installed. From a batch system orientation, most systems now offer an on-line, real-time capability. This change in orientation changes the response time requirements when a problem occurs. In a batch environment, a solution was usually found to resolve a problem in the short-term until a permanent solution could be found. The user was often not aware that a problem had actually occurred. In an on-line, real-time system, a problem is usually immediately apparent to the user. If the problem causes the system to crash, a solution must be found to allow the system to be brought back up again and for processing to resume. Problem management is the catchall term used to describe the plans and actions that need to be in place to ensure timely, continuous and accurate operation of the computer facility.

The first section of this chapter describes the control perspective for including information systems problem management as one of the basic building block elements of information systems. This section also describes the relevance of this subject area to the skill set and knowledge requirements of the Level 1 and Level 2 auditor. Causes of exposure are described, as are the more common types of control which act upon these causes of exposure. The types of exposure which may occur as a result of a deficiency or breakdown in the control structure are then discussed. Finally, the audits to be performed are described in terms of relevant objectives and frequency.

CONTROL PERSPECTIVE

A key attribute of a well-controlled information systems organization is the ability to deliver consistent, high-quality and timely service. Problems in information systems processing are a normal part of the business. Often, the difference in the level of performance between information systems installations is the ability to manage problems. Successful installations have the proper processes in place to assure high quality operations by not repeating previous mistakes, by fixing problems based on business priorities and by detecting problems before they escalate into major issues.

SCOPE OF INFORMATION SYSTEMS PROBLEM MANAGEMENT

The scope of information systems problem management spans the spectrum from the point where a potential problem may occur to the situation where a problem has actually happened. Problems can occur in hardware, software and/or telecommunications and can originate from actions or omissions on the part of the in-house organization or a vendor. Specific controls must be put in place to prevent, detect and correct these problem situations.

Problems can also be classified according to the urgency with which they must be resolved. A "crashed" on-line system problem affecting hundreds or perhaps thousands of users (or customers) clearly demands more immediate attention than a tape drive malfunction where the work can be flipped to another drive.

The scope of information systems problem management includes the need for escalation procedures to ensure that the right people in the organization (and potentially in a vendor's organization) know about the problem and are activating the necessary resources to deal with the problem in a timely manner.

LEVEL 1 AUDITOR — SKILL AND KNOWLEDGE OBJECTIVES

Overall Objective

Know the control points in an information processing problem management methodology and be able to execute an audit program to attest to the adequacy of the methodology.

LEVEL 2 AUDITOR — SKILL AND KNOWLEDGE OBJECTIVES

Overall Objective

Be able to design audits to attest to the adequacy of the technology to achieve the appropriate control objectives related to information systems problem management, based on an understanding of the related technology.

CAUSES OF EXPOSURE

The causes of exposure in the area of information systems problem management are as follows:

- Untimely response.

- Preventable errors.

- Undetected errors.

- Unrecoverable errors.

- Recurring problems.

Untimely Response

In order for problems to be dealt with, someone should be held accountable for the timely resolution of specific problem areas. The next step in timely resolution is to ensure that there is a mechanism in place to inform the designated individuals once a problem has occurred. Finally, these individuals must have at their disposal the facilities needed to deal with the problem.

There are three areas within information systems that require problem management:

- Hardware.
- Software.
- Telecommunications.

In terms of mainframe hardware, the vendor is usually responsible for problem resolution. Typically, the maintenance contract calls for an engineer to be on site to fix the problem within a set number of hours (usually two to four). In some large installations there may be a systems engineer on site. Many vendors now have remote diagnostic capabilities where not only is the problem identified by the mainframe but is relayed to the vendor's control center for resolution. The problem can be fixed from a remote area or an experienced engineer from the local office can be dispatched. There is, of course, a control issue when remote diagnostics and remote fixes are applied.

The issue of service performed after business hours should be examined. Contractually, it is possible to have the basic level of service extended to after business hours. This can be expensive and may not be necessary. However, if the service is provided on a time and materials basis there may not be a guaranteed response time. This could mean that the problem is not fixed in time for the beginning of the next business day.

For peripheral hardware (terminals and PC workstations) it is common to have an in-house technical support team that is responsible for installation and trouble shooting. Problem correction is usually contracted to an external supplier.

The resolution of application software problems falls under the category of system maintenance (see Chapter 7). The responsibility for system maintenance usually falls to the project team dealing with the system causing the problem. However, in some organizations there is a system maintenance group with global responsibility for all software maintenance. Either situation is acceptable assuming that there are adequate resources and adequate documentation.

For system software, the systems programmer is the first line of defense but, for more complex problems, the vendor may have to become involved.

In the area of telecommunications there should be a network control function within computer operations charged with the responsibility for resolving network problems. The delineation of responsibility between network problems and problems with devices attached to the network is one that can cause accountability problems. There should be a clear statement of scope of responsibility and accountability given to both the network control function and to the terminal/workstation support group.

Preventable Errors

Preventative maintenance programs for hardware "involve inspections, tests, and routine replacement of components at regular intervals."[1] "Generally, maintenance is performed by an outside vendor: either the equipment manufacturer or an independent service organization."[2]

In terms of software, preventative maintenance means being aware of the cumulative effect of changes made to the system. It also involves anticipating the point at which the system should be streamlined or made the subject of more stringent testing before the introduction of the next release into production.

For telecommunications, knowing the condition of the lines and being able to monitor for gradual deterioration in the quality of the signal on the line are essential to having adequate preventative measures in place. Once a deterioration has been detected it is often possible to have corrective action taken before the user even notices the problem.

---

[1] Mair, William C., Wood, Donald R., Davis, Keagle W. *Computer Control & Audit* (Altamonte Springs, FL: The Institute of Internal Auditors, 1978).
[2] Ibid.

Undetected Errors

Worse than not being able to prevent a problem from happening is the situation where a problem does occur but is not detected. In terms of hardware operation, the computer operator has responsibility for recognizing any hardware malfunction message which may appear on the console log. The vendor's operating system is responsible for interrogating the status of work performed and ensuring that the hardware units (such as CPU, disk drives, tape drives and printers) are performing according to specification.

For batch application systems, the production control group is the first line of defense to detect problems in the operation of the system. The application system itself must have been built with proper controls to allow for the detection of errors. For on-line systems, the user may be the first person to detect a problem. The user's procedures must give clear instructions on what to do when a problem is detected. The network control group may also be involved in the early stages of detection. Reliance on the vendor is again required when addressing the detection of system software problems. The first line of defense for these types of problems is the systems programming group.

For telecommunications, the diagnostic and error detection capabilities of the network operating system is crucial. The network control group has the responsibility for taking action once an error condition is detected and reported.

For all organizational functions there should be a clear understanding of their responsibilities once an error is detected. In judging the adequacy of the error detection mechanisms in place, the services of a Level 3 auditor (i.e., a technical specialist) may be required, particularly when dealing with system and network software.

Unrecoverable Errors

In order to recover from an error there must be a way of eliminating the effects of the condition that caused the problem. In application system software, this is frequently achieved by backing out the erroneously processed transaction. Where the cause of the problem is more extensive (for example, the loss of a disk drive), there is a need for effective backup and recovery procedures. In general, unrecoverable errors are a result of being unable to get back to the position just before the problem occurs. Often, unrecoverable errors are related to undetected errors in the sense that once an error is discovered, too much time has elapsed to be able to do anything about it.

Most errors are recoverable to some degree given enough time and money. However, an error is classified as unrecoverable if extraordinary and expensive procedures must be used to effect the recovery.

Recurring Problems

Once a problem has been fixed, it should not be expected to occur again, at least not within the established mean time between failures (MTBF) for the failed component. Recurring problems are usually a symptom of a more serious management problem. It is important that failures are recorded and an analysis is conducted at periodic intervals to determine if there is any kind of trend developing with respect to recurring problems. When a trend is identified it is important that the underlying cause is identified and rectified.

For hardware and telecommunications, recurring problems may be the result of a lack of preventative maintenance. For software, recurring problems may be a result of poor testing. In all cases there is a management issue that should be dealt with.

CONTROLS

Applicable controls intended to prevent, detect and/or correct the causes of exposure just described as relevant to the area of information processing problem management are as follows:

- Preventative maintenance.

- Defined responsibilities.

- Quality assurance.

- Vendor controls.

- Notification procedures.

The Institute of Internal Auditors

Preventative Maintenance

As a concept, preventative maintenance for hardware is well understood. From experience it is known that physical components usually break down after a specific period of time in service. One important aspect of preventative maintenance is to replace these components just as they are approaching this service threshold and before they actually break down. Another aspect of preventative maintenance is to conduct regular inspections so that wear and tear can be recognized before the point where failure takes place. The hardware vendor (or third-party contractor) is usually responsible for hardware maintenance. When reviewing the adequacy of the maintenance agreements, the existence of a preventative maintenance schedule followed up with detailed records on the life span of individual components is an important consideration.

Preventative maintenance for software is more difficult to define. However, there is a stage in the life cycle of any software product where the number of changes made to the system over the years has made the software vulnerable to error. Once this stage is reached, it may be necessary to retrofit the system through a form of system re-engineering in order that the system may be further modified and its productive life extended.

Defined Responsibilities

Areas of responsibility must be clearly defined. Earlier in the chapter the primary responsibility for hardware, software and telecommunications problem identification and resolution was defined.

The performance of each of these areas should, in part, be determined by the results achieved in problem management.

Quality Assurance

Quality and the incidence of problems are inversely related. Therefore, an investment in quality control will reduce the cost of dealing with errors as they arise. There is a distinction between quality control and quality assurance. Quality assurance is the overall process of assuring quality whereas quality control is one distinct step in the process.

A quality assurance function ensures that there are sufficient review points (one of which could be termed the quality control checkpoint) in the operational process and that there are appropriate standards in place. In information systems, the operational process may be system development, system maintenance, computer operations, network operations, and so forth. What is important is that someone is charged with the responsibility of reviewing these operational processes on an ongoing basis and making recommendations for how the process can be improved. In many organizations, quality assurance is an inherent part of management's responsibilities. In other organizations, there is a quality assurance function established to assist management in the conduct of their responsibilities. The size of the organization is very often the determining factor in which approach is used. However, it is important that quality assurance be in place in some form.

Vendor Controls

Many of the ways to detect problem conditions depend upon diagnostic features existing within the vendor's hardware and software. Where these features do not exist or are inadequate for the purpose, a significant exposure may exist. Vendor controls tend to be technical in nature and it is beyond the scope of this text to go into detail on any particular aspect of these controls. A Level 3 auditor (technical specialist) will be required to examine these controls in detail and determine their adequacy. Suffice it to say that these controls indicate when there is a problem with a hardware device, with the operating system, with the network control system and with the interaction among and between any of these three components and with the application systems designed and developed to run on the vendor's hardware.

Many vendors are now promoting the concept of unattended operations with all diagnostic tests being performed electronically and the results of these tests being sent to a remote location for the appropriate action to be taken. This approach has enormous potential for cost effective operations. It is also true to say that although the type of diagnostic software being used will become as accurate as an expert in the field (we will discuss expert systems later in the text), the fact remains that this software is embryonic at the present time and great care should be taken to ensure that the vendor has a successful track record in the use of this software before any reliance is placed on it. There is also the issue of system security to be considered when the vendor has a direct link into an organization's mainframe. Remote diagnostics and attendant free operation is definitely the wave of the future. However, there are a number of control issues that should be recognized and addressed.

Notification Procedures

Once a problem has occurred and the responsible party is searching for a solution, anyone who will be affected by the problem should be informed. All users should be notified of the extent of the problem and when a solution is likely to be applied. Notification procedures should be formalized to the extent that notification is automatic and does not depend on someone taking the initiative to inform the users. Where a lengthy outage is expected, the users should be given periodic updates of the status of the problem.

Within notification procedures are the issues of escalation and containment. If the person responsible for fixing the problem cannot find a solution or requires the help of others either inside or outside the organization, it may be necessary to invoke escalation procedures in order that the right levels within the organization(s) are dealing with the issues. Once again, the escalation procedures should be formalized and not left to chance.

Containment is required when a problem occurs that has the potential to affect a wide audience but can be restricted to a small group. Very often the trade-off is between *some* aggravation spread across a large population versus *a lot* of aggravation for a localized few. Poor response time across the entire system caused by problems in one application is an example of this type of situation. A decision should be made as to whether to suspend the problem application and relieve the problem for the majority but cause significant problems for the users of the application, or to let everyone in the system share some of the pain. These types of decisions cannot generally be formalized; each one should be dealt with on its own merits. Escalating the problem to a higher authority is often required in this type of situation. The escalation procedure can and should be formalized.

TYPES OF EXPOSURE

For each of the causes of exposure and resultant types of exposure, there should be application and system controls in place to prevent, detect and/or recover from the occurrence of any type of problem. However, the last line of defense is problem management (such as the process of taking action once a problem has or is about to occur). If the information systems problem management system breaks down, the front line controls which act directly upon individual causes of exposure will be of little value. Management cannot afford to treat control deficiencies and problem occurrences on an individual basis. Management must take the "big picture" approach and be in a position to assess the cumulative effect of control deficiencies and problem occurrences. It is this big picture approach that information systems problem management is all about.

CONTROL EVALUATION TABLE

The Control Evaluation Table for information systems problem management is illustrated in Figure 8.1. The evaluation numbers in this table continue to be subjective and should be adjusted based upon the conditions that exist in individual organizations.

However, the content of this table is somewhat different from that in previous control evaluation tables. Each of the types of exposure has been marked as being likely to occur (or classified as a "2") if there is a breakdown in the control structure. This notation is a result of the fact that the other controls in place to prevent, detect and/or correct the type of exposure from occurring are not being given due consideration because the organization is not properly managed to respond. However, in practice, the completion of the Control Evaluation Table continues to be in two parts:

- During detailed information gathering where, from the review of available documentation and the results of personal interviews, the key to reliance on individual controls and the "overall control rating (design)" are determined.

- During the execution of the audit program where, as a result of various audit tests, the strength of individual controls is fully assessed and the "overall control rating (tested)" is determined.

AUDIT APPROACH

An assessment of the adequacy of the information systems problem management system should probably be a cumulative assessment based on the results from a number of audits. Problem management, as discussed in this chapter, has many different organizational facets. It would be difficult to construct an audit program to adequately address the many varying issues. The ultimate auditee is really the organization as opposed to any particular line manager. The individual audits that will contribute to this cumulative assessment are as follows:

- **The data center audit** where the management of operational and network problems can be assessed.

- **Change control audits** where the control over software changes can be assessed.

- **Application system operational audits** where the exercise of the controls built into the application can be assessed. Controls within the user departments and the data center are included in the scope of an application system audit.

- **Application system development audits** where the adequacy of the controls built into the system can be assessed.

The audit assessment on the adequacy of information systems problem management should be done on a yearly basis and probably as part of an overall assessment to senior and executive management on the adequacy of the information systems function in the performance of its corporate mandate.

Figure 8.1 — Control Evaluation Table
Information Systems Problem Management

CAUSES OF EXPOSURE

CONTROLS	Untimely Response	Preventable Errors	Undetected Errors	Unrecoverable Errors	Recurring Problems
Preventative Maintenance	2	3	2	1	2
Defined Responsibilities	3	2	3	2	2
Quality Assurance	2	2	2	3	2
Vendor Controls	2	2	2	2	2
Notification Procedures	3	1	2	2	1
Overall Control Rating - Design					
Overall Control Rating - Tested					

EXPOSURES

	Untimely Response	Preventable Errors	Undetected Errors	Unrecoverable Errors	Recurring Problems
Erroneous Record Keeping	2	2	2	2	2
Unacceptable Accounting	2	2	2	2	2
Business Interruption	2	2	2	2	2
Erroneous Management Decisions	2	2	2	2	2
Fraud and Embezzlement	2	2	2	2	2
Statutory Sanctions	2	2	2	2	2
Excessive Costs	2	2	2	2	2
Loss or Destruction of Assets	2	2	2	2	2
Competitive Disadvantage	2	2	2	2	2

KEY TO RELIANCE ON CONTROL
3 - High reliance
2 - Moderate reliance
1 - Control has only a peripheral effect on the cause of exposure
Blank - No significant impact

KEY TO OVERALL CONTROL RATING
3 - Strong control
2 - Moderate but adequate control
1 - Inadequate control

KEY TO DEGREE OF CERTAINTY OF OCCURRENCE IN THE EVENT OF AN INADEQUATE CONTROL STRUCTURE
3 - Virtually certain
2 - Probable
1 - Possible
Blank - Very unlikely

9
INFORMATION SYSTEMS CONTINGENCY PLANNING

INTRODUCTION

The term "contingency planning" is most commonly used to refer to the plans and procedures put in place to counter a prolonged downtime at an organization's central data center. The events leading up to the use of the contingency plan would be classified as a major catastrophe. Generally, localized problems in the data center or problems of a temporary nature are not covered by a contingency plan, with the possible exception of a lengthy, full-scale blackout of electrical power. More typically though, a contingency plan involves finding alternative arrangements to normal information systems processing.

The first section of this chapter describes the control perspective for including information systems contingency planning as one of the basic building block elements of information systems. This section also describes the relevance of this subject area to the skill set and knowledge requirements of the Level 1 and Level 2 auditor. Causes of exposure are described, as are the more common types of control which act upon these causes of exposure. The types of exposure which may occur as a result of a deficiency or breakdown in the control structure are then discussed. Finally, the audits to be performed are described in terms of relevant objectives and frequency.

CONTROL PERSPECTIVE

Many organizations are in the position of being totally dependent on their computer systems for the ongoing operation of their business. Without at least the basic operation of certain "mission critical" systems, these organizations are no longer viable as going concerns. The amount of time that these organizations can function without these critical application systems varies from organization to organization, but can be measured in days for many large organizations. When a disaster occurs, the days have a way of going by very quickly.

For these reasons, every information systems department should develop and maintain a disaster recovery plan (or contingency plan) for all information systems that are critical to the ongoing operation of the business. The objective of the plan is to provide continuity of business processes in the event that a disaster befalls the primary information systems processing environment. The plan must provide for business continuation which will meet the ethical and legal obligations to the owners, customers, suppliers and employees of the business.

SCOPE OF INFORMATION SYSTEMS CONTINGENCY PLANNING

Information systems contingency planning includes the following subtopics in its scope of activities:

- Preliminary planning.

- Establishing the information systems contingency planning sections.

- Testing the plan.

- Maintaining the plan.

Preliminary Planning

There are a number of questions that need to be answered when doing the preliminary planning for information systems contingency planning:

- What application systems are critical to the organization?

- How long can the organization survive without these critical applications?

- What is the minimum hardware configuration that these applications can run on?

- Where are the main users of these critical applications principally located?

- Are there any special supplies required by these applications (for example, special stationery)?

- Under what conditions would the organization revert to the contingency planning arrangements?

- Are there any other factors that need to be considered which would prevent the orderly recovery of a critical application?

Once the answers to these questions have been determined, it is possible to look at various alternatives for contingency planning. The basic requirement is to be able to recreate an operating environment for the critical parts of critical applications. Notice that this operating environment need not be for all applications or even for all parts of the critical applications. There are many applications which have no bearing on the ongoing viability of an organization. Certainly, the absence of these systems will cause problems and inconvenience but, in reality, the organization will be operating in crisis mode anyway as a result of the catastrophe (the situation that caused the need to resort to the contingency plan in the first place). Problems and inconveniences will be the order of the day and the basic ingenuity and resilience of human beings will usually be sufficient to overcome these conditions. This is not the case with critical applications. However, not all parts of critical applications are critical. For example, there may be periodic reports that can be dispensed with. As long as the data have been properly captured, these reports can be produced at a later time or simply bypassed for the period in question.

Once the critical parts of the applications have been determined (including how long the organization can survive without these systems), it should be possible to map out the alternative approaches that are available for contingency planning.

The location of the users of the system is important as is the question of whether the users' access to the system is in batch or on-line mode. On-line systems are much more difficult to accommodate from a contingency planning perspective because of the telecommunications implications.

The need for special supplies or other special requirements must also be known in advance so that they can be made available at the alternate processing site.

The next step in the preliminary planning process is to identify various processing alternatives that will accommodate the requirements just listed. There are a number of these alternate processing environments each with its own advantages, disadvantages and cost structure:

- **Revert to manual procedures.** In certain situations it may be appropriate to simply go back to the manual process that was in place before the introduction of the computer application system. The problem with this approach is one of volume (the computer system was probably put in place because the manual effort was not keeping up with the business requirements) and the availability of staffed trained in the manual procedures (after a while no one remembers how the old system used to work). The advantage of this approach is that it is inexpensive and quick to enact. In many situations this is the first approach to be adopted in the face of a catastrophic situation. Only when the magnitude of the problem is clear are other alternatives considered.

- **Enter into a reciprocal processing arrangement.** This approach used to be quite popular. The idea was to enter into some form of agreement with another organization that had a similar processing configuration. If one site experienced a failure, the critical systems could be moved to the other organization until the first facility was up and running. The problems with this approach are fairly apparent. Things change over time. Installations that appear to be similar on the surface are probably somewhat different. The gulf between the two organizations almost certainly widens over time. What also changes is the availability of the excess capacity which is fundamentally implied in these types of reciprocal arrangements. If excess capacity is not available, it will not be possible to absorb the work from the other organization.

The conventional type of reciprocal arrangement is on an informal basis between two organizations in the same geographical area with similar processing environments. These types of arrangements are, at best, of questionable value and usually only pay lip service to the idea of contingency planning. However, if the agreement is formalized and the processing changes taking place in both organizations are taken into account and tested, then this type of approach may be a cost effective way of providing a disaster recovery scenario.

- **Use the services of a disaster recovery service.** There are a number of organizations that are in the business of offering disaster recovery facilities. The extent of the facilities that are available is usually directly dependent on what the organization is prepared to pay. The range of services spans the spectrum from a "cold" site that offers a raised floor and electricity, to a "hot" backup site that comes with a full configuration ready to take over from the principal site at a moment's notice.

  The type of service needed depends on the criticality of the application systems to the ongoing viability of the organization. A "hot" backup facility is relatively expensive but may be fully cost justified for some organizations who just cannot afford to go through any significant downtime in their computer operation. The entire issue goes back to understanding what the exposure is and making sure that the cost of the controls put in place is commensurate with the risk of loss.

- **Establish a duplicate processing site.** A significant number of large organizations have developed second sites in order to ensure that not all of their computer processing "eggs are in one basket." Neither installation is intended to be capable of running all applications for the entire organization, but each installation has the capacity to run the critical parts of the critical applications for the entire organization.

Once the type of contingency planning arrangement has been determined, the conditions under which this arrangement would be invoked needs to be determined and documented. The person in the organization that has the authority to make the call for a move to the contingency planning arrangement needs to be identified. That person, as well as a backup person, should be made known to the rest of the organization.

The procedures to make the move to the contingency planning arrangement have to be thought out and documented. In order for the contingency plan to work, certain key elements must be in place. Contingency planning is an ongoing state of operation for an organization. Certain procedures, such as the proper backup and storage of data files, must be in place and should be followed at all times. Without these elements in place, the contingency plan will not work.

The final element to be thought about in preliminary planning is testing. Contingency plans have a way of becoming redundant very quickly. Things change so quickly in a computer processing environment that it is easy to forget to update the contingency plan. Regular testing is the only effective way of ensuring that the plan stays current with the needs of the organization.

Establishing the Information Systems Contingency Planning Sections

A contingency plan needs to be properly planned and documented. The sections which should be included in the contingency plan are as follows:

- Contingency plan overview.

- Contractual arrangements.

- Contingency operating configuration.

- Critical functions of critical applications.

- Invocation conditions.

- Contingency procedures.

- Key personnel.

- Contingency operating procedures.

- Testing strategy.

- Restoration procedures.

- Insurance.

The contingency plan overview is a summary of the contingency plan arrangements and encompasses, in summary form, all of the details in the other sections of the plan.

If there are any contractual arrangements with third parties, they are spelled out in this section of the plan. Contractual arrangements are necessary if a reciprocal arrangement forms the basis of the contingency plan. Similarly, if a disaster recovery service bureau is to be used, there should be a description of the contractual arrangement for this service. The hardware vendor(s) may also be asked to undertake certain contractual responsibilities in the event of a disaster at the primary data center.

If the intent is to move the contingency operating configuration to an alternate processing site, the configuration should be described. This configuration must be able to run the basic application set defined as critical for the ongoing viability of the organization. This basic application set is by no means static. Therefore, it is important that the contingency operating configuration be reviewed on a regular basis and updated as required.

Perhaps the most important part of the contingency plan is to identify the critical functions of the critical applications. Again, this is an area that is subject to change and must be reviewed regularly and updated as required. When an organization faces the type of catastrophe that requires it to revert to a full-scale contingency plan, there are inevitably compromises that have to be made in terms of how the business is run. This is also true in the information systems area. It is unlikely that the contingency plan will accommodate business as usual. In fact, economically it is probably inefficient to plan to operate all systems on a business-as-usual basis.

Once the basic shape of the contingency plan has been put in place, the contractual arrangements have been formalized, and the configuration required to operate the identified critical business functions has been determined, the question is, "Under what conditions will the contingency plan be invoked?" Not every problem, even a major problem, will cause the invocation of the contingency plan. Usually, the principal criteria for determining whether or not to invoke the contingency plan is time. In other words, "How long will the main processing facility be out of commission as a result of the catastrophe?" Some organizations may be able to wait several days before having to go to the contingency plan; others may have to commit within hours. It is important to reach a decision before a catastrophe occurs. Decisions that are made rationally have a greater chance of being correct than those made in the midst of a major crisis.

Contingency procedures describe the mechanics of moving to the contingency planning arrangement. The key elements to be considered are people, data (both system and business data), telecommunications and supplies.

There will be a need to have people on-site at the contingency processing facility who know how the applications run. Backup procedures and off-site storage must be in place in order to ensure that the correct versions of the application systems and business data are available for processing. In critical on-line applications, the business data may be transferred on an ongoing basis to the contingency processing site so that there is a mirror image of the data in both the principal and the contingency processing sites. Processing can then be flipped to the contingency site very quickly with little loss in processing time. The alternative (and more common approach) is to load the programs and data on the contingency site computer and then start to operate the systems. This can take a significant amount of time, depending on the requirements of the organization.

Having the systems up and running at the contingency processing site is one thing. Being able to get the input transactions to the system and information back out to the users is quite a different matter. The telecommunications aspect of on-line systems presents quite a problem for contingency planning. Duplicate networks going to both the primary and contingency processing sites are expensive and may not be justified under the circumstances. Other alternatives are to make arrangements with the telephone company to have all lines terminate at a central location. The purpose of this is that the lines can be re-routed from this location to the contingency processing site rather than the principal processing location, which would be the destination in normal times. Dial backup is another approach that can be used to get to the contingency processing site. The telecommunications issue requires a great deal of thought when constructing the contingency procedures.

There will be a number of key personnel required to ensure that the contingency procedures work when invoked. These personnel will include computer operators, systems programmers, application programmers (potentially) and users. It is important that these individuals understand their responsibilities in the event of a move to the contingency processing environment. Documented procedures and adequate training are key elements in ensuring that these responsibilities are thoroughly understood.

Once the transition to the contingency processing arrangement has taken place, the contingency operating procedures take the place of the regular operating procedures. Computer operations and the users will certainly be impacted. Input times for the submission of data may be different, sign-on to on-line systems may be different, and report distribution may be different. There are so many facets of the operation that may be different that it is often useful to focus on what does not change rather than on what does change.

The other groups that will be affected are the system programmers, network operations and the application programmers. The implications of working in this new environment need to be considered and documented. Once again, documentation, communication and training are key elements to success in any contingency plan.

The only way to know if the contingency plan will actually work in practice is to test it. A testing strategy is, therefore, a key part of the contingency planning documentation. Contingency plan testing will be covered in detail in the next section of this chapter.

The contingency processing arrangement is a temporary one. At some point it will be necessary to move back to the principal processing environment. Very often the restoration procedures required to effect this move back to the principal processing site are overlooked. Ensuring that the data is restored at the correct level is one of the key challenges of the restoration procedures. Even during operation in the contingency arrangement it is important to continue to take regular snapshots of the data (business, system and administrative) so that they can be restored back on the primary site when necessary.

Transition procedures for the users also should be in effect when the move is made back to the principal processing site. This is particularly true for on-line users for the same reasons that cutting over to the contingency site was such a problem — lines have to be switched, users have to dial into the correct system, and so forth.

All of the elements of a contingency plan cost money to execute. Insurance is a key element in any contingency plan. As discussed in Chapter 5, insurance is a "last line of defense" to protect an organization against a catastrophic loss which cannot be absorbed and cannot be absolutely protected against. An insurance policy should be considered to cover the cost of moving to the contingency planning arrangement and subsequently moving back to the principal processing site. The cost of the premiums for this type of coverage will depend on the quality of controls in place to prevent a catastrophe from happening.

Testing the Plan

Testing of the contingency plan should be conducted in three steps:

1. First of all, the contingency plan should be reviewed for completeness against a conceptual view of the elements that should be included. The previous section of this chapter listed the various elements that form a reasonable conceptual view of a contingency plan. The intention of this review is to ensure that the entire issue of contingency planning has been thought out. It also ensures that

the organization knows what it is trying to protect against and has the measures to continue operation in the event of a disaster.

2. Once the overall contingency plan has been reviewed and found to be adequate, individual elements of the plan should be tested. For example, tests should be conducted to ensure that the off-site storage arrangements for data files are working properly and that the stored files are able to support the enactment of the contingency plan. The availability of processing capacity at the contingency site is also important. Periodic reviews should be conducted to ensure that the capacity thought to exist does, in fact, still exist.

3. Finally, the entire contingency plan should be practiced on a regular basis (for instance, once every six months) and maintained in contingency operating mode for several days. Only in this way can an organization be sure that the contingency planning arrangement will work in practice. One question which frequently arises is whether this part of the test should be called on a surprise basis. It is the opinion of the author that, except in unique situations, a surprise test is not required. Keep in mind that reverting to the contingency planning arrangement is going to cause significant strain on the organization; the only reason for putting the organization through this strain is to test out procedures which everyone hopes will never be needed anyway. Adding the additional strain of a surprise test is probably not worth the benefit of seeing the enactment of the contingency procedures in as close to an actual situation as possible.

Maintaining the Plan

In a computer environment, things change almost constantly. New applications are developed, existing applications are changed, new hardware is employed, existing hardware is upgraded or discarded and new telecommunication facilities are employed. The contingency plan is intended to mirror the environment and ensure that the critical parts of critical applications can be run. This infers that whenever the applications or the environment change, the contingency plan must change accordingly. Rather than trying to update the plan on a continual basis, it probably makes more sense to review and update periodically, perhaps every quarter or six months.

LEVEL 1 AUDITOR — SKILL AND KNOWLEDGE OBJECTIVES

Overall Objective

Know the areas that must be covered by information systems contingency planning and the methods used to ensure an adequate level of control in this area.

Preliminary Planning

Know the elements of preliminary planning and be able to assess the plans put in place against established criteria.

Establishing the Information Systems Contingency Planning Sections

Know what each planning section should contain. Be able to assess whether or not the actual sections are adequate.

Testing the Plan

Be able to conduct the necessary audit tests to assess the adequacy of the Information Systems Contingency Plan and, from the results of the tests, be able to determine and document where control weaknesses exist.

Maintaining the Plan

Know the rights and responsibilities of ownership of the Information Systems Contingency Plan and the maintenance process which should be in place to ensure that the contingency plan is kept up-to-date.

LEVEL 2 AUDITOR — SKILL AND KNOWLEDGE OBJECTIVES

Overall Objectives

Be able to design and execute audits which can attest to the adequacy of information systems contingency planning. Be able to relate the level of information systems contingency planning to the issue of risk management for the corporation.

Preliminary Planning

Be able to establish the criteria against which the preliminary plan should be assessed. Be able to factor in the elements of preliminary planning into other audits and arrive at an overall opinion on the adequacy of the planning process from the results produced from these audits. Be able to construct an audit program to assess the adequacy of any software used in the preliminary planning process.

Establishing the Information Systems Contingency Planning Sections

Be able to set the criteria for the adequacy of content for each of the planning sections and be able to design an audit program to measure the actual plan against the established criteria. Understand the role that technology will play in each of the planning sections and be able to assess the adequacy of the planned role against what is achievable and desirable.

Testing the Plan

Be able to design the necessary audit tests to assess the adequacy of the Information Systems Contingency Plan including tests designed to assess the adequacy of the role of technology in the contingency plan. Be able to make use of available technology in designing and conducting audit tests of the Information Systems Contingency Plan.

Maintaining the Plan

Be able to determine the implications of changes in technology to the Information Systems Contingency Plan and be able to assess whether or not the plan is properly maintained to reflect these changes in technology.

CAUSES OF EXPOSURE

The causes of exposure in the area of information systems contingency planning are defined somewhat differently from those in previous chapters. Contingency planning is in fact a control used to offset the exposure resulting from a catastrophic occurrence such as fire, storm, earthquake, flood or sabotage. For the purposes of this chapter, the causes of exposure are derived from potentially serious weaknesses in the contingency plan. Similarly, the controls section of this chapter will focus on the controls which contribute to a strong and effective contingency plan. Therefore, with this variation in mind, the causes of exposure relating to information systems contingency planning are as follows:

- Incomplete functionality.

- Inadequate access.

- Untimely cut-over.

- Insufficient supplies.

- Inadequate hardware.

Incomplete Functionality

The reason for having a contingency plan is to ensure that the organization can continue to function in the event of a catastrophic occurrence at the principal processing site; a catastrophe that would make it impossible to run application systems that are considered critical to the organization. The contingency plan must, therefore, be able to run the critical parts of critical applications.

There are a number of reasons for incomplete functionality. It may be that the missing function was not considered critical when the plan was first put together. This may have been an error or it may be that the need for the application or function has changed since the last time the plan was updated. The function may have just been developed within a brand new system or added to an existing system. Again, the problem stems from inadequate maintenance of the plan.

Inadequate Access

The subject of telecommunications has already been extensively discussed in this chapter. If an on-line user cannot get access to the contingency processing site and needs such access to perform a critical function, there is a major weakness in the contingency plan. In certain cases the contingency plan reverts to a centralized data entry function when operating in a contingency arrangement. This is acceptable as long as the procedures are in place to get the input from the source location to the central location so that the input can be processed in a timely manner. Another variation on this theme is to move to regional input from branch input. Once again, this is an acceptable alternative as long as the infrastructure is in place to transfer the work effectively.

New on-line applications and/or new on-line users can also impact the adequacy of the access to the contingency planning arrangement.

Untimely Cut-over

When a catastrophe occurs there is usually a great deal of panic and indecision. In turn, this can lead to actions not being taken when they should have been. The decision to cut over to the contingency planning arrangement will undoubtedly have an impact on the entire organization. Making an unnecessary move will cause a great deal of disruption and unnecessary cost. On the other hand, if the move is not made in time, there will be even more pressure to get the system up and running before more time is lost.

There are many factors to be taken into consideration before "turning on" the contingency plan. Someone within the organization who is in a position to consider these factors should be held responsible for deciding when to go to the contingency plan. This person must then communicate this decision to all those involved in the cut-over process.

Insufficient Supplies

It is not just computer cycles and telecommunications lines that are required to make a contingency operation successful. The usual computer supplies of stationery, tapes, and disks must be available. Tapes and disks are commodities that can be readily obtained. Customized stationery usually has a long lead time. For this reason, contingency arrangements must be in place to get the stationery to the contingency processing site as required.

Inadequate Hardware

Having just said that it takes more than computer cycles to make a contingency plan, it is also true that sufficient computer cycles must be in place to run the applications required as part of the contingency plan. It is difficult enough to handle capacity planning at the regular processing site without also having to worry about the contingency processing site. However, the reality is that the whole contingency plan rests on the fact that there is enough of the right types of hardware to run the applications. Given the rate at which applications, system software and hardware change, it is a major exercise to ensure the compatibility between the contingency processing environment and what is required to run the critical applications.

CONTROLS

Applicable controls intended to prevent, detect and/or correct the causes of exposure just described as relevant to the area of information systems contingency planning are as follows:

- Documented procedures.

- Defined responsibilities.

- Training.

- Regular review and update.

- Regular testing.

Documented Procedures

The essence of successful contingency planning is to have all aspects of the plan properly thought out and documented. Too often, the details of the contingency plan are left to chance, and only the broad overview of the plan is worked out in any detail. The expectation is that it will be a straightforward matter to "fill in the blanks" when the occasion demands. The rationale for this thinking is that there should be only "satisfactory" effort put into a contingency plan given that it is a plan for something which is not expected to happen and for which there are many controls in place to ensure that it does not happen. The reality is that a crisis situation is not the time to be figuring out the details of a broad-based contingency plan. There will be enough details to be worked out without having to deal with issues which could have been easily resolved beforehand. The ideal situation is to look upon the execution of a contingency plan as a "two-minute drill" where the procedures are clearly defined and everyone knows what they are supposed to do.

The Institute of Internal Auditors

The documented procedures should describe a broad overview of the contingency plan followed by a detailed description of the roles and responsibilities of everyone involved in the execution of the contingency plan. Procedures describing the operational characteristics of the contingency planning arrangements should be described in detail along with the repair procedures for bringing the systems back to the primary processing site.

Defined Responsibilities

There will be a number of people involved in the execution of any contingency plan — from the person (or committee) who makes the call to go to the contingency plan, to the operators who will run the systems at the contingency processing site. The roles and responsibilities of these individuals and their alternates should be documented and communicated.

A key individual in all of this is the person who has responsibility for the development and maintenance of the contingency plan. This responsibility varies between organizations. Many organizations place this responsibility with the data security officer. In other organizations it is part of the responsibilities of the executive in charge of information systems or with the responsibilities of the computer operations manager. In these latter situations, the responsibility will almost certainly be delegated to someone else (probably a staff member) within the organization. The point to be made here is that the responsibility for contingency planning should not be treated casually. There is a great deal of time and effort in putting together a contingency plan, not to mention keeping the plan up-to-date and properly tested. The amount of work needs to be kept in mind when assigning the responsibility for contingency planning.

Training

Having defined the roles and responsibilities of the individuals involved in the contingency plan, the corporate expectations of these individuals must be clearly communicated in the form of training. Given that these roles and responsibilities will have to be carried out in a time of crisis, it is important that everyone fully understands what is expected of them and knows how they should fulfill these expectations. Training sessions should be put on for everyone involved in the execution of the contingency plan.

Regular Review and Update

As has been noted many times throughout this chapter, the contingency plan in any organization making use of information systems technology will be subject to ongoing change as a result of changes in hardware, software and/or communications. At regular intervals, or whenever a significant change is known to be taking place, the contingency plan should be reviewed and updated. Documented procedures, defined responsibilities and training must all be reviewed and changed where appropriate.

Regular Testing

The only way to really know if the contingency plan works is to test it in a live setting. This means switching over to the contingency processing arrangements (whether manual or computerized) and running in this fashion for a period of time before reverting back to the primary processing location.

The results of the test should be documented, weaknesses noted and corrective measures taken. If the results from the test prove to be unsatisfactory, it may be necessary to make the corrections and repeat the test. Given the disruption to the organization from having to process under contingency conditions, repeating the test should be avoided, if at all possible.

TYPES OF EXPOSURE

Listed below are the types of exposure which can occur as a result of the inadequacy or failure of the system of control to prevent the occurrence of a cause of exposure in the area of information systems contingency planning.

The Institute of Internal Auditors

Erroneous Record Keeping

Contingency planning requires that the organization have an alternate method of processing available. Incomplete functionality, untimely cut-over and inadequate hardware could all result in a situation where it is not possible to maintain accurate records.

Business Interruption

The entire purpose of contingency planning is to avoid business interruption stemming from a catastrophic occurrence at the primary computer processing facility. Any of the causes of exposure could result in business interruption.

Erroneous Management Decisions

The treatment of this type of exposure in terms of information systems contingency planning will be handled a little differently from previous chapters. The reason is that contingency planning is, in and of itself, all about management decisions. Having a contingency plan put in place is a significant management decision. Many large organizations do not have a contingency plan. Their belief is that the cost of such a plan is not warranted in light of the risks involved. Their faith is pinned on the strength of the controls in place to prevent a catastrophic occurrence from happening or, in some cases, the fatalistic view that a catastrophe that is sufficient to wipe out the computing facility will wipe out the rest of the organization with it. It should be noted that an information systems contingency plan is only one part of the puzzle. All other departments should also be thinking about what to do in the event of a catastrophe in their working location. This is typically not done.

Once the decision has been made to put a contingency plan in place, the next step is to decide on the scale of the contingency planning arrangements. The scope spans the spectrum from reverting to manual procedures all the way to operating a dual data center.

The next decision point is when the catastrophe occurs. At what point should the switch be pulled and the contingency planning arrangement be activated? As was previously discussed, this is a major decision. If it is too soon, the organization goes through unnecessary inconvenience and cost; too late and one simply adds to the trauma of the situation. A decision then should be made on the timing for moving back to the primary processing facility.

Each of these decision points has considerable bearing on the operation of the organization. An error at any point can have significant repercussions throughout the organization.

Excessive Costs/Deficient Revenues

There is no doubt that having a contingency plan in place results in additional costs. These costs could only be considered excessive if the risks to the organization were less than the costs incurred. Similarly, when it is necessary to invoke the contingency plan, additional costs will be incurred. These costs would usually not be considered excessive given the alternative of not being able to function. The absence of a contingency plan in the face of a catastrophic occurrence at the primary computer processing facility will almost certainly result in excessive costs to just try and keep the organization going. Revenues will almost certainly be adversely impacted.

Loss or Destruction of Assets

By definition, there will have been a loss of destruction of assets if a contingency plan is activated. The intent of the contingency plan is to ensure that there are suitable replacement assets to take the place of those that were destroyed. Incomplete functionality may be a result of not having sufficient replacement assets (in this case, software programs).

Competitive Disadvantage

One of the main purposes of a contingency plan is to minimize competitive disadvantage in the event of a catastrophe. Any weakness in the contingency plan could result in additional competitive disadvantage over and above that which could be expected to happen given the circumstances.

CONTROL EVALUATION TABLE

The Control Evaluation Table for information systems contingency planning is illustrated in Figure 9.1. The evaluation numbers are subjective and should be adjusted based upon the conditions which exist in individual organizations. Note that, in practice, the completion of the Control Evaluation Table is in two parts:

- During detailed information gathering where, from the review of available documentation and the results of personal interviews, the key to reliance on individual controls and the "overall control rating (design)" are determined.

- During the execution of the audit program where, as a result of various audit tests, the strength of individual controls is fully assessed and the "overall control rating (tested)" is determined.

AUDIT APPROACH

There should be a specific audit activity focused on the adequacy of the information systems contingency plan. This audit should be timed to coincide with the periodic test of the contingency plan. The audit assessment should be in three parts:

- An assessment of the adequacy of the approach to contingency planning. As previously mentioned, some organizations take the approach that it is not economically justifiable to put a formal contingency plan in place and that management will assume the risk of a catastrophic occurrence at the principal data center. At the other extreme is the situation where a dual data center is established so that a catastrophe at either site will not cause complete failure of the organization's computing capacity. Between these two extremes are a myriad of different variations. What the auditor needs to assess is the appropriateness of whatever arrangement is in place to the needs of the organization. A risk assessment should be carried out where, should such a catastrophe occur, the causes of exposure are identified, the risk of their occurrence is estimated and the financial cost to the organization is calculated. From this assessment the auditor can determine the general level of adequacy of the contingency plan put in place.

- Individual components of the contingency plan can be tested for compliance with the level of expectation of senior management of what should be in place to counter a prolonged downtime at the principal computer facility. The contingency procedures can be reviewed for completeness, clarity and relevance. The backup and off-site storage arrangements can be tested for timeliness and completeness. The contractual arrangements with any external vendor (particularly those providing alternate computing facilities) can be reviewed to ensure that everything is in place should there be a need to call on these services.

- Finally, the results of the contingency plan test can be reviewed and comments can be made to senior management.

Figure 9.1 — Control Evaluation Table
Information Systems Contingency Planning

CAUSES OF EXPOSURE

CONTROLS	Incomplete Functionality	Inadequate Access	Untimely cut-over	Insufficient Supplies	Inadequate Hardware
Documented Procedures	2	2	2	1	1
Defined Responsibilities	1	1	2	2	2
Training	1	2	2	2	
Regular Review and Update	3	2		2	2
Regular Testing	3	3	3	3	3
Overall Control Rating - Design					
Overall Control Rating - Tested					

EXPOSURES

	Incomplete Functionality	Inadequate Access	Untimely cut-over	Insufficient Supplies	Inadequate Hardware
Erroneous Record Keeping	2	1	2	2	2
Unacceptable Accounting	3	3	3	3	3
Business Interruption	2	2	2	2	2
Erroneous Management Decisions	1	1	1	1	1
Fraud and Embezzlement	1	1			
Statutory Sanctions	1	1	1	1	1
Excessive Costs	2	2	2	2	2
Loss or Destruction of Assets	2		2		
Competitive Disadvantage	2	2	2	2	2

KEY TO RELIANCE ON CONTROL

3 - High reliance
2 - Moderate reliance
1 - Control has only a peripheral effect on the cause of exposure
Blank - No significant impact

KEY TO OVERALL CONTROL RATING

3 - Strong control
2 - Moderate but adequate control
1 - Inadequate control

KEY TO DEGREE OF CERTAINTY OF OCCURRENCE IN THE EVENT OF AN INADEQUATE CONTROL STRUCTURE

3 - Virtually certain
2 - Probable
1 - Possible
Blank - Very unlikely

10
INFORMATION
PROCESSING
OPERATIONS

INTRODUCTION

Information processing operations act as the "factory" of the information systems department. Whereas most information systems activities are project based, those in information processing operations are very much on a day-to-day, repetitive basis. However, this is not to say the planning attributes that have been stressed in previous chapters are any less important in information processing operations. The function of information systems processing is to supply the organization with accurate, timely and complete information. Application systems may be the vehicles that deliver the information but it is information systems operations that supply the network of highways to allow the vehicle to reach its intended destination.

The first section of this chapter describes the control perspective for including information processing operations as one of the basic building block elements of information systems. This section also describes the relevance of this subject area to the skill set and knowledge requirements of the Level 1 and Level 2 auditor. Causes of exposure are described, as are the more common types of control that act upon these causes of exposure. The types of exposure which may occur as a result of a deficiency or breakdown in the control structure are then discussed. Finally, the audits to be performed are described in terms of relevant objectives and frequency.

CONTROL PERSPECTIVE

Organizational responsibility for information processing operations is usually the mandate of the computer operations group within the information systems department. As can be seen from the organization chart shown in Figure 10.1, the scope of responsibilities for the computer operations group is very broad and deals directly with many security and control issues of interest to the auditor.

The correct operation of the hardware and software systems is an important element in the control process for large and small system installations. The computer operations control structures must ensure the validity of the input, the accuracy of the processing, and the completeness and timeliness of the output. In addition, the computer operations group acts as custodian for a large percentage of the organization's electronic data and is, therefore, responsible for the safety and integrity of these data.

SCOPE OF INFORMATION PROCESSING OPERATIONS

Information processing operations includes the following subtopics in its scope of activities:

- Library management (logical and physical).

- Scheduling.

- Quality control.

- Planning.

- Operations.

- Input/output control.

- Performance monitoring.

- Backup and recovery.

Library Management (Logical and Physical)

The custodial aspects of all of the libraries are the responsibility of computer operations. Typically, the libraries contain system data (either application software or system software) and should be subject to the same level of data security controls as other types of data files (see Chapter 5). The number of libraries and the interaction between libraries is usually a factor of change control procedures which are discussed in greater detail in Chapter 7. So far, the control structure being described has been of a logical nature (software driven). However, the computer operations group should also be held responsible for the physical management of these libraries. For example, the physical movement of library members between test and production libraries should be under the control of the change control group within computer operations. Libraries should be backed up to tape on a regular basis. This should be scheduled by the production control group and executed by computer operations. The security administrator(s) should establish the access structure to the various libraries.

In addition to the logical control structure, there is also the physical control structure that should be looked at. In addition to software libraries there are physical libraries to be maintained. The most significant of these libraries is the tape library. Tapes are used for a number of purposes including as a storage medium for backup purposes. Tapes must be cataloged and stored so that they can be retrieved when required. Tapes, because of their portability, are the ideal media for the storage of backup files. Therefore, there will typically be both an on-site and off-site tape library. The on-site library will contain the files that are required for immediate processing (usually that day's processing) and scratch tapes to be used for various purposes including system backups. The off-site tape library will contain files that may be required for recovery purposes (i.e., backup files), files that are required for later processing (or year-end processing) and files for historical record purposes (i.e., month and year end files). There are a number of housekeeping duties which should be performed to ensure that the tape files maintained in the library are still readable. Tape cleaning at regular intervals and copying files onto fresh tapes after a specified period are examples of this type of housekeeping duty.

Scheduling

The predominant use of computer time in most organizations is for production jobs. The responsibility for job scheduling belongs to the production control group. There should be a separation of duties between the group that is responsible for running the jobs (i.e., the computer operators) and the group responsible for scheduling and submission of jobs (i.e., the production control group). The jobs that are run in the production environment should be authorized prior to execution. Even when emergencies arise, as happens when reruns or special processing are required, the work should be authorized by someone other than the computer operator. To make scheduling effective, there must be a formal review of all variances from authorized schedules. The operating system is able to provide information on the jobs that were run (such as the console log or some electronic variation thereof). This log of actual jobs should be compared to the authorized schedule on a regular basis and signed by the production control supervisor.

Given the complexity of the job streams run by many organizations and the interaction that exists between jobs both within and between job streams, it is usual to find that the scheduling activity has been automated. When this is the case it may be necessary to engage the services of a Level 3 auditor (i.e., a technical specialist) to attest to the adequacy of the controls over the addition, modification and deletion of jobs within the various job streams.

Quality Control

Quality control is part of a quality assurance program and is a "point-in-time" activity designed to ensure that quality of the input and output is such that the users' expectations will be met. The monitoring of key activities is the essence of a quality control program.

The data control area within computer operations is usually responsible for quality control over data (for instance, input and output). Quality control over processing is a joint responsibility between the application development group, the technical services group, the network control group and the computer operations group with some involvement from the production control group. Quality control over development activities is discussed fully in Chapter 7.

The data control responsibilities under the heading of quality control are fairly straightforward: to make sure that the input to the various application systems is complete, accurate and timely and that the output reports from these systems are similarly complete, accurate, timely and properly distributed to the correct users.

Performance monitoring of on-line response time is also a part of quality control. The network control group, computer operations and the technical services group have joint responsibility for ensuring that on-line response time is consistently within the parameters set by the organization. Performance problems within an on-line system can be caused by a number of different factors, including line, software, job mix and applications problems. A team approach is required to achieve the required level of quality control.

Planning

When talking about information processing operations, planning usually means capacity planning. An organization should have a five-year forecast of expected growth for both the hardware cycles required and the network configuration. Hardware cycles are commonly expressed in MIPS — millions of instructions per second — but sometimes in terms of the number of on-line transactions per second of throughput. The technical services group is usually given the mandate to put the capacity plan in place, although in some organizations, there is a dedicated group for this task. In order to plan effectively, an organization must know its current capacity and its plans for growth. Another complicating factor is the rapid rate of change in all aspects of the technology. The cost of hardware is decreasing in terms of price and performance. Any organization that is seriously committed to capacity planning should develop a relationship with its principal vendors so that future direction of the hardware is understood, at least in conceptual terms. Very often, through signing a non-disclosure agreement, an organization can be given a specific insight into what the technology will look like in the next few years and can factor this information into their plans.

Within computer services, the other aspects of planning that are common to all areas within the information systems department still must be done. These aspects include the planning that is involved for growth in staffing levels, for keeping the staff members current with the latest technology, and for taking advantage of new or emerging technologies

Operations

Computer operations are responsible for successfully running the jobs which are either authorized through the job scheduler or are submitted manually by the production control group or by an authorized user (which includes the application and system software groups). In a batch environment, the computer operators role is relatively straightforward. Jobs that are submitted for processing will funnel through defined channels, usually through the production control group or directly to the computer operators. Jobs are then submitted to the system and released for processing by the operator.

In an on-line, interactive environment, the users are able to submit jobs at will. This is becoming the standard type of operation, particularly in large organizations. The computer operator's role in this type of environment is to ensure that system performance is not degraded as a result of a bad mix of jobs from the users. Maximizing throughput from the available resources is one of the key responsibilities of computer operations. Suspending jobs for future release is one possible approach to achieving this goal.

In addition to these resource optimization activities the computer operator is also responsible for certain physical activities.

- Mounting and dismounting data files (usually tape files but also disk packs).

- Loading paper into the printer.

- Aligning forms on the printer.

- Responding to decisions requested by the operating system.

- Responding to decisions requested by the application programs.

- Maintaining job accounting records.

- Performing routine maintenance.

- Responding to hardware and software failures.

Generally, computer operations will operate on a shift basis, with many large organizations working 24 hours per day over three shifts. The work load in each of the shifts tends to be quite different. The day (or prime) shift has the on-line, interactive work and quick turn-around jobs. The night shift does the batch work that is distributed to the users in time for the start of business the next day. The night shift is used for backups and other system maintenance activities. In reviewing computer operations it is important to recognize the difference in each of these shifts and to ensure that each shift is properly reviewed. It would be wrong to assume that the conditions seen in one shift are representative of all shifts.

Input/Output Control

Input/output controls are the domain of the data control group within computer operations. In a batch environment this role is readily definable. Input is received from the users, batched and converted (usually keypunched) into computer readable format, edited by the computer, balanced and then submitted for processing. Output is received in printed form and checked to ensure that it is complete (the application system should provide the balancing tools and an inventory of reports produced) before being distributed to the users.

In an on-line environment the on-line user takes over much of the responsibility of the data control group. The application system is still required to edit and validate the input being submitted for processing. Printed reports may be spooled directly to the users' location in which case it is the users' responsibility to ensure that the output is complete and that any control totals balance.

Performance Monitoring

Hardware has a defined capacity to process work. Whether defined in MIPS (millions of instructions per second) or transactions per second there is an expectation that the hardware will process a certain amount of work in a given period. Unfortunately, there are other factors, usually related to the amount of access required for input/output devices, which influence this capacity to process work. Degradation in performance can be caused by hardware or software malfunctions and by a poor mix of jobs running at the same time causing contention (and wait time) for access to certain input/output devices.

Three issues are important in performance monitoring: recognizing that there is a problem, determining what is causing the problem and deciding what to do to fix the problem. In order to recognize that there is a problem, there should be a standard measure of acceptable performance and a method of tracking to this level of performance. Once a problem has been recognized, there should be diagnostic methods and tools available to pinpoint the problem area. The resolution of the problem depends on the cause. However, there should be operational procedures in place which give direction on the course of action to be taken when particular types of problems do occur.

Backup and Recovery

In Chapter 9, the subject of information systems contingency planning was covered in detail. Contingency planning deals with a prolonged downtime at the primary processing facility. An important part of contingency planning are the backup procedures which should be in place on a regular basis within the computer operations facility. The backup files are then used for recovery procedures where the backed up data is restored to the appropriate files and libraries so that processing can resume at a particular point in time.

The backup files and recovery procedures are not only used in the event of a catastrophic occurrence at the primary processing facility. In fact, this use of backup and recovery procedures should be used only on rare occasions, hopefully only when testing the contingency

planning arrangements.   The more common use of backup and
recovery procedures is where a localized problem has occurred and it
is necessary to recreate a file or library member at a particular point,
or at the latest point prior to the occurrence of the problem situation.
In an on-line situation the back-up procedures should have "before
and after" images of the records being updated with the recovery
procedures being able to recreate all files to the point just before the
problem arose. The intent of the backup and recovery procedures in
this situation is to ensure that the users have to re-enter only a
minimum amount of data.

LEVEL 1 AUDITOR — SKILL AND KNOWLEDGE OBJECTIVES

Overall Objective

Know the various functional areas that comprise information processing operations and the control issues that affect each of these areas.

Library Management (Logical and Physical)

Know the logical and physical aspects of library management (including the control issues associated with each aspect). Be able to execute
an audit program to assess the adequacy of control over each of the
various issues.

Scheduling

Know the control issues relating to scheduling in an operational
environment and be able to execute an audit program to determine the
adequacy of the scheduling process.

Quality Control

Know the control issues relating to quality control over all aspects of information processing operations. Be able to execute an audit program to determine the adequacy of control exercised over this issue.

Planning

Know the process that should be in place to effect proper planning over information services operations and be able to assess the process that *is* in place against that which *should* be in place.

Operations

Know the various job functions that comprise information processing operations and the control issues that are relevant to each of these job functions.

Input/Output Control

Know the various job functions that comprise information processing input/output control and the control issues that are relevant to each of these job functions.

Performance Monitoring

Know the key elements of information processing operations which should be subject to performance monitoring. Know the benchmarks against which these key elements should be measured.

Backup and Recovery

Know the control issues and processes associated with backup and recovery in an information processing operations environment.

The Institute of Internal Auditors

LEVEL 2 AUDITOR — SKILL AND KNOWLEDGE OBJECTIVES

Overall Objectives

Be able to design and execute audits which can attest to the adequacy of information processing operations. Be able to relate control weaknesses in specific functional areas to the overall scope of information processing operations and either expand the scope of audit activity or call for increased controls in particular areas.

Library Management (Logical and Physical)

Be able to design a specific library management audit program and factor a library management audit into other related audits (such as a data center audit).

Understand the technology that drives the logical aspects of the library management system and the control issues which need to be addressed as part of a review of this technology.

Understand the technology that drives the physical aspects of the library management system and the control issues that need to be addressed as part of a review of this technology.

Scheduling

Understand the technology in use to automate the scheduling process. Be able to design an audit program to attest to the adequacy of the controls inherent in this technology and the manner in which this technology contributes to the overall control over the scheduling process.

Quality Control

Understand the technology in place to effect proper quality control over the operational process. Be able to structure audits to assess the adequacy of the controls inherent in this technology and the manner in which this technology actually contributes to an effective quality control program.

Planning

Understand the technological implications of the planning process. Be able to factor theses implications into the audit program dealing with planning for information systems processing.

Operations

Understand the technology associated with each of the job functions relating to information processing operations. Be able to determine the implications of a control weakness in any one of these technologies to the control structure surrounding each of these job functions.

Input/Output Control

Understand the technology associated with each of the job functions relating to information processing input/output control. Be able to determine the implications of a control weakness in any one of these technologies to the control structure surrounding each of these job functions.

Performance Monitoring

Be able to relate the key elements of information processing operations that should be subject to performance monitoring to the technology which is in place. Be able to make use of technology when auditing compliance with established performance criteria.

Backup and Recovery

Understand the technology associated with backup and recovery from a number of different perspectives (on-line, real-time systems, batch systems, distributed systems and so forth) and the control implications from each perspective.

Be able to design audits which address the control issues for each of the different perspectives identified.

CAUSES OF EXPOSURE

Causes of exposure in the area of information processing operation prevent the work of the data center from being done in a complete, accurate and timely manner. The causes of exposure are as follows:

- Physical disasters.

- Human error.

- Hardware failure.

- Software failure.

- Network failure.

- Capacity problems.

- Recovery failures.

Physical Disasters

Physical disasters include fire, flood, wind, earthquake, sabotage, etc., all of which would create some degree of interruption to the operation of the data center and consequently to information processing operations. The subject of physical disasters and corresponding controls is dealt with in detail in Chapter 5 when discussing information systems security and will not be dealt with further in this chapter. For this reason, physical disasters and environmental controls are excluded from the control matrix presented in Figure 10.2.

Human Error

Information processing operation is the result of a complex series of interactions between hardware, software and the network. All of these are under the control of a number of organizational groups both inside and outside (the user community, including application developers) the data center.

Any number of situations can be caused by human error. The wrong file(s) may be used as input to a job, file(s) may be erroneously deleted, unbalanced batches of input may be submitted for processing, printed reports may not be produced or may not be distributed, and system or application error messages may go unnoticed.

Hardware Failure

In a typical information processing facility (such as the data center), there are many different hardware components. Failure in any component may be obvious (for instance, a tape unit fails to ready a new tape mount) or may not be apparent to the computer operator (such as a disk controller malfunction resulting in dropped blocks of data being sent to the disk device). There are also situations where there is clearly something wrong but the real extent of the problem is not immediately apparent (such as console messages from the operating system warning that something is wrong). What looks like a hardware problem may in fact be software related (such as an error in the system generation when defining the hardware configuration to the operating system).

There must be controls in place to deal with each of these eventualities. Beyond the point of recognizing that a failure has taken place, there should be a defined process for having the problem resolved; this could include calling the vendor support engineer or the systems programmer.

Software Failure

Software failure may stem from either application software or system software, or, in some cases, from the interaction between the two.

Problems resulting from a software failure may manifest themselves through an abend mechanism with a code indicating the nature of the problem or may provide a console message indicating that a problem has occurred. Once again, there should be a defined procedure in place to address the occurrence of a software problem.

Network Failure

The responsibility for monitoring the behavior of the network belongs to the network control group. The manifestations of problems with the network are varied — response time may be degraded, "junk" may appear on the screen, and access to an on-line application may be lost. The reasons for the problems can be equally varied — physical problems with the lines, physical problems with the controllers or modems connecting the terminal devices to the line, problems with the terminal devices, problems with the emulation software that allows a workstation to look like a terminal, problems with the network management software, and so forth.

The network control group should have the ability to monitor the traffic going through the network and be able to spot potential problems. Often, line degradation can be detected and repaired before the users become aware that there is a problem. Procedures that are designed to resolve problems which do occur should be in place. The telephone company, the systems programming group and the application development group may all be involved in the resolution of the problem. In some cases the users are even involved in the resolution exercise, particularly when the problem is with a physical device at the users' end and resetting the device will solve the problem.

Capacity Problems

Where there is more work to be processed than there is capacity for, the result is invariably degraded performance to all applications. Capacity problems are a management problem. Ideally, the processing capacity requirements will be thought out in advance and hardware upgrades will be made in time to handle the increase in the volume of transactions. The practical reality in many organizations

The Institute of Internal Auditors

is that hardware upgrades are only made when there is a crisis and the justification for the upgrade is based on the ongoing problems with the day-to-day information processing operations. This type of "we have no other choice" approach to capacity planning can be avoided. Increases in capacity stem from two sources — an increase in transactions from existing applications and an increase in transactions resulting from the implementation of new systems. When business volume is expected to increase, this should be factored into the information systems capacity plan through the regular business planning cycle and incorporated into the information strategy (see Chapter 4). When new applications are being developed, the implications of these transactions on the current hardware capacity should be factored into the business case under "ongoing cost of operation." If these simple measures are followed, capacity planning becomes an ongoing exercise within the organization and not one that is reserved for crisis management.

Recovery Failures

When a problem does occur and a solution has been identified, there may be cases where it is not possible to apply the solution because of a missing ingredient. For example, the solution may be to revert back to a previous version of an application program because the current version is causing major problems. If this previous version is not available, there is a recovery failure. In practice, a recovery failure usually means that the "best" solution to the problem is not available and that another solution must be found and applied. This takes time and undoubtedly increases costs to the organization.

The solution to recovery failures is anticipation. By identifying the risks to which the data center is exposed, the organization can put in place the controls which allow recovery from the occurrence of one of these risks thereby minimizing the possibility of recovery failure.

CONTROLS

Applicable controls intended to prevent, detect and/or correct the causes of exposure just described as relevant to the area of information processing operations include:

The Institute of Internal Auditors

- Environmental controls.

- Policies and procedures.

- Training.

- Vendor controls.

- Application controls.

- Capacity planning.

Environmental Controls

Environmental controls are aimed directly at physical disasters and are dealt with in Chapter 5. These controls must be in place to prevent any physical disruption to the process of work within the data center. Similar to the associated cause of exposure (i.e., physical disasters), environmental controls are not shown in the control evaluation table for information processing operations. It is, however, covered in the corresponding control evaluation table in Chapter 5.

Policies and Procedures

Service levels and the methods of achieving these service levels should be documented in the form of a policies and procedures manual for the data center. Policies and procedures that are properly thought out and documented are essential for the smooth operation of information processing operations. With the many demands which are placed on the data center on a daily basis and the opportunity for unforeseen problems, it is simply not possible to manage on a entirely reactionary basis. The people who work in the data center need a basis on which to respond when a problem does occur. The policies and procedures manual provides this foundation for action.

The policies and procedures manual should describe the organization of the computer operations department and the responsibilities of each group within the department. Work flows for the submission of work should be described, including the control points in the work flow. Of particular interest to the auditor will be the segregation of responsibilities within the data center to ensure that no one person has end-to-end control over the input, processing and output of any transactions.

Problem resolution and escalation procedures should be described and, for each application system, there should be a list of all operator error messages and the names of the people to be contacted in the event of a problem. Backup and recovery processes should be described, as should the preventative maintenance schedule of activities.

Training

Information processing operations is a complex mix of many different activities. Although few of the activities, by themselves, are particularly difficult, the combinations and changes that can happen in a day are considerable. This means that the employees involved in the operation have to be well trained in their roles and responsibilities. Technology is changing constantly, rapidly and significantly. An organization cannot just invest in technology and the technologist. The employees who will be responsible for operating the technology must also be trained.

For each person in the computer operations department there should be a training program in place on both new technologies and on new applications that will be introduced into the data center in the foreseeable future.

Vendor Controls

A large part of the environment within which information processing operations takes place is provided by external vendors, particularly the hardware vendor. The hardware, operating system, network management system and data base management system are all typically provided by an external vendor. When something either goes wrong with these products or the products detect that something else within the operation is going wrong, there should be effective communication of these facts to the operator. An organization is dependent on the adequacy of the controls installed by the vendor for a large percentage of the processing that takes place on a regular basis within the data center. Attesting to the adequacy of these controls usually requires the services of a Level 3 auditor (i.e., a technical specialist).

Application Controls

From a software perspective, application controls should be considered as complementary to vendor controls in that, in combination, they should provide a complete picture of information processing operations as they take place within the computer. The application controls that are relevant to information system processing are those that interface or report to the operators of the system. The application system should make sure that the correct files are being used and that the input is balanced. It should also provide sufficient information on the output that is produced so that someone can ensure that all of this output is being received. Chapter 11 deals with application system controls in detail.

Capacity Planning

As previously stated, capacity planning is an ongoing activity and not something that should only be done once a year or when a capacity crisis has struck. Capacity increases result from increased transaction in existing systems and incremental transactions as a result of new systems. The increase in business transactions for existing systems should be planned for in the regular business planning cycle. The capacity requirements of a new system should be factored into the business case justification for the new system. However, there is still a need for someone to be assigned to take these increases in transaction volumes and project what the increase means to the hardware and network capacity. Given the changes that are taking place almost constantly in the technology arena, it is essential that the person who is responsible for capacity planning be conversant with the state-of-the-art as it exists within the environment chosen by the organization. Proposals for hardware and network upgrades should be presented for approval to senior management in time to have the capacity in place before it is needed. This approach allows management to fully understand the need for the additional capacity and to test out other approaches, thereby ensuring that the organization is getting the best return on its investment. The alternative is to wait until the last minute when a crisis is developing and be forced into an upgrade because there seems to be no other choice.

TYPES OF EXPOSURE

Listed below are the types of exposure which can occur as a result of the inadequacy or failure of the system of control to prevent the occurrence of a cause of exposure in the area of information processing operations.

Erroneous Record Keeping

All of the causes of exposure relating to information processing operations can result in erroneous record keeping. Human error related to file management can cause the wrong file to be updated; hardware failure may cause a "bad" record to be written to the accounting file(s); software failure may result in a logic error which causes the wrong record to be updated or the right record to be updated incorrectly; network failure may cause an incomplete transaction to take place because the network fails midway through a transaction; capacity problems sometimes result in strange circumstances as the system becomes overloaded with the transactions that are submitted for processing; a recovery failure may prevent the resolution of any of the previously defined problems.

Unacceptable Accounting

Erroneous record keeping may result in unacceptable accounting depending on the nature of the error. Typically, however, only application system errors will result in unacceptable accounting by not having the correct checks and balances built into the system.

Business Interruption

Any failure which causes the operation to halt its processing can result in business interruption to some degree. Unless the organization is unusually dependent upon its computer operation for day-to-day processing, the level of business interruption that is contemplated in this chapter (i.e., as an outage of varying degrees but of short duration) will be more of a nuisance than a major business problem. A prolonged outage of computer resources as discussed in Chapter 9 is an entirely different matter.

Erroneous Management Decisions

Insufficient information from the vendor or from the application systems may result in erroneous management decisions. When a problem has arisen or is in the process of developing, management needs enough information upon which to base their actions. Insufficient information may mean that a decision is not made because the problem is not noticed or is not clearly understood. It may also result in the wrong decision being made. Human error covers a whole host of potential problems, some of which could, in certain situations, result in erroneous management decisions.

Excessive Costs

When a problem occurs that cannot be handled under business-as-usual policies and procedures, excessive costs may occur. In information processing operations the reality of the matter is that problems will occur. Therefore, the budgeted operating costs of this function should include the capacity to deal with routine problems. Excessive costs occur when the problem is not routine and/or does not have a set policy or procedure to deal with it. Correspondingly, all of the causes of exposure have the ability to generate excessive costs if they cannot be dealt with in the normal course of business.

Loss or Destruction of Assets

The inability to recover from a problem will result in a loss of assets. Typically, a loss of assets will refer to data that are now recognized as a major corporate asset. If it is not possible to electronically recover data after a problem has occurred, it will probably be necessary to try and recreate the data using other means (such as from manual records, previously printed reports, data from other systems, and so forth). The extent of the loss of assets will depend on the nature of the problem and the availability of other means to recreate the data.

CONTROL EVALUATION TABLE

The Control Evaluation Table for information processing operations is illustrated in Figure 10.2. The evaluation numbers are subjective and should be adjusted based upon the conditions that exist in individual organizations. Note that, in practice, the completion of the Control Evaluation Table is in two parts:

- During detailed information gathering where, from the review of available documentation and the results of personal interviews, the key to reliance on individual controls and the "overall control rating (design)" are determined.

- During the execution of the audit program where, as a result of various audit tests, the strength of individuals controls is fully assessed and the "overall control rating (tested)" is determined.

AUDIT APPROACH

The primary audit attesting to the adequacy of information processing operations is the data center audit. In Chapter 5, the data center audit was named as one of the principal audits for attesting to the adequacy of information systems security. This dual function of the data center audit stems from the dual role of the data center which functions as the custodian for most corporate data and the factory function which turns data into information.

The data center audit is usually conducted on an annual basis and is a compliance audit based on the policies, practices and procedures of the data center. From the perspective of information processing operations, the audit is conducted to provide management with assurances that the data center can and will continue to process work in an accurate, timely and complete manner. The first step in this audit should be an evaluation of the adequacy of the documented policies and procedures manual. The scope of information processing operations as presented earlier in this chapter can be used as a template for assessing the adequacy of the content of the policies and procedures manual. If the manual is found to be deficient, management should be informed and the appropriate remedial action taken. As previously stated, the smooth operation of a data center should not be left to reactive decision making; documented policies and procedures, along with adequate training, allow for consistent decision making under the pressure of production conditions.

Once the policies and procedures manual has been reviewed, the audit should measure compliance with these procedures, always remembering that in a multi-shift environment, each of the shifts must be reviewed separately. The areas to be reviewed include production control, data control and computer operations. The technical services group is usually left to a separate audit under the direction of a Level 3 auditor. In the production control area the issues to be addressed include control over the scheduling of jobs and the control over the allocation of resources to individual jobs, which is also the responsibility of the production control group. Control over input and output is the thrust of the data control group audit. Particular attention should be paid to procedures used to correct problems in either input or output. In computer operations, the focus is on the handling of work and the actions taken to identify and resolve problems.

In all of the individual reviews, attention should be paid to the adequacy of information which is fed to management on what is happening within the computer operations group overall. Statistical information on jobs run, transactions processed, file space used and available and CPU usage should all be part of a regular report to management.

Figure 10.1 — Computer Operations Organization Chart

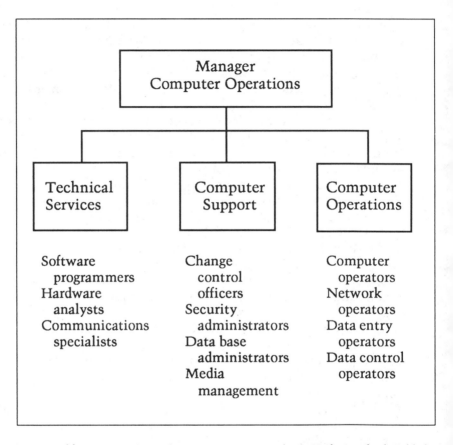

**Figure 10.2 — Control Evaluation Table
Information Processing Operations**

CAUSES OF EXPOSURE

CONTROLS	Human Error	Hardware Failure	Software Failure	Network Failure	Capacity Problems	Recovery Failure
Policies and Procedures	3		1	2	2	2
Training	3				2	3
Vendor Controls	2	3	3		2	2
Application Controls	2		3			2
Capacity Planning	1	1	1	1	3	
Overall Control Rating - Design						
Overall Control Rating - Tested						

KEY TO RELIANCE ON CONTROL

3 - High reliance
2 - Moderate reliance
1 - Control has only a peripheral effect on the cause of exposure
Blank - No significant impact

KEY TO OVERALL CONTROL RATING

3 - Strong control
2 - Moderate but adequate control
1 - Inadequate control

EXPOSURES

	Human Error	Hardware Failure	Software Failure	Network Failure	Capacity Problems	Recovery Failure
Erroneous Record Keeping	2	2	2	1	1	3
Unacceptable Accounting	1	1	2	1	1	1
Business Interruption	1	1	1	1	1	1
Erroneous Management Decisions	2	2	2			
Fraud and Embezzlement						
Statutory Sanctions						
Excessive Costs	2	2	2	2	2	2
Loss or Destruction of Assets	1	1	1	1		3
Competitive Disadvantage						

KEY TO DEGREE OF CERTAINTY OF OCCURRENCE IN THE EVENT OF AN INADEQUATE CONTROL STRUCTURE

3 - Virtually certain
2 - Probable
1 - Possible
Blank - Very unlikely

11
APPLICATION SYSTEMS

INTRODUCTION

In Chapter 6, the subject of system development is dealt with in detail. What differentiates the content of Chapter 6 from this chapter relates to the issue of process versus content. Chapter 6 deals with process; the system development process that should apply to all application systems. This chapter deals with the content of specific application systems. Clearly, the subject of system development and application systems are related. In order to develop application systems that meet the defined needs of the user, on time and within budget, there should be a formal methodology in place which provides sufficient review points for the user and senior management to sign off before proceeding to the next phase of the project. The subject of system development as discussed in Chapter 6 concerned the details of this formal methodology and showed how to audit for the presence of an effective methodology. This chapter deals with the next step — to describe the controls that should be present in any production computer system. The chapter focuses on how to ensure an adequate control structure is actually developed into application systems as they are being built. It also deals with attesting to the adequacy of the control structure from an ongoing operational standpoint.

The first section of this chapter describes the control perspective for including application systems as one of the basic building block elements of information systems. This section also describes the relevance of this subject area to the skill set and knowledge requirements of the Level 1 and Level 2 auditor. The causes of exposure are described, as are the more common types of control which act upon these causes of exposure. The types of exposure which may occur as a result of a deficiency or breakdown in the control structure are then discussed. Finally, the audits to be performed are described in terms of relevant objectives and frequency.

The Institute of Internal Auditors

CONTROL PERSPECTIVE

"The proof of the pudding is in the eating." This adage is certainly relevant to application systems. Adherence to a formal methodology does not guarantee a well-controlled application system, although with proper control review points, the risk of implementing a system which has poor controls is considerably reduced. The point is that the auditor must look beyond the formal methodology to what is actually happening on an application system by application system basis.

It is also a reality that many application systems to be audited were developed without the benefits of a formal development methodology and, therefore, do not have the formalized control structure that one would expect to find had a methodology approach been used. Where there is no formalized and documented control structure, the auditor must be able to document a reasonable facsimile of the control structure before designing the audit program to verify the existence and adequacy of anticipated controls. The creation of a documented control structure will take place during detailed information gathering (see Chapter 3) and will be derived from interviews with the users of the system and with the technical staff responsible for the maintenance and operation of the system. When the information to document the control structure is incomplete, the auditor should make note of the omission and factor the appropriate tests into the design of the audit program. However, in order to proceed with detailed information gathering, the auditor should assume the type of control structure that should be in place, given good business practice, and evaluate these assumptions when the audit program is executed.

If we can accept that the primary mission of any information systems department is to develop, implement and operate the application systems for the user constituency, then application system integrity is crucial to business success or failure. There should be a set of controls in place that ensures that the system processes and the logic perform according to the specifications each time the system is run.

SCOPE OF APPLICATION SYSTEMS

Application systems include the following subtopics in its scope of activities:

- Basic systems analysis.

- Application design.

- Functionality.

- Input, processing, output and storage.

- Business purpose.

- Business risks.

- Controls identification.

- Testing.

The auditor must understand all aspects of each application system being audited. The scope of an application system does not change based on whether or not the system was developed using a formal methodology. However, where a formal methodology was used to develop the system, there should be sufficient documentation to allow the auditor to piece together the scope of the system fairly easily. If a formal methodology is not employed, the auditor will need to use alternate means (such as interviews with users and with technical staff, a review of systems and user documentation, and so forth) to gain an adequate understanding of the scope of the system.

The starting point for the audit of any application system should be during the system development stage. Much of the material in this section of the chapter is organized to reflect this ideal situation. However, as many practicing auditors will attest, it is frequently the case that an ongoing application system that is to be audited was not subject to audit as the system was built. This places the auditor in the position of having to recreate, in the limited time available, much of the material that would (and should) ordinarily be generated through the system development process. Therefore, the material in this section is relevant whether or not the system was subject to audit as it was being developed given that the auditor must, in any case, arrive at answers to the background issues that are the subject of this section.

Basic Systems Analysis

The intent of basic systems analysis is to lay out the problem definition and the most beneficial solution, supported by a business case. In terms of conducting an application systems audit of a production system, the auditor must have a clear understanding of the business issues and problems addressed by the system.

Within the framework of the formal methodology used within this text, basic systems analysis occurs in the general design and feasibility analysis phase of development (see Chapter 6 for more detailed information on this phase of development). The audit requirements from basic systems analysis should come straight from the documentation prepared as the system was being developed. In the absence of available documentation, either as a result of insufficient compliance with the methodology or the total lack of a methodology, the auditor should interview the users to determine the basic business functions that are intended to be addressed by the system and the flow of information between the system and the user.

The end result of either the audit review of the documentation produced during the system development process or the interview process conducted with the end users of the system should be as follows:

A description of the business or system problem: "Solutions looking for problems to solve" and "if it ain't broke, don't fix it" are two adages that describe what many users believe often happens in the information systems field. The reason for this belief is that the business problem and the eventual solution often do not seem like an appropriate fit. This is frequently the result of an inadequate definition of the business problem. Notice that the task says "business or system problem." It is worth spending a few moments on the distinction between these two types of problems. A business problem inhibits the organization's ability to do either the type or volume of business it wants to do. A system problem inhibits the organization from doing the type of business it wants to do, the way it wants to do it. A system problem may be procedural (for instance, a manual procedure that cannot deal with the current volume of transactions), or technical (the data base/file architecture does not support the level of ad hoc reporting required by management) or both.

During system development, a systems analyst will be assigned the task of preparing the basic systems analysis. The responsibility of the systems analyst is to define the real problem, which is not necessarily the apparent problem. In other words, the need for a particular report from an existing system may only be the tip of the iceberg. The real problem may be an architectural problem concerning the ability to access data in different ways.

Given that the eventual objective is to have the approval to solve the identified problem, the definition of the business or system problem must be in business terminology and not wrapped up in technological mumbo jumbo.

A description of the existing environment: A process flow or data flow (or both depending on the standards within the organization) of the existing function should be prepared. The intention here is twofold: clearly, to understand what is currently happening but, perhaps more importantly, to be able to simplify the process before deciding how to automate it. Too often, the analysis is constrained by what is taking place today, and the process rather than the business intent becomes the focus.

A description of the selection process for the system as it is currently installed: Once the real problem has been described and the business process simplified, it should be possible to identify a number of possible solutions during the development process. Packaged software has some pros and cons but it is certainly a viable alternative for many types of systems. In identifying possible solutions it is necessary to specify cost, implementation time frame, complexity to implement and any other issues that are relevant to the final selection process. The auditor should ensure that alternative solutions were investigated and tested against pre-selected criteria. The solution selected should be the one that best meets the needs of the organization at the time the selection is made. This recommended solution should be supported by a business case which lays out the costs and benefits of the proposed solution.

When auditing an ongoing application system which was not previously the subject of a development audit, the installed solution is usually a given. Even in the case of serious control deficiencies it is usually very difficult to overturn a decision that has been made and implemented. The only recourse open to the auditor is to insist that the control structure be strengthened and comment to senior management on the way the selected decision was actually made.

Application Design

Application design is a technical function which takes the business solution defined in general analysis and feasibility and produces a technical solution that will fit within the operating architecture of the organization. The overall system is progressively broken down into manageable entities which can be accurately specified. Data base design is also done during application design. It may be that the data base already exists and only needs to be updated by the data elements used within the system to be built (if they do not already exist). Alternatively, it may be necessary to undergo substantial data base design work where there is nothing presently in place.

Audit and control issues are fleshed out as the application is designed. In the analysis phase, the causes of exposure that need to be controlled can be defined. However, it is only after the application system has been designed that ways to control the causes of exposure can be determined.

The test plans for systems acceptance testing should be drawn up at this stage of development. Refer to Appendix A (Systems Acceptance Testing) for a full description of what this preparation entails.

Once again, it should be possible for the auditor to draw on the material produced when the system was developed. However, if this material does not exist, the auditor must talk to the technical resources responsible for maintaining the system and reconstruct the application design from these interviews and from a review of available technical documentation.

Functionality

Too often, a new system simply automates an existing procedure which may previously have been entirely manual or served by a system which, for whatever reason, is no longer considered adequate. The problem with this approach is that the opportunity to simplify the process is missed. Ideally, the underlying rationale for all activities within the existing process (both manual and automated) for all users should be identified. It is very likely that a number of redundant, or at least inefficient, activities will have been found to have been introduced into the process over time. This is only to be expected as more and more changes are retrofitted to the original framework.

The functionality of an application system should be mapped to a specific business intent and should be designed to streamline delivery of this intent. What does this mean in practical terms? The level of sophistication of a particular system and associated functions should be reflective of the culture and needs of the organization. Some organizations pride themselves on the level of sophistication of their systems and believe they derive a business advantage from this sophistication, while other organizations want the basic functionality at the lowest price possible while still meeting the business needs. The analysts and designers who are putting the system functionality together need to understand these corporate nuances if they are to meet the overall organizational requirement of effective and relevant systems.

An interesting development in recent years concerning the functionality of application systems is the entire concept of ad hoc reporting and data-driven system development. Previously, system development was very much a process-driven exercise with all focus on the activities to be automated. Recently, it has been recognized that the information systems group is very good at building the overall framework for application systems. At the same time, the group is consistently unable to provide the responsiveness to change required by the user once they have seen the potential of what the system can do for them. Therefore, rather than have the information systems department held responsible for the entire system, it is suggested that they only be held responsible for populating the data base (or data capture, validation, and storage). This would allow the users to go against the data base with powerful ad hoc report writers which can provide the users with any report they desire provided that the data exists. The concept of data driven development is discussed in more detail in Chapter 14.

When conducting an audit of an ongoing application system, the auditor should be aware of the business functions being addressed by the system. He or she should be able to assess the implications of both the changes that have taken place in the business functions as well as those having taken place in the functionality of the system to ensure that the system continues to provide an adequate level of support to the business function.

Input/Processing/Output/Storage

Once an application has been analyzed and designed, specific controls are applied to act on the causes of exposure which have been identified as relevant to this application. Some of these controls will be generic across all applications.

Application controls can be conveniently categorized into those that deal with: (1) input, (2) processing, (3) output and (4) storage. While the control objectives remain the same, the specifics are different between on-line, real-time systems and batch systems. On-line systems are dealt with in detail in Chapter 15. In this chapter, only the principal differences between on-line and batch controls will be highlighted.

Input controls: The control objective of input controls is to ensure that all input is authorized, timely, complete and accurate before being processed. Input controls can be both procedural (i.e., manual) and automated.

- **Input authorization** is achieved in different ways depending on whether the system is on-line or batch. In an on-line environment, the user should be required to go through an identification and authentication process just to get into the system. Beyond this point of entry, the application system should determine the type of input the user is authorized to initiate. In some cases there is a separate authorization screen which is used by the initiator's supervisor to verify the input transaction before it is passed to the processing module. In other cases (probably the majority), once the application system has verified that the user is authorized to input a transaction, the transaction is passed directly to the processing module.

In a batch system, the user manual should specify when a certain type of input requires authorization. The input form should provide space for the signature. Authorization on the input document should be verified by data control before the documents are keyed. Input documents should be batched and a batch slip should be used to identify the input document or system and the user submitting the batch. The slip should contain the date, batch number and batch control totals. Users should maintain batch logs and batching procedures should be included in the user manual. Batch verification should be built into the application system.

- **Completeness and accuracy** — checks of this type should be part of the input validation performed by the application system. This is typically referred to as input editing. Input edit checks can be thought of as having two elements: (1) at the batch level, and (2) at the individual transaction level. Sequence checks, control total reconciliation, hash total checks, crossfoot and balance, and record counts are all controls to ensure that there is nothing missing from the batch (and that nothing has been added to the batch). Valid character tests, checks for missing data, valid field checks, tests on the validity of input codes, cross checks between data elements, limit tests, tests for zero, reasonableness tests and check digits are all examples of individual transaction tests to ensure that the data within the transaction is valid for subsequent processing.

The input validation controls should produce certain reports which can be used by the data control group and/or the users to verify that the input has been correctly submitted for processing. Batch balance reports, error reports, and exception reports should be produced by the edit routines. The intent and content of each of these reports is as follows:

The Institute of Internal Auditors

- **Batch balance report:** Where batch control totals are entered, the application system sums the control fields, compares the calculated totals with input totals, and prints out agreements and variances. If a batch is out of balance, all items in the batch should be listed. If the program does not compare calculated totals with input totals, all batches and their totals should be printed.

- **Error report:** Each input item with one or more erroneous fields should be shown on this report. If an item has more than one erroneous field, each error should be identified. Code numbers or letters should only be used when limited space precludes the use of an English error message. If error codes must be used, users should be provided with a document that decodes the error message. Although the error report can be combined with the transaction list, a separate report is preferable.

- **Exception report:** This report lists entries that do not pass complete editing rules in the application system. The person responsible for the data must determine whether the item (such as a salaried employee with fewer than eight hours accounted for in one day) was in error. Unusual items that may not be in error (for example, all accounts payable checks exceeding $5,000) should also be reviewed. Although the exception report can be combined with the transaction report, a separate report is preferable.

Processing controls: The control objective of processing controls is to ensure that the input transactions are properly applied to the appropriate data base records and files. The processing controls should produce certain output reports which can be used by the data control group and/or by the users to verify that the processing has taken place correctly. Transaction reports and master file change reports should be produced by the application system. The intent and content of each of these reports follows:

- **Transaction report:** In this report, important data fields of every valid transaction in a processing cycle are listed.

- **Masterfile change report:** This report shows the status of every master file item before and after it is changed. If the master file items have fields for current or accumulated transaction values, changes to these fields need not be shown on a master file change report. For example, if the accounts receivable master file contains a year-to-date record of purchases, the master file item need not be printed on the master file change report each time a purchase is made.

There are a number of other processing controls which should be mentioned:

- **Program-to-program controls:** An application system may consist of several discrete programs which are linked together to form a system. Control is passed from one program to the next as processing progresses through the system. To guard against hardware, software, and program errors, control totals and record counts should be passed from program to program. These controls need to be printed only if an error is detected.

- **File verification:** If the operating system or other utility software does not verify the data in the file labels used by an application system, this data must be verified by the application. The retention period on scratch tapes must be checked to ensure that the data on saved files is not destroyed.

- **File labeling:** Header and trailer labels (records) should be used on all files. Depending on what the operating system permits, the header or trailer record should contain specific data characteristics:

  - File name and number.
  - Creation date or cycle.
  - Retention period or purge date.
  - Tape reel or disk pack number.
  - Sequence number, if the file is larger than one tape reel or disk pack.

- **Checkpoint and restart:** The equipment, power or system may fail in the middle of a run. In a batch system, the run is usually started over. However, when the run is expected to last more than one hour, checkpoint/restart techniques that allow the application system to be restarted from a defined point in the run (i.e., from the point of the last checkpoint) should be used.

  In an on-line system, it is mandatory that the system be able to recover at any point of failure with a minimum of re-keying on the part of the users. It is simply not acceptable to have to go back to start-of-day processing.

Output controls: The control objective of output controls is to ensure that the files and reports to be produced by the application system are actually produced and, in the case of printed reports, are distributed to the correct destination. Output controls include report formats, output forms control, error corrections and run-to-run totals.

- **Report formats:** All reports, including data center control reports, must have meaningful names, and report and page numbers must be printed on every page. The effective date of the data in the report must appear in the report heading. All columns of data should have meaningful titles. However, if space limitations require the use of cryptic abbreviations, definitions of the abbreviations should be printed on the first page of the report for users.

- **Output forms control:** Pre-numbered forms should be used to control the use of output forms. The application system should also print a number of the form and maintain a count of the number of forms printed. Logging and control procedures should be specified in the user manual. For example, logs should record the first and last number used, any spoiled forms, and missing numbers, if any. The person responsible for forms control should subtract the first preprinted number used from the last. Similarly, the first number printed by the application system should be subtracted from the last one printed. The two should be compared and any discrepancies should be resolved.

- **Error corrections:** Errors should be placed in a suspense file and all uncorrected errors should be printed. The user manual should explain the cause of each type of error as well as error correction procedures.

- **Run-to-run totals:** If totals are carried forward from one run to the next (such as year to year totals), the system should print beginning- and end-of-run totals on reports. Control instructions should specify the procedures for verifying the accuracy of the run-to-run data.

Storage controls: The control objective of storage controls is to ensure that the application data is securely controlled between and during executions of the application system. Data may be stored on tape or disk. More commonly, given the move to data base systems, the application system data is stored on disk. Storage controls are intimately related to information systems security. Access controls, retention policies and backup and recovery procedures are all part of storage controls.

The auditor must ensure that an adequate control structure is designed into the system. It is an established fact that the cost of retrofitting controls is more expensive after the system has gone into production. The control structure should be comprehensively documented as part of the system development audit review. When an audit is conducted of the system after it has been installed in production, the focus is on ensuring adherence to the controls that were put in place and attesting to the fact that the control structure is adequate in light of production conditions. What may have seemed like a strong control structure during the development phase may not withstand the realities of the operational environment within which the system operates. When this is the case, additional or compensating controls will have to be implemented.

Business Purposes

Technology is a tool used to facilitate the achievement of management's objectives of profitability, continuity of business, protection of assets, competitiveness, productivity and management effectiveness. Application systems are typically the means by which technology is applied to the business. Therefore, it should be possible to identify the need for a particular application system by going back to the strategic plan for information systems (or the information strategy). Given that a primary goal of the information strategy is to map to the corporate business plan, the business purpose of any application system should be readily identifiable. The question is really whether or not the application system is meeting these business functions once it has been developed and implemented. Two approaches to answering this question are available to the auditor: (1) a post implementation review and (2) a full application audit. Both of these approaches will be discussed later in this chapter when dealing with the issue of audit approach to application systems.

Business Risks

The management of risk is a key managerial responsibility in any business. Building, implementing and operating application systems brings with each of these functions a degree of risk which varies between applications and between organizations. The key point is to be able to identify what the risks are and to assess these risks in the context of an individual organization.

In building an application system, the risk factors are the technology being used, the importance of the functionality of the application system to the organization, the size of the development effort and the complexity of the functionality within the application.

When new technology is being used, the risk factor is high because of the learning curve that the organization must go through to become familiar with the new technology. It is probable that there are few if any people on the project team who are experienced with the technology. Finding and fixing errors can be a major problem in this type of environment as an unusual amount of reliance has to be placed on the vendor of the technology.

The importance of the functionality to the business is an obvious risk factor. Any delay in implementation may seriously affect the organization. At the same time, a hasty implementation, with many attendant problems, may be even more serious.

The size of the development effort and the complexity of the business functions being automated provide many challenges to the project management of an application development. The project management effort of a large and varied project team requires considerable communication between the various groups to ensure consistency between the deliverables from each of the groups. One approach to this problem is to have an integration manager on the project along with a project manager. Where the project manager is responsible for the project schedule and budget, the integration manager is responsible for the quality and consistency of the various deliverables from the different project groups. All developments of application systems should have dedicated user involvement. However, this is even more crucial where complex business functions are involved. The choice of user participation may be limited in this type of situation. The other side of this problem, of course, is that the individuals who have the required business expertise are also key members of the day-to-day operation in the user department.

The risks in implementation are basically concerned with whether or not the application system has been sufficiently developed and tested to be implemented into the production environment. Pilot tests and parallel runs are approaches that minimize the risk at implementation time. However, there are cases when neither of these techniques can be used. Reliance on adequate acceptance testing is the only way to reduce risk in this type of situation.

Once an application system has been implemented the risk is that it will not function according to the business requirements either functionally or technically (slow response time, too expensive on hardware cycles). Once again, adequate acceptance testing is a key control. System maintenance and change control procedures (see Chapter 7) are key to ensuring that the application system continues to operate in a risk controlled manner.

Controls Identification

Within the methodology to develop systems there should be tasks that deal with the identification of specific causes of exposure and related controls, both of which should be clearly spelled out in the system documentation. The user manual(s), the data center manual for production and data control and the programming documentation should have the control structure for the relevant application system clearly documented. It is from this documentation that the auditor is able to gain an initial assessment of the adequacy of the control structure. When the causes of exposure and controls are not clearly documented, the auditor must spend additional time in defining what both of these issues are, otherwise the controls review will be performed in a vacuum. However, where there is no clear documentation on the causes of exposure and related controls, the auditor should question management on the reasons why any controls which do exist were designed into the system. It may be that the controls were based on a generic assessment of requirements for the type of system being developed without due consideration of the organization's specific use of the system. When this situation exists, there can be some basic weaknesses in the control structure that will need to be addressed.

Controls Evaluation

The method of controls evaluation for specific application systems is to identify the causes of exposure to which the application system is suspect. The controls which act to prevent, detect or correct the occurrence of any of these causes of exposure should then be identified. The evaluation measures the effectiveness of the control structure to prevent, detect or correct the occurrence of a cause of exposure. Where the controls structure is not considered to be 100 percent effective (a common occurrence), the evaluation must take into consideration the likely outcome (or the exposure) of the occurrence of a cause of exposure given the presence of the control structure. A business decision then needs to be made as to whether or not to add new controls or enhance existing ones. The Control Evaluation Table shown in Figure 11.1 can help in this exercise.

Testing

Application systems should be tested when they are first developed and when any changes are made to them subsequent to their introduction into the production environment. Appendix A (System Acceptance Testing) provides a complete discussion on this topic.

LEVEL 1 AUDITOR — SKILL AND KNOWLEDGE OBJECTIVES

Overall Objective

Know the development phases for application system development and the level and type of audit involvement required in each phase.

Basic Systems Analysis

Know the basic steps in the systems analysis process. Have an understanding of the principal control points which should typically be addressed in this phase of development. Be able to identify control weaknesses from the deliverables produced from the analysis phase of the development life cycle. Know the principles of structured analysis and the role of CASE tools in the analysis process.

Application Design

Know the component parts that make up a business application system (application software, data base management system, network control software) and be able to differentiate between the levels of control required for each component.

Functionality

Be able to identify the business functions being automated and equate the system controls to the manual controls which were in effect prior to the automation of the system. Be able to determine if the functionality within the system is consistent with what the user was asking for.

Input/Processing/Output/Storage

Know the basic controls governing input/processing/output/storage for both on-line and batch systems.

Business Purposes

Be able to determine if the system meets the business purposes for which it was developed.

Business Risk

Know the factors which contribute to business risk in application systems and be able to assess how well these risks are being managed.

Controls Identification

Be able to identify the control structure within an application, including the identification of environmental controls which lie outside the application but which contribute to the overall control over the application.

Controls Evaluation

Be able to evaluate the adequacy of controls within an application system.

Testing

Be able to conduct and evaluate both compliance and substantive tests for all aspects of an application system.

The Institute of Internal Auditors

LEVEL 2 AUDITOR — SKILL AND KNOWLEDGE OBJECTIVES

Overall Objectives

Be able to identify the required level of control for different types of application systems and design and execute audit programs accordingly.

Basic Systems Analysis

Be able to identify control weaknesses from the deliverables produced from the analysis phase of the development life cycle and relate these control weaknesses to the broader scope of the system of internal control, if applicable. Be familiar with the application of structured walk-through techniques and be able to participate in a walk-through to ensure that proper controls are being built into the system. Be able to specify audit requirements where a continuous auditing subsystem is to be built as part of the overall system.

Application Design

Be able to establish an appropriate control structure for application systems based on risk to the organization. Be able to factor in the findings of environmental audits (for example, operating system audits, network control system audits, DBMS audits) into the control structure of systems under development. Be able to develop an audit program for the ongoing audit of the application system once it is in production.

Functionality

Be able to determine if the functionality within the system is consistent with corporate requirements. Be able to differentiate between the functionality provided by conventional software development and that provided by specialized technologies. Be able to develop audit procedures accordingly.

Input/Processing/Output/Storage

Be able to relate the controls over input/processing/output/storage to the technology being used and to the overall level of control within the operating environment.

Business Purposes

Be able to determine if the system meets corporate requirements and fits in with the corporate strategy.

Business Risks

Relate the business risk that is inherent in individual applications to the broad spectrum of business risk within the entire operation. Be able to break down the elements of business risk and to direct audit resources to individual elements to more fully assess the extent of any particular business risk.

Controls Identification

Be able to formulate the scope of individual audits to determine and assess the adequacy of controls within an application.

Controls Evaluation

Be able to evaluate the overall level of control within an application system (including environmental and application system controls).

Testing

Be able to design, conduct and evaluate both compliance and substantive tests for all aspects of an application (including environmental systems).

CAUSES OF EXPOSURE

The causes of exposure in the area of application systems are as follows:

- Business objectives not met.

- Operational problems.

- Excessive maintenance.

- Input errors.

- Processing errors.

- Output errors.

Business Objectives not Met

The intent of an application system is to meet the business needs and objectives of the organization. This intent is usually achieved by meeting the defined needs of the various user departments. However, there are instances where the defined needs of a particular user are not consistent with the business objectives. If there is no effective means of prioritizing the system development or system maintenance activity, the "squeaky wheel" user may receive a disproportionate amount of scarce information systems resources. Prototyping can also lead to systems being "overbuilt" from a functionality standpoint as the user keeps asking for more functionality to be prototyped. In effect, the system to be built is never defined and keeps on being something of a moving target.

Typically, neither the user's needs nor the corporate business needs are typically met by an application system. There are a number of reasons why application systems become inappropriate to the needs of the business: poor analysis and/or design of the system; the system functionality does not keep pace with the business requirements; or the hardware cannot process the increased growth in use of the system.

For whatever reason, an application system that fails to meet the business objectives for which it was developed must be analyzed and a decision made on the most appropriate corrective course of action. It may be appropriate to do nothing given the relative importance of this application versus others within the organization. Alternatively, it may be appropriate to commit resources (hardware, software and/or people) to correct the problem to whatever degree makes business sense. The 80/20 rule (where 80 percent of the benefit can be had for 20 percent of the effort, the remaining 20 percent of benefit requires considerably more proportionate effort) applies equally well to application systems as it does to other parts of the business. The upgrade, or downgrade in the event of overbuilt functionality, should be the subject of a business decision based on costs and benefits.

Operational Problems

The application system may incur unforeseen operational problems. These problems may be directly attributable to software problems in the application, which is the subject of the next cause of exposure (i.e., excessive maintenance), but may also be caused by a poor fit between the application system and the organization. It is this latter area that is the focus of this particular cause of exposure.

The users of the system should be well trained in the use of the system and in what is available from, and expected by, the system. When this training does not take place as part of the implementation methodology, experience suggests that operational problems are almost certain to occur. There are other instances where the operational problems start to show up in areas which should not be directly affected by the introduction of a new application system or by enhancements made to an existing system. One obvious example is where a new or enhanced application system causes degraded performance in on-line response for other applications. The impact on supposedly unimpacted areas is often more subtle than this and can cause considerable disruption and consternation to the organization until the root cause of the problem is identified. An impact analysis is one approach of trying to anticipate any adverse reactions to a new or enhanced application by the various operational groups within the organization, including those that are not directly impacted by the implementation. Appendix B, as its title suggests, gives a full description of how to conduct an impact analysis.

Excessive Maintenance

The level of maintenance that is applied to an application system usually grows as the application system ages. However, some new application systems experience an inordinate amount of maintenance in the first year because of poor analysis, or design, or development. It may also be a result of rushed implementation where a number of subsequent phases are required to provide the originally promised functionality. Management should be made aware of instances where this level of maintenance is required, particularly if it is happening on a recurring basis.

Even where a system has been well developed and maintained over the years (unfortunately, not a common occurrence), there is a point in every system's life where the effort required to maintain the system is out of line with the benefits to be obtained from any one change. However, the cumulative benefit of the system to the organization may still be considerable. At this point in the life of an application system several alternatives are available: (1) do nothing and continue to incur excessive costs for all maintenance activities; (2) build a new system from the ground up using the functionality of the old system as the baseline; (3) restructure the code of the old system to make it more maintainable; (4) completely re-engineer the application to take advantage of new data base structures as well as structured design and development techniques. The decision on which alternative to take should be based on an economic analysis of the expected value of the system to the organization over time.

Input Errors

Input errors which are allowed through the editing process can have a potentially devastating impact on an application system. All processing subsequent to the edit routines within an application system usually assumes that only valid data are now being handled. Consequently, little revalidation is performed and the erroneous input is applied to the master files and/or to the report files. To correct a problem of this type it is often necessary to take special custom coded routines to "cleanse" the master files of the erroneous data. These "cleansing" routines, in themselves, present significant control problems as they must usually be written in a rush and used with little testing. In certain situations, the organization may find that the cure is worse than the original problem.

The key is to have stringent edit checks in place and to ensure that these checks are fully tested. It is also advisable to have reasonableness checks in the processing and reporting sections of the system to track resulting situations that theoretically cannot happen, or that seem suspect.

Processing Errors

As with the occurrence of undetected input errors, the effects of a processing error can be devastating. The adage "garbage-in, garbage-out" has been revised to look more like "garbage-in, gospel-out." Once processing has taken place, there is a strong urge to accept the output as correct because the computer says it is. In other words, "computers do not make mistakes." The implied assumption is that the processing logic was fully tested and is correct. It is important to take every possible measure to ensure that this is a correct assumption. With computers now providing mission critical applications to many organizations, the drive for defect-free software will become even more appealing.

Output Errors

Output errors are often the manifestation of input and/or processing errors, but can also be caused purely as a result of erroneous processing in the output modules. Another complicating factor with output processing is the reliance on the vendor's software for much of the processing. It is the vendor's software in the form of the operating system and associated subsystems that must ensure that records are properly written to the data base and that any errors are trapped and reported back to the application system. The application system must then have routines which can deal with these erroneous conditions. Similarly, the interaction of the printers attached to the hardware processor is controlled by vendor-supplied software.

CONTROLS

Applicable controls intended to prevent, detect and/or correct the causes of exposure just described as relevant to the area of application systems are as follows:

- Steering committee(s).

- Development methodology.

- Audit review and quality assurance.

- Testing.

- Impact analysis.

- Change control procedures.

Steering Committee

The steering committee should be comprised of senior executives from the primary application user departments. The mandate of the steering committee is to:

- Approve the allocation of resources for individual application system development on the basis that they are consistent with the information strategy and are supported by a strong business case.

- Monitor the progress of each application development project and act as the approval mechanism when projects need to move from one phase of the development methodology to another with a concomitant increase in financial expenditures.

- Reset priorities when the need arises.

The steering committee should meet regularly with a formal agenda and minutes should be taken. It is also advisable for the executives on the steering committee to make an investment in time and money to become familiar with technology and its current and potential role within their organizations. Too often, the steering committee is a rubber stamp mechanism for the information systems department. This situation arises because of a lack of knowledge on the basics of managing an information systems function on the part of the steering committee and, consequently, a total dependence on the advice of the information systems department.

Development Methodology

This subject is dealt with in detail in Chapter 6. Suffice at this point to say that a development methodology is a formalized approach for pulling the three inherent components of application system development (people, plans and processes) together into a logical, structured regimen so that they are transformed into a successfully developed and implemented application system. Development methodologies break down the system development life cycle (SDLC) into manageable phases (and constituent tasks) with appropriate project control and management review points to ensure that the development is still on track before proceeding to the next phase of development.

An adjunct to the development methodology is the post-implementation review. The post-implementation review is typically conducted about six months after an application system goes into production. The objectives of the post-implementation review are as follows:

- To ensure that the system, as implemented, meets the functional specifications as defined in the feasibility study and business case.

- To identify changes which need to be made to make the system more effective.

- To ensure that the benefits in the business case are being achieved or are likely to be achieved in the foreseeable future.

- To identify ways in which the development process can be improved through the experiences of developing the application system under review.

To ensure an impartial review, the post-implementation review should be conducted by a group that is separate from the original developers and users. The audit group or quality assurance group are likely candidates to conduct the review.

Audit Review and Quality Assurance

The roles played by the audit department and the quality assurance group (where one exists) are similar but different. The audit function, as discussed in Chapter 3, is part of the management control structure but is an independent observer and reviewer of the internal control system within an organization. The quality control function is also part of the management control structure but is an inherent part of this structure as opposed to an independent observer. The quality control function is responsible for recommending controls within the development methodology and for taking an active part in ensuring that controls are properly designed into the system. Although their corporate mandates are different, the benefits that both roles bring to the development process are considerable.

Testing

Testing is the key to all aspects of the integrity of an application system. Frequently, however, testing is only considered to be relevant to the program development phase. This is not necessarily the case. It is possible, through the use of structured walk-throughs and prototyping, to test the analysis, design and program specification aspects of the development process. Testing is also a key control in the area of program change control procedures. Appendix A presents a full description of application system acceptance testing.

Impact Analysis

The introduction of a new system may have a significant impact on an organization quite beyond what was anticipated in the analysis phase of the systems development life cycle. Unless the impact of an implementation is identified and planned for, the effects may extend throughout the organization and be difficult to control because the underlying cause is not understood. An impact analysis, which is conducted after the system is built, assesses how the system will affect the organization after it is implemented. Appendix B offers guidelines on how and when to conduct an impact analysis, who should conduct the study, and its role in the systems development life cycle.

Change Control Procedures

When dealing with application systems it is not sufficient to look only at the development process. During the life span of an application, the maintenance effort will probably greatly outweigh the original development effort. Change control procedures are intended to ensure that changes to the application system are documented, approved, properly tested and migrated into the production environment in a controlled fashion. Chapter 7 deals with system maintenance and change control in detail.

TYPES OF EXPOSURE

Listed below are the types of exposure which can occur as a result of the inadequacy or failure of the system of control to prevent the occurrence of a cause of exposure in the area of application systems.

Erroneous Record Keeping

Input errors, processing errors and output errors can all lead to erroneous record keeping.

Unacceptable Accounting

As with erroneous record keeping, input errors, processing errors and output errors can lead to unacceptable accounting in certain circumstances.

Business Interruption

If business objectives are not met there is a chance of business interruption. Input errors, processing errors and output errors can lead to business interruption in extreme cases where the problem is particularly severe and the application system is mission critical.

Erroneous Management Decisions

The information emanating from a computerized application system has an implied guarantee of accuracy. Management decisions are often made based on this implied infallibility. Input errors, processing errors and output errors can all result in erroneous management decisions by providing "bad" information which is then taken at face value and acted upon.

When business objectives are not met and the information to be provided by having met these objectives is critical to some forms of management decision making, erroneous management decisions could result.

Excessive Costs/Deficient Revenues

All causes of exposure could result in excessive costs:

- Input errors, processing errors and output errors all have to be corrected.

- The business objectives that are not being met will have to be achieved in some other way. It may be that the business objectives were, in fact, to decrease costs or increase revenues.

- Operational problems have to be investigated and addressed.

- Excessive maintenance has to be paid for.

Loss or Destruction of Assets

Input errors, processing errors and output errors could all result in the loss or destruction of assets if there is no way to completely correct the results of the error.

Competitive Disadvantage

The degree of competitive disadvantage an organization could experience through the occurrence of a cause of exposure is dependent on the importance of the application to the organization. If business interruption occurs, the organization will be competitively disadvantaged. For that reason, the same ratings are given in the control evaluation table for competitive disadvantage as for business interruption.

CONTROL EVALUATION TABLE

The Control Evaluation Table for application systems is given in Figure 11.1. The evaluation numbers are subjective and should be adjusted based on the conditions that exist in individual organizations. Note that, in practice, the completion of the Control Evaluation Table is in two parts:

- During detailed information gathering where, from the review of available documentation and the results of personal interviews, the key to reliance on individual controls and the "overall control rating (design)" are determined.

- During the execution of the audit program where, as a result of various audit tests, the strength of individuals controls is fully assessed and the "overall control rating (tested)" is determined.

AUDIT APPROACH

The audit approach to application systems is varied. The objectives of an audit of an application system are:

- To ensure that the system meets the business objectives it was developed to achieve.

- To ensure that there is adequate control over input, processing and output.

- To ensure that there is adequate change control over the introduction of new versions of the system.

These objectives are very broad in scope. Ensuring that business objectives are being met implies that the users understand how to use the system and are, in fact, using the system to their advantage. Control over access to data and access to specific functions within the system is implied by having good control over input, processing and output as are the controls over the communication network that provides the link between the user and the system in an on-line environment. Being able to maintain the system through the presence of adequate documentation and trained professionals is part of the effective change control procedures. Application system audits should be considered in two ways:

- When the system is being developed.

- Once the system is running in production.

System Development Audit

Audit involvement begins with a review of the development methodology currently in force and the reporting to management of any shortcomings or omissions. The auditor should then develop a checklist of audit department activities, requirements and outputs for each of the development phases. This checklist should be presented to the systems development group so that a protocol can be established whereby the auditor is made aware of significant events regarding the development of new application systems. The auditor must also establish criteria for determining which application systems under development will be reviewed.

The number of developing applications to be reviewed largely depends on the ratio of auditors to development staff. The auditor is usually unable to review all developing applications. Therefore, factors such as budget allocation, the criticality of the application to the operation of the organization, and the financial reporting and legal aspects of the application must all be considered in the evaluation.

An application system development review is basically a compliance audit based on the methodology currently in force. The audit is designed to assure management that:

- The application is being developed to meet the defined, approved needs of the user.

- The application is being developed on schedule and within budget.

- The application contains sufficient controls over input, processing and output.

Production Application System Audit

In order to audit the effectiveness of the operation of an individual application system, the auditor must understand the adequacy of the controls within the environment in which the system operates. Any deficiencies in this environment must be assessed in light of their implications to the application system being audited. The environmental audits which should be reviewed before conducting an application audit are as follows:

- The data center audit (see Chapters 5 & 10).

- The system maintenance and change control audit (see Chapter 7).

- The system software/environmental control programs audit (see Chapter 12).

- The data management audit (see Chapter 13).

- The data base management/data dictionary audit (see Chapter 14).

- The telecommunications network audit (see Chapter 15).

The amount of work to be reviewed may seem excessive, but it is important to know the strengths and weaknesses of the production operating environment within which the application system is being run. Many of the controls within the application interact with environmental controls. The strength of the application control is only as strong as the environmental control allows it to be.

Once the control structure of the environment has been analyzed and any weaknesses identified and understood, the auditor is in a position to look at an individual application system in depth. Even here, there are portions of other audits which can be combined to create an audit program for a specific application system:

- The data center audit as it relates to the handling of input, output and the network operation for the application system. Controls over the processing aspects as conducted by the computer operators, production control, data control and network operations should all be reviewed for compliance with the expected level of control.

- The data security audit in terms of the controls in place to protect the data processed by the application system from unauthorized disclosure, modification or destruction, whether accidental or intentional. The data security audit will have determined the adequacy of the control structure over data files in general. The question is "are these controls in place and functioning for the application system under review?"

- The information systems contingency planning audit to the extent that it deals with this specific application system.

- The system maintenance and change control procedures audit to confirm that changes to the application system being audited are being handled in a manner that is consistent with the previously audited change control procedures.

In addition to the controls which are predominantly focused on the data center, the auditor should also review the use of the application system within the user department. Control over passwords, the use of reports, the presence of authorization and approval controls, division of duties, the presence of backup material for recovery purposes, and the training and rotation of personnel are all controls which should be present in the user department.

Ideally, as has been stressed throughout this chapter, the controls structure should have been defined and documented during the system development process for the application system being audited. When this is not the case, the auditor must go back to first principles and reconstruct the control structure before designing and executing the audit program.

Figure 11.1 — Control Evaluation Table
Application Systems

CAUSES OF EXPOSURE

CONTROLS	Business Objectives Not Met	Operational Problems	Excessive Maintenance	Input Errors	Processing Errors	Output Errors
Steering Committee	3					
Development Methodology	2	1	1	2	2	2
Audit Review & QA	2	2	2	2	2	2
Testing	2	2	2	3	3	3
Impact Analysis	2	2	1	1	1	1
Change Control Process		1	2	2	2	2
Overall Control Rating - Design						
Overall Control Rating - Tested						

EXPOSURES

	Business Objectives Not Met	Operational Problems	Excessive Maintenance	Input Errors	Processing Errors	Output Errors
Erroneous Record Keeping				3	3	3
Unacceptable Accounting				1	1	1
Business Interruption	1			1	1	1
Erroneous Management Decisions	1	1		1	1	2
Fraud and Embezzlement						
Statutory Sanctions						
Excessive Costs	2	2	3	2	2	2
Loss or Destruction of Assets				1	1	1
Competitive Disadvantage	1	1		1	1	1

KEY TO DEGREE OF CERTAINTY OF OCCURRENCE IN THE EVENT OF AN INADEQUATE CONTROL STRUCTURE

3 - Virtually certain
2 - Probable
1 - Possible
Blank - Very unlikely

KEY TO RELIANCE ON CONTROL

3 - High reliance
2 - Moderate reliance
1 - Control has only a peripheral effect on the cause of exposure
Blank - No significant impact

KEY TO OVERALL CONTROL RATING

3 - Strong control
2 - Moderate but adequate control
1 - Inadequate control

12
SYSTEMS SOFTWARE/ ENVIRONMENTAL CONTROL PROGRAMS

INTRODUCTION

Application systems operate within an environment that consists of both hardware and software. It is the area of software that will be addressed in this chapter. This software is generically called systems software and comes under the domain of the technical services group within computer operations. Specifically, systems (or software) programmers are responsible for this software.

By nature, the environment (in general) and systems software (in particular) are vendor specific. With the increasing advances in technology, the complexity of the tasks to be mastered by the system programmers is becoming greater, resulting in an ongoing degree of specialization among system programmers. The area of systems programming has been one the auditor has been reluctant to tackle because of this degree of complexity and specialization.

What we attempt to do in this chapter is to provide an overall insight into the areas of interest for the auditor, but from the perspective of how systems software interacts and affects the operation of application software, which is the usual area of interest for the auditor. A detailed description of the methods of auditing specific elements of systems software is outside the scope of this text. A Level 3 auditor (technical specialist) is required to undertake specific systems software audits having received training and gained experience in the use of these "brands" of software.

The first section of this chapter describes the control perspective for including systems software/environmental control programs as one of the basic building blocks of information systems. This section also describes the relevance of this subject area to the skill set and knowledge requirements of the Level 1 and Level 2 auditor. Causes of exposure are described, as are the more common types of control which act upon these causes. The types of exposure which may occur as a result of a deficiency or breakdown in the control structure are then discussed. Finally, the audits to be performed are described in terms of relevant objectives and frequency.

CONTROL PERSPECTIVE

Every computer system incorporates one or more operating systems along with various utility or service programs. These systems and programs are essential for the proper and continuous operation of application systems. Proper management of the systems software function significantly improves performance. Sound control structures, in concert with effective program security administration, reduce business risk.

The focus of concern within this text continues to be the application system. The rationale for this focus is that the application system, not the hardware or systems software, serves the business. A useful analogy is to think of a car when it first comes off the assembly line. The car has great potential to provide transportation, but without gasoline and a driver, it can go nowhere. However, the car itself must be a safe and reliable vehicle, otherwise the gas and the driver will be unable to realize the potential of the car, and the driver may even be at risk by using it.

In this instance, a computer is exactly the same. The hardware and software delivered by the vendor have great potential. Application systems represent the gasoline in this analogy and the users of the organization, through the articulation of their business needs, represent the drivers. However, just as the car has to be reliable and safe to use, the computer (or the hardware and system software) must be reliable and secure.

SCOPE OF SYSTEM SOFTWARE/ ENVIRONMENTAL CONTROL PROGRAMS

System software/environmental control programs include the following sub-topics in their scope of activities:

- Operating systems.

- System software library management.

- Segregation.

- Performance.

- Support.

- Product specifics.

Operating Systems

It is necessary to understand the differences and the relationships between the operating system and the other systems that run on the computer. In its purest sense, the operating system is the vendor-supplied software that is used to provide an interface between application software and the hardware devices that are attached to the computer (such as MVS, VM, DOS in an IBM environment; Guardian in a Tandem environment; and VMS in a DEC environment). The instructions to the operating system are usually in the form of some kind of job control language (JCL). The JCL tells the operating system what application to run and the files that the application wants to use and/or create. In some cases the JCL has to be specific about the characteristics of these files, including specifying the location of the file. In other cases, the operating system can work this out for itself. The operating system will load the application system that is to be run and will start the application. As the application requires resources (for example, data from a disk or tape file, input from a terminal, to write to a file or printer, and so forth), a request is sent from the application to the operating system. The operating system takes care of the request and passes the resource and control back to the application system. When any computer processing problems occur in the application system, the operating system software takes over and provides for an orderly resolution of the problem. This usually means aborting the application with an error message and moving on to the next job to be run.

What has just been described is the pure definition of an operating system. Another way of defining an operating system is that any software that is not considered an application system is part of the operating system. Included in this definition would be compilers, utilities, data base management software, network management software, data security software and any other software which make up the processing environment.

Perhaps the best way to resolve this definitional problem of "what is the scope of the operating system?" is to include all system utility programs and compilers but exclude the rest. The rationale for this suggestion is that the software recommended for exclusion is the subject of separate audit activity, whereas it would be very difficult to isolate the utilities and compilers from the operating system and make them the subject of a separate review.

System Software Library Management

In Chapter 7, the concept of application program libraries and the controls over movement to, from and between these libraries are discussed. In the area of system software, similar issues arise. System software is really a collection of computer programs that is organized into libraries for system management purposes. What is stored in each of these libraries, who has access to the libraries and what documentation exists to describe the activity that takes place within each library are all issues of concern to the auditor.

Test and production versions of these libraries should exist. New versions of the operating system are provided by the vendor on an ongoing basis. These new versions must be tested before being used in production. This is especially important in the case of system software. In application software, a programming error will usually only impact the users of the application. This is not the case with system software. System software is part of the environment that supports all application systems. Therefore, a system software error can potentially impact all application systems.

The same issues of ownership and custody, discussed as relevant to application system libraries, are also relevant to system software libraries. Custody is an easy issue to resolve. As with most system data files (which are what libraries really are), custody is in the hands of the computer operations group. Ownership is a trickier issue to deal with. Usually, the owner of a piece of software is the principal user of that software. However, in essence, the entire organization uses systems software. The other candidate for ownership is the technical services group or, more specifically, the systems programmers. The argument for ownership being given to this group goes back to the rights of ownership, which is to determine who can read, write, add and delete the software. The technical support group will certainly have a major say in these rights of ownership. Another argument for giving ownership to the technical support group is that they are generally the only ones in the organization who have the skill levels to make intelligent decisions about what should happen to systems software.

It is the belief of the author that the technical support group should be the owner of the system software libraries. However, it is critical that the procedures surrounding the use of these libraries be documented and the activity within these libraries be supported by an audit trail which is reviewed at regular intervals by management.

Segregation

The tools provided by system software are, of necessity, extremely powerful. There are a number of powerful utilities provided by the software which are required in the course of the overall management of the operating environment. The ability to view and change files, to circumvent barriers to access, to copy and delete files and to manipulate systems as they are processing are all features which are available within any operating system software. These tools are necessary. A high degree of control over their use is also required. Unfortunately, it is this dichotomy between operating expediency and proper control that poses such a dilemma to the auditor. Compounding the problem is the aura of mystique that surrounds all aspects of systems software. The auditor should not be misled into believing that the systems software area rightfully has rules of its own when it comes to proper control. Many of the basic techniques that have been introduced in the application software area are equally applicable to systems software. One of these techniques is segregation.

There should be segregation between the test and production environments. The systems programmers should not, except under strictly controlled conditions, have access to the production environment. Certainly, there should not be carte blanche access to this environment. Too often, the systems programmer seems to treat the production operating environment as his or her private domain. This should not be allowed. The only situations in which direct access should be permitted are in cases of emergencies. If there is an emergency, there should be a follow-up procedure in place. This ensures that any action taken is documented and that there is a managerial review process to ensure that the action taken and the number of instances of such occurrences is appropriate for the organization. Systems programmers should not have access to application systems and should not be able to take over the duties of the computer operators.

Performance

One of the principal duties of the systems programmer is to maximize the throughput of the computer. Given the complexity of both the hardware and software that is in place in many organizations today, this is not a trivial task. Many jobs are automatically scheduled. Many others are on-line systems which must be up and running all day. Contention for resources and basic system overhead are two of the principal reasons for poor performance. One of the issues for the auditor is that the basic system overhead may include several control features (such as maintaining a log of systems activity). These control features are often discretionary and can be turned off by the systems programmer. Clearly, the auditor needs to know when this action has been taken or is being contemplated. Whether or not such action is appropriate will depend on what the organization is trying to protect against and how important the feature is in maintaining an adequate level of control. The key point is that the decision on whether or not to turn off a control feature should be made after having taken the control implications into account and not just as a hasty reaction to poor performance.

The systems programming group should have system monitoring tools available and should be actively monitoring and tracking the performance of the system in order to anticipate performance problems. This leads into the area of capacity planning which is usually a responsibility of the technical support group (unless there is a special group devoted to this activity). Effective capacity planning will prevent many instances of poor performance resulting from inadequate hardware capacity.

Support

The in-house systems programming function is the first line of defense for any problems with the systems software/environmental control programs. However, what frequently happens is the systems programmer isolates the reason for the problem and the area within the operating system where the problem is occurring but requires assistance from the vendor to actually fix the problem permanently. The systems programmer may suggest a solution until a permanent, vendor-supplied repair (or fix) is available.

From the auditor's perspective, the control over the application of these fixes is important. Vendors routinely issue tapes of fixes to be applied to their operating systems software. Frequently, the problem encountered by an organization has been previously encountered somewhere else. A fix may already have been identified and put on one of these program temporary fix (PTF) tapes which are either issued automatically to all users of the software or are available on demand. The question is, "should all fixes be applied or only those that have been identified as being relevant to the organization?" The suggested approach is to apply all fixes on the tape even although there is some validity in the argument that the fixes themselves may introduce problems not previously experienced. The vendor, however, is more inclined to be responsive to problems where the software is at the current revision level, including temporary fixes. The key issue is to ensure that the systems software is properly tested before being moved to the production environment. An acceptable way of performing this testing is to use the new version of the operating system for the in-house system development group.

Most vendors have user groups, one of which is usually devoted to the systems programming aspects of their software. An organization should investigate the benefit of being a member of such a group. In general, there is a great deal of value in being a member because of the sharing of ideas and problems with others in a similar environment.

Product Specifics

Each organization will have a fairly unique set of software products which constitutes its systems software/environmental control programs. There will be an operating system in use, along with various utility programs, compilers and other software products. Although the products will vary, the purpose of these products is fairly uniform across installations. The purpose served by these products is as follows:

- Act as the interface between the application systems and the hardware.

- Provide the interface between the computer (hardware and software) and the operators.

- Detect error conditions and relay this information to the operator.

- Maintain activity logs and produce reports of such activity as required.

- Provide tools to investigate and correct problem conditions.

- Provide the tools that are required to effectively manage the operation of the system (such as performance monitors, disk space utilization statistics, and so forth).

It is crucial for auditors to understand the system software that is in place within their own organizations and to relate the use of such software to the specific functions being performed.

LEVEL 1 AUDITOR — SKILL AND KNOWLEDGE OBJECTIVES

Overall Objective

Know the elements which comprise systems software/environmental control programs, the control objectives for each element and the audit approach to attest to the adequacy of control within each element.

Operating Systems

Understand what operating systems are, how they differ from application systems, how they fit into the total information systems environment, and how they interface with other systems and systems controls.

Systems Software Library Management

Know the various libraries associated with systems software and the principles of effective management control over the use of these libraries. Be able to execute an audit program designed to attest to the adequacy of control over the management of the systems software library.

Segregation

Understand the need for proper segregation in a systems software environment and know the roles and responsibilities that should be in place to ensure that the control objectives related to segregation of duties are being met. Of particular interest in this area are the roles and responsibilities of the systems programmers.

Performance

Know the basic principles by which systems performance can be enhanced and the control tradeoffs which can be made in pursuit of improved performance.

Support

Understand the support requirements in a systems software operation, including the various levels of support and escalation procedures that should be in place. Be able to execute an audit program to measure the adequacy of the support policies and procedures that are currently in place.

Product Specifics

Know the software products that are included in the systems software environment and the basic functions that each of these products performs.

LEVEL 2 AUDITOR — SKILL AND KNOWLEDGE OBJECTIVES

Overall Objectives

Be able to design and execute audit programs to attest to the adequacy of the level of control over systems software/environmental control programs. Be able to determine when the scope of individual audits needs to be expanded in light of individual control deficiencies. For example, be able to fully assess the implications of individual control weaknesses on other parts of the operation.

Operating Systems

Recognize potential weaknesses in operating systems controls or in the administration of operating systems. Be able to develop and conduct tests of these controls.

System Software Library Management

Be able to design an audit program to attest to the adequacy of control over the management of the systems software library. Understand the technology in place to effect systems software library management and be able to factor this use of technology into the appropriate audit programs.

Segregation

Understand the technology in place to assist in effecting proper segregation of duties. Be able to factor the use of this technology into an audit program designed to ensure that proper segregation of duties exists in the systems software environment.

Performance

Understand the technology in place to effect improved performance of systems software. Be able to design and execute an audit program to attest to the accuracy of the results produced by this technology.

Support

Relate the support policies and procedures to the other facets of the systems software control infrastructure, such as library management, performance and segregation. Be able to rate the overall acceptability of the level of support within the systems software organization.

Product Specifics

Be able to design and execute audits of individual products as well as factor these products into other audits dealing with the systems software environment.

CAUSES OF EXPOSURE

The causes of exposure in the area of systems software/environmental control programs are as follows:

- Inadequate control structure.

- Poor control over utilities.

- Mismanaged implementations.

- Poor vendor support.

- Unlimited system access.

Inadequate Control Structure

The adequacy of the control structure within systems software depends to a large degree on the vendor. What is required from the systems software is proper management reporting on which activities are taking place and who requested those activities. Over the years many auditors have expressed dissatisfaction with the control structure within most systems software. The feeling is that there are too many ways around the controlled management approach to running the system, and that these "backdoor" approaches provide insufficient audit trails. The response from the vendors is that these alternative approaches are required for expediency in the event of an operational problem and that, if they did not have these features, they would be operating at a competitive disadvantage with other operating system vendors. The only solution to this problem is for the marketplace to insist that adequate controls be built into systems software and for the marketplace to make adequate controls a major selection criterion in the purchase of system software. Until this economic force is applied to the problem, systems software will continue to put operating expediency in front of control considerations. The marketplace has to show that it is willing to pay for adequate controls and will not, in fact, purchase products that not do have an adequate control structure

The other side of this problem is that many of the control features that do exist within system software are optional and can be turned off by the systems programmer. The usual argument for turning these control features off is that performance will improve given that the control feature usually requires additional processing cycles. As previously stated in this chapter, the decision to turn off control features within systems software should not be a hasty reaction to poor performance.

Poor Control Over Utilities

One of the principal areas of concern to auditors with regard to system software is the use of utilities. Part of the package of system software supplied by the vendor is a collection of utility programs that allow various forms of manipulation of data and storage. Utilities that copy, delete, merge, sort, move and change files are all standard to most sets of system software. There are also utilities that allow computer memory to be changed dramatically when an application system is running. Although necessary, these utilities are very powerful, particularly if they can be run in some form of privileged state where the common forms of audit trails are (or can be) turned off or circumvented. It is necessary to have controls in place that limit the use of these utilities and provide adequate reporting when they are used.

Mismanaged Implementations

When a new version of the operating system is to be introduced or changes must be made to correct problems, it is important that the implementation goes well. Errors in the operating system are likely to affect all applications and are, therefore, extremely disruptive to the organization.

As new versions of the operating system arc introduced it is conceivable that applications which currently work will cease to do so. This may be because of an error in the operating system, but is more often the result of incompatibility between the application system and the new version of the operating system. The general trend in operating system software is to require closer adherence on the part of application systems to the protocols established by the operating system. Where an application system previously made use of weakly controlled features of the operating system, it is likely that the new operating system will force a change.

There may also be instances where the systems programmers have made custom changes to the operating system. These changes will not be in the new release of the systems software. A decision must be made on whether to retrofit these changes to the new version or to go with the new version without the changes. Whatever approach is taken, there is a need for significant amounts of testing.

Communication of the fact that a new or amended version of the operating system is to be installed is important, as is complete testing of the new or amended version. The testing must include the interaction of the operating system with all application systems.

Poor Vendor Support

Many problems that occur in systems software have to be referred to the vendor for resolution. Usually, the systems programmer is able to solve a problem and will send the vendor any available information (usually in the form of a core dump). Until the problem is solved, there is always the chance that the problem will reoccur and cause an attendant disruption in operation. In extreme cases, the entire operation may be disabled until the vendor can supply a solution.

Responsive vendor support is, therefore, a key element in the overall control structure for systems software. There should be contractual agreements in place with the vendor for support as well as escalation procedures should the first line of support fail to solve the problem in an acceptable time frame.

Unlimited System Access

In previous chapters it has been stressed that the application system programmer should not have access to production data of any kind (for instance, business, system or administrative). Does, or should, the same rule apply to systems programmers? The answer is essentially "yes," but with some refinements. There is no question that the scope of responsibility for the systems programmer encompasses the entire computer operation, including both test and production environments. This scope of responsibility implies that the systems programmer needs access to both environments. What is not implied by this scope of responsibility is that the systems programmer is above and beyond the control structure that is in place for the rest of the organization. On the application side, the individuals who do have access to production data are subject to review of their activities. This should also be true on the systems software side of the operation. Policies and procedures governing access to the production environment should be in place.

Included in these policies and procedures should be a regular management review of activities performed by the systems programmers with follow-up on unusual activities.

The bottom line is that the system programmers should not be given carte blanche access to system resources. Their work should be structured in a controlled manner so that the principal responsibilities can be carried out expeditiously but also in a manner which is consistent with the control objectives of the organization.

CONTROLS

Applicable controls intended to prevent, detect and/or correct the causes of exposure just described as relevant to the area of system software/environmental control programs are as follows:

- Policies and procedures.

- Control reports.

- Segregation.

- Testing.

Policies and Procedures

As discussed throughout this chapter, the systems programmer should operate in a controlled environment but still have the facilities available to get the job done. In order to achieve this balance between operational requirements and control, the role of the systems programmer needs to be fully thought out and documented. There must be a management process in place to ensure that these responsibilities are being carried out in a manner which is consistent with the defined approach.

There should be documented policies and procedures covering the area of systems software/environmental control programs. The concept of policies and procedures has been accepted for many years on the application systems side of information systems. This has not necessarily been the case on the more technical issues of operating systems software. This is a situation that needs to change. There appears to be no reason why a policies and procedures manual cannot be created for the management of the systems software environment within an organization.

Part of the policies and procedures manual should be a section on system maintenance and change control. The same basis used for application systems should be used for systems software. Changes to systems software should be properly documented, approved by management, fully tested and migrated into the production environment in an orderly fashion. This clearly implies that the systems programmers should go through a controlled process when changing any aspect of the production environment. In situations where emergency action must be taken, there should be a follow-up procedure to put the appropriate documentation in place. Although the specifics and scope of systems software differ from that of application systems, the same fundamental control issues and techniques exist.

Control Reports

The operating system is capable of tracking all activity that takes place in the system. However, for a number of reasons, this does not guarantee that the operating system environment is well controlled.

- There are a number of ways in which the tracking mechanism can be altered or even turned off.

- Another problem is trying to interpret what is really going on from the data provided by the operating system.

Ideally, a number of control reports should be designed to extract the information from the data provided by the operating system. This information is necessary to describe the activities taking place in the system. Special focus should be on certain powerful utilities, including who used them and what they were used for.

These control reports should also provide information on the control features that are present within the system. The reports should also indicate which control features have been turned off.

There is no question that the design of these reports requires particular technical expertise. Even the interpretation of the reports usually requires a broader range of technical knowledge than most people possess. If there is a data security officer in an organization, this individual should receive the control reports and be able to interpret them. In the absence of a data security officer, the computer operations management team should receive the reports. Evidence of frequent review of these reports should exist regardless of who the reports are sent to.

Segregation

The work of the systems programmer should be segregated from that of the computer operations group and from the application programming group. The systems programming group should not be in a position to initiate and run production systems, nor should it have access to the source or object code of individual application systems.

There should be a test environment for systems software that is distinct from that of the production environment. Procedures should be in place to control the migration between these two environments.

Testing

Given the widespread implications of new or enhanced systems software to all applications that run within the computer environment, exhaustive testing is essential. There are various levels of testing for systems software that are similar to application system testing. Unit and system testing should be performed by the technical support group (i.e., the systems programmers). Acceptance testing should also be conducted by the technical support group, but with heavy involvement from both the computer operations group and the application development group.

A testing plan should be formulated and distributed to all affected parties. In this way it should be possible to elicit from the other groups any peculiarities with the interface to the current version of the systems software. As mentioned earlier in this chapter, it is possible for application systems to stop working when new systems software is introduced. The chance of this type of problem occurring can be minimized by distributing a list of the changes being introduced along with the new version of the systems software to all "users" of the operating system.

TYPES OF EXPOSURE

Listed below are the types of exposure which can occur as a result of the inadequacy or failure of the system of control to prevent the occurrence of a cause of exposure in the area of systems software/ environmental control programs.

Erroneous Record Keeping

The systems software controls the interface between the hardware and the application systems software. If a problem goes undetected, either by the systems software itself or by the operator, there is a chance of erroneous record keeping.

Unacceptable Accounting

It is conceivable that the use of utility programs combined with a lack of adequate control reports may result in unacceptable accounting.

Business Interruption

Problems with system software tend to affect a wide range of application systems. The degree of business interruption will depend on the importance and level of dependency of the organization on its application systems.

Fraud

The uncontrolled presence of powerful utilities which can change the contents of data files could result in fraud. Clearly, there would need to be collusion elsewhere in the system in order to realize a tangible benefit from this unauthorized use of a utility. However, the possibility does exist, particularly if the level of control reporting is not adequate.

Excessive Costs

Problems with systems software tend to be expensive to correct because many application systems are involved. It is not just the cost of fixing the system software problem, it is also the impact that this error may have had on the application systems and the subsequent cost of fixing the damage.

Loss or Destruction of Assets

System software is by nature very powerful and can, through the use of various powerful utilities, be used to damage any data which exists within the computer environment. Correspondingly, destruction of data is destruction of a major corporate asset.

CONTROL EVALUATION TABLE

The Control Evaluation Table for system software/environmental control programs is given in Figure 12.1. The evaluation numbers are subjective and should be adjusted based on the conditions that exist in individual organizations. Note that, in practice, the completion of the Control Evaluation Table is in two parts:

- During detailed information gathering where, from the review of available documentation and the results of personal interviews, the key to reliance on individual controls and the "overall control rating (design)" is determined.

- During the execution of the audit program where, as a result of various audit tests, the strength of individuals controls is fully assessed and the "overall control rating (tested)" is determined.

AUDIT APPROACH

Level 1 and Level 2 auditors should, at a minimum, know the makeup of the environment (hardware and software) within which all application systems are run within their organization. The auditors should also have a technical appreciation of the principal function that each hardware and software component performs within the environment. This is not to say that Level 1 and Level 2 auditors are expected to be technical specialists. This technical specialist function, and the audits of the specifics products which demand this level of expertise, belongs to the Level 3 auditor. However, the Level 1 and Level 2 auditors should be encouraged to attend at least the introductory training courses dealing with the primary elements of the computing environment within their organization.

The reason for this training is so the Level 1 and Level 2 auditors will be able to read the reports from the audits of specific products and relate the findings to the audits that they are conducting. Weaknesses in the operating system/environmental control programs may require that compensating controls be built into application systems. For example, where the management control reports from the operating system do not report on unsuccessful attempts at logging onto a specific application, the application may have to be designed to incorporate this feature.

The scope of this text does not address the audits of specific products. However, emphasis should be placed on ensuring that adequate controls exist within the operating system environment, including proper control over the use of powerful utilities and proper control over the setting of audit trail switches so that adequate management reporting is provided. The principles of control which have developed over the last 15 years with respect to application systems can be used in large measure for the control of systems software/environmental control programs.

Figure 12.1 — Control Evaluation Table
Systems Software/Environmental Control Programs

CAUSES OF EXPOSURE

CONTROLS	Inadequate control structure	Poor control over utilities	Mismanaged implementations	Poor vendor support	Unlimited system access
Policies and Procedures	2	2	2	2	2
Control Reports	1	2		1	2
Segregation	1	2	1		3
Testing	2		3	2	
Overall Control Rating - Design					
Overall Control Rating - Tested					

KEY TO RELIANCE ON CONTROL
3 - High reliance
2 - Moderate reliance
1 - Control has only a peripheral effect on the cause of exposure
Blank - No significant impact

KEY TO OVERALL CONTROL RATING
3 - Strong control
2 - Moderate but adequate control
1 - Inadequate control

EXPOSURES

	Inadequate control structure	Poor control over utilities	Mismanaged implementations	Poor vendor support	Unlimited system access
Erroneous Record Keeping	2	2			2
Unacceptable Accounting	2	2			1
Business Interruption	1	1	1	1	1
Erroneous Management Decisions					
Fraud and Embezzlement	1	1			1
Statutory Sanctions					
Excessive Costs	1	1		1	
Loss or Destruction of Assets	1	1			
Competitive Disadvantage					

KEY TO DEGREE OF CERTAINTY OF OCCURRENCE IN THE EVENT OF AN INADEQUATE CONTROL STRUCTURE
3 - Virtually certain
2 - Probable
1 - Possible
Blank - Very unlikely

13
DATA MANAGEMENT

INTRODUCTION

A great deal has been said and written about "data as a corporate resource" and the need for proper management of this resource. It is useful to reflect on what these statements actually mean. The first issue to be tackled is whether or not this is a new phenomenon. From the earliest days of computer processing, the term "data" has been in common use to the point where "computer processing," "data processing" and "information processing" are interchangeable terms. Data has always been a corporate resource but, until recently, an untapped one.

A resource is something that can be drawn upon to provide a desired product or service. What management has realized in the last few years is the need for information to run the business. Also, many organizations, particularly in the services sector, compete on the strength of the information they can provide to the customer. Although several services may be performed, the tangible product to the customer is information. The accuracy, completeness and timeliness of the information is a major competitive issue.

In terms of running the business, the last few years have been characterized by more intense competition in the marketplace, a more educated consumer and shorter product cycles. Based on available information, organizations are deciding what products to market, when, where and how to market them and to whom. This information is derived from externally gathered data (such as the state of the economy, market surveys, trends in the financial markets, and so forth) and from internally gathered data (for instance, sales reports, historical precedents and productivity analysis). The result is that businesses find themselves to be information driven.

Therefore, in order for an organization to be successful, it must understand the nature of the information which drives the business and then ensure that the raw data which provides this information is captured and readily available for analysis in various forms. A good analogy is the comparison with mining for coal. It is clearly much easier to mine coal that is close to the surface rather than having to build coal shafts underground and provide the cumbersome, costly (but necessary) infrastructure to ensure safe mining. It is the same way when "mining" through data to obtain information. If the data are not readily accessible it will be necessary to build various levels of support before information can be retrieved, if it can be retrieved at all. This chapter covers the management issues that surround the translation of raw data into usable information.

The first section of this chapter describes the control perspective for including data management as one of the basic building block elements of information systems. This section also describes the relevance of this subject area to the skill set and knowledge requirements of the Level 1 and Level 2 auditor. Causes of exposure are described, as are the more common types of control that act upon these causes of exposure. The types of exposure that may occur as a result of a deficiency or breakdown in the control structure are then discussed. Finally, the audits to be performed are described in terms of relevant objectives and frequency.

CONTROL PERSPECTIVE

In order to more efficiently utilize data on a organization-wide shared basis, the management and cataloging of data have become an important science in information processing. The efficient, economical and proper use of data in the information age is a critical element in the efficient conduct of business.

"Data resource management" is the term used to describe the methods of managing the corporate data resource in a way that will provide the required information in the most effective manner.

The three inherent principles in data resource management are :

- Focus on the data.

- Separate the data from its uses.

- Structure the data for varied access.

It is essential that the data within the corporate data base are maintained securely, accurately and completely.

In addition, the corporate data base in a mature "data driven" organization will become the heart of the organization. It is essential that proper control is exercised over who has access to the data base. Issues dealing with the ownership of data, usage of data and custodianship must all be addressed.

SCOPE OF DATA MANAGEMENT

Data management includes the following subtopics in its scope of activities:

- Identification.

- Classification/logical data view.

- Organization/ownership.

- Distribution.

- Protection.

- Integrity.

Identification

As stated earlier in this chapter, for an organization to be successful it must understand the nature of the information that drives the business and identify the source of that information (i.e., the raw data). The identification element of data management is concerned with identifying the required data items, including the source of each item, its characteristics and relationships with other data items. This is easier said than done. In fact, the work performed during the identification stage will have a profound impact on the other activities associated with data management.

The information used within an organization can generally be categorized as either external or internal. Table 13.1 shows the type of information that would typically fall into each category. It is apparent that some of this information, particularly on the external side of the equation, is not suitable for computerization, at least not in the traditional sense.

Identification, therefore, entails the preparation of the corporate data model. This is best achieved through interviews with the department heads of each of the functional areas within the organization. The questions to be posed and answered are, "What type of data influences this functional area?" and "What information is required to successfully operate and manage the area?" After all the interviews have been completed, the collection of data items must be analyzed and distilled into a form or model that is understandable, acceptable and presentable to the management of the organization. This analysis will include a determination of the source of the data, its characteristics, interrelationships with other data items and its source. The corporate data model that is created must then be compared to the data that is currently held and maintained. The difference between what is currently available and what is ultimately required becomes the basis for the data collection aspect of new application system development.

Numerous Computer Aided Software Engineering (CASE) tools are available to help formulate and maintain the corporate data model. CASE tools have also been developed to help reverse engineer the current file structures. Reverse engineering is a process whereby the current file structures are analyzed by a software product that is designed and developed for this purpose. The output from the software product is typically a schematic of the data structure showing the various interrelationships between data elements. Once this schematic has been developed, there are products currently being developed that will be able to edit the schematic to produce a final product which can then undergo a "forward-engineering" process. This forward-engineering process will automatically generate the necessary tables and structures for the data base management system in use within the organization. There are a number of products presently available that have achieved some success in this forwared-engineering approach.

Classification/Logical Data View

In the description of the preparation of the corporate data model, the point was made that individual application systems should be developed to populate the data model with data values. The development of these application systems takes on what is referred to a "data-driven approach to system development."

The traditional approach to developing information systems has been to focus on the processes to be performed. This is particularly true when dealing with operational systems. The drawback to this approach is that subsequent information needs that are of a tactical or strategic nature are not generally considered when designing a process-oriented system. If these information needs do arise, it is usually a scramble to draw together the required data from sources which were not designed to be accessible to ad hoc enquiries. In many cases the information requests go unanswered either because the source data do not exist or it would be too costly and/or time consuming to custom build software to meet the request. In this "information age" the inability of many conventional systems to yield complete, timely and accurate information is a major disadvantage. What is required is a focus on data and information requirements when planning and building systems. Data items should be incorporated into a corporate data model that is reflected (typically through an integrated data dictionary) in the application systems and inquiry routines that are written to convert this data into information.

There has been considerable debate over the relative merits of the data-driven approach to system development versus the process-driven approach. In reality, both methods are used. When performing the general design and feasibility phase of development, the analyst will most likely use a data flow diagram (DFD) to model the process flow of data. While this is happening the data administrator should also be preparing the entity-relationship (ER) diagram. There are two different ways in which the ER diagram can be prepared — the bottom-up method and the top-down method. The bottom-up approach (or normalization process) starts with the data elements that are known to exist because of their presence on reports, form, screens and computer files. This is typically the approach that is used when data modeling in individual application development. Top-down data modeling starts with a high-level view of the functions of the organization and the data elements that drive the organization. This approach is more commonly used for corporate data modeling. The proper way to perform data modeling is to use the top-down approach initially and then apply the bottom-up, normalization process to the attributes in the entity and relationship sets resulting from the initial approach.

An entity is an object about which the organization wishes to store information. Each entity has attributes and relationships to other entities. The first step in the ER approach is to identify entities, relationships and attributes. The next step is referred to as translation (or mapping). This involves taking the ER model that has been developed to this point, applying several sets of rules to rationalize the design and arriving at a logical data model. Once the logical data model has been designed it is possible to move onto the next step which is the physical design of the data model. Whereas the conceptual data model is independent of any data base management system (DBMS) software, and the logical data model is only somewhat dependent, the physical data base design is very much DBMS software dependent.

The subject of entity-relationship modeling is a discipline in itself. What has been described to this point is, of necessity, a thumbnail sketch of the activities that take place during the development of an entity-relationship model. Readers who are interested in pursuing this subject in detail should refer to the work of P. Chen, E.F. Codd, C. Date, Chris Gane and James Martin.

Within the scope of this text it is sufficient for the auditor to recognize that entity-relationship modelling is a technique for ensuring that data can be accessed in the most flexible manner. This flexibility, in turn, allows changes to the data aspects of the application system to be made relatively easily, as opposed to the major efforts which were previously the norm in situations where changes were required to the attributes or relationships between data entities or elements. What the auditor should be looking for is the incorporation of these ERM techniques into the methodology for application system development.

Organization/Ownership

From an organizational standpoint there are two distinct dimensions to data management:

- The business dimension of identifying the data which are relevant to the organization, the source of these data, the method of data capture and the interrelationship which these data items have with each other.

- The technical dimension of storing data on computer-readable media in a form which is readily accessible to the business needs of the organization. The technical dimension includes the data base administrator function. This person is responsible for translating the logical view of the corporate data model (as developed by the data administrator) into a physical form on computer-readable media while still providing the required business functionality. Data base administration is also concerned with the integrity of the data on the data base, performance issues relating to accessing data and the various security issues associated with the data base, including backup and recovery.

Given the nature of these organizational considerations there are now three interested parties in the development of any computer system:

- The data administrator who is responsible for the integrity of the conceptual and logical view of the corporate data base and, typically, the custodianship of the data dictionary.

- The system development group that is responsible for developing the program logic which will turn data into information.

- The data base administrator who is responsible for the physical representation of the data base and the performance of the data base once it is in production.

It is important that these responsibilities are clearly communicated to (and understood by) the three parties involved. The development methodology in use must be modified to reflect this split in responsibilities.

In terms of ownership, the data base administrator has ownership of the corporate data model and the data dictionary. However, the ownership of the data in the data bases which comprise the corporate data model belongs to the principal users. The data administrator may be called upon to arbitrate on contentious questions of ownership between competing groups.

Distribution

An added dimension to the problem is the wide distribution of data within the organization. With the emergence of end-user computing and the proliferation of microcomputers, corporate data may be spread across many different physical data bases each with its own format, update rules and state of completeness. Although end-user computing has many benefits and should be encouraged, it also should be controlled. An organization cannot afford to have its various user departments going off in different directions in the pursuit of information. If this is allowed to happen, the current problems in the data processing environment with data integrity, data duplication, data maintenance and availability will be minuscule in comparison to the problems that will exist in an uncontrolled end-user computing environment.

Data consistency and data redundancy are the principal concerns in a data distributed environment. There should continue to be a single version of any data element even although the element may be distributed across different hardware platforms. This implies that there should be control over the updates to all data elements. Through the update process, it must be ensured that all versions of the data element are updated at the same time. Cooperative processing is a form of distributed processing through the integration of various levels of processing capability across multiple hardware and software platforms. The concerns of data consistency and data redundancy also exist in a cooperative processing environment. There should be an overall data architecture in place that looks at the corporate data model in its entirety. Distributed processing, in any of its manifestations, should not be allowed to become a reason for taking a piecemeal approach to data management.

Protection

Data management is a corporate responsibility. Perhaps the biggest change in the concept of data protection stems from this corporate view of data as opposed to the more parochial view that was taken when data files were associated with individual applications. It is no longer sufficient to deal with protection of data at an application level. A control model should be built to address the issues of data protection for the organization. This control structure should reflect a top-down view of data management. Issues of data ownership, levels of access, integrity of the data base, backup and recovery must all be dealt with as part of this control model. The control model should reflect a hierarchy of activity starting with the role of the person having the overall responsibility for the management of the control model (usually the data security officer) and ending in the maintenance roles which must be performed.

Maintenance is concerned with making changes to the corporate data model, reflecting these changes in the data dictionary and ensuring that they are properly communicated to all parties who have a need to know the current status of the corporate data model. With the degree of data independence that can be achieved in today's data base management systems, changes to the data base should necessitate minimal changes to application programs. However, the addition of new data items and changes or deletions to existing data items must be accorded the same level of control as currently surrounds changes to application systems. Therefore, the principles of change control that have been applied to application programs (such as segregation of duties, proper testing, proper migration procedure and a documented audit trail) must be applied to changes in the definition of the data used by these programs. Prior to the separation of programs and data, the data definitions were embedded in the programs. Controlling changes to the programs inherently meant controlling changes to the data definitions. This is no longer the case when the definitions are maintained externally from individual application programs. See

Chapter 7 for a detailed description of the principles of system maintenance and change control.

It is important to understand the distinction between owners of data (or those with update authority) and users of data (those with inquiry access only or limited update authority). The computer operations group is the custodian of all data. They ensure that proper monitoring is performed and that backup and recovery procedures are in place and functioning. On the question of data ownership, the data administrator should be in a position to arbitrate any dispute between rival users.

Integrity

Integrity implies a lack of errors in the content of the data bases that comprise the corporate data model. There are a number of integrity checks that can be made to minimize the incidence of error. Referential integrity checking, domain constraints, non-key dependency constraints, consistency of redundant information and constraints on derived data are the most frequently encountered types of integrity constraints that should be tested for. For additional information, see Flaatten et. al., *Foundations of Business Systems*, (Orlando, FL: Dryden Press, 1989), 419-425.

Referential integrity checks ensure the validity of the value of a data element within a data base, where the data element is also the key to another data base record (such as a foreign key) or table. For example, in a payroll record there may be a deduction code. Deduction codes may be contained in a separate data base. The deduction code in the payroll record must refer to a valid record within the deductions table, otherwise a referential integrity violation will occur.

Domain checking concerns the adherence of the data values to the attributes that have been established for a data element. Attributes concern the length of the data element, the nature of the content (for example, numeric versus alphanumeric) and any specific values that the data element is restricted to.

Non-key dependency is concerned with the relationship between data elements within the same data base. For example, in a payroll application, only certain classes of employees may be eligible for pension benefits. Unlike referential integrity, where the data base management system can be asked to ensure data integrity, non-key dependency is the responsibility of the application system.

If there is a need to retain redundant data there is a requirement to update all of these data at the same time. Two problem situations quickly come to mind when trying to retain the integrity of redundant data — distributed systems and system failure. When the redundant data are spread across different hardware platforms, the data base management system must be able to commit the updates to all systems before considering an update transaction to be complete. This implies that all systems are networked together and the DBMS is able to maintain data integrity across all platforms. This is not always the case and, in fact, tends to be the exception rather than the rule. System failure may occur between updates of redundant data elements. Similar to the situation with distributed systems, the update cannot be considered to be complete until all data items have been updated. The application systems that use these data elements must be developed to perform updates to all the data elements. The backup and recovery procedures must be able to return all of the redundant data elements back to the same values that existed before the system failure.

Constraints on derived data is a system performance issue. A particular value, such as hours worked in a month, may be obtained (or derived) from a cumulation of many records, such as daily time sheets. The choices are to either maintain redundant data, such as the accumulated hours worked and the individual daily hours worked, or to go through the exercise of reading all the constituent records and calculating the hours worked from these records. Neither of these alternatives is intuitively correct. Each decision must be made in light of the circumstances that exist at the time.

LEVEL 1 AUDITOR — SKILL AND KNOWLEDGE OBJECTIVES

Overall Objective

Know the issues relating to data management from both a technical and a management perspective. Be able to differentiate between the two (for instance, ownership versus custodianship and logical versus physical views of data).

Identification

Know the process by which the data elements that comprise the corporate data model are identified and incorporated into the data dictionary. Be able to factor this knowledge into an audit of the development of a new system that uses some or all of these data elements.

Classification/Logical Data View

Be able to classify data elements according to the view of a particular end user (known as a sub-schema or "logical data view"). Be able to factor this knowledge into an audit of a data driven system development.

Organization/Ownership

Know the responsibilities of the data administrator function (including those as an arbitrator in cases of dispute over data ownership). Be able to execute an audit program to ensure compliance with the responsibilities as defined for this function.

Distribution

Know the issues that are associated with distributed data management. Be able to execute an audit program to determine if an appropriate level of control is being exercised over the entire corporate data base.

Protection

Know the issues that need to be addressed when designing to protect data from unauthorized access. Be able to review a proposed design and comment on the adequacy of the controls built into the design.

The Institute of Internal Auditors

Integrity

Know the principles of preserving the integrity of the data across the data base and the steps by which this objective is achieved.

LEVEL 2 AUDITOR — SKILL AND KNOWLEDGE OBJECTIVES

Overall Objectives

Be able to design and execute audits that address the control issues relating to data management from both a business and a technical perspective.

Identification

Be familiar with reverse and forward engineering techniques that are used to identify and classify data elements within the corporate data base. Be able to design an audit to comment on the completeness and accuracy of the data element identification process.

Classification

Understand the methods used to depict the classification of data (including the use of normal forms) and any technology used to assist in this classification exercise. Be able to audit the accuracy and completeness of a diagrammatic representation of a data schema and sub-schema and the use of these representations in the development of computer systems.

Organization/Ownership

Understand the issues that must be resolved by the data administrator. Be able to perform an audit on the completeness and appropriateness of the roles and responsibilities assigned to this function.

Understand the relationship between the diagrammatic representation of data (schema and sub-schema) and the descriptive language employed by the data base management system. Be able to perform an audit to ensure consistency between the two representations.

Distribution

Understand the technology that is required to keep control over a distributed data base. Be able to design and execute audits that will provide sufficient coverage and information to determine if an appropriate level of control is being exercised over the entire corporate data base.

Protection

Understand the various levels of protection that can be designed into a data base application (such as file, record, field, user type, and so forth). Understand how this level of protection is activated. For instance, does it go through the data base management system, or is it built into the application?

Integrity

Understand the features of the data base management system that are designed to preserve the integrity of the data across the data base. Be able to design tests that cover all conditions where the integrity of the data may be compromised.

CAUSES OF EXPOSURE

The causes of exposure in the area of data management are as follows:

- Ignorance.

- Inflexibility.

- Lack of integrity.

- Redundancy.

- Lack of accessibility.

Ignorance

The entire essence of data management is the recognition by management that data is a corporate resource and should be managed as such. When this recognition does not exist, management will remain ignorant of the benefits that can be realized by harnessing data for the benefit of the organization. The recognition of data as a corporate resource leads to the development of different types of systems, such as decision support systems, expert systems and executive information systems. These can have a more direct bearing on the bottom line of an organization than the more traditional, transaction processing systems.

The management of data requires an investment of resources (time and money) by an organization. Part of this investment is in the preparation of the corporate data model and the adoption of new data-driven or information engineering techniques for the development and maintenance of application systems. Just as importantly, however, is the training and education of the executives of an organization into the possibilities offered by effective data management. If data management is left as the private domain of the technicians (or the information services department) many of the potential business benefits will be lost because the technicians simply do not have the breadth of vision into what is possible with effective data management.

An antidote to ignorance is communication. Once the corporate data base has been established and rules have been developed about who has access to what, there must be procedures which clearly define how to make use of this data base. The first hurdle to be overcome is communicating to potential users what data exists. Tools must then be provided to enable the user to gain access to selected data items in a manner that is conducive to obtaining the necessary information. The provision of query languages that provide flexible access to the data base and that allow "what if" conditions to be presented and answered are being implemented in many organizations. An area of great potential is the ability to interface selected data items with business software tools (such as spreadsheet applications, trend analyzers, and so forth.). This allows for a more meaningful presentation of the extracted information.

Inflexibility

Businesses change over time, as do the ways of doing business. Application systems have typically had great difficulty keeping pace with the rate of business change. One of the principal reasons for this inability to meet changing requirements has been the inflexibility of being able to access the data base. Before the emergence of data base management systems, the data were tied very closely to application systems. The emergence of data base management systems promoted the separation of data from specific uses. This is the theme of "data independence" that was described earlier in the chapter. However, before the emergence of relational data bases, the access to data followed predetermined paths which had to be predefined to the data base management system.

If there was a need to add or change a data element, there most often was a requirement to change the application system given that the prespecified path to the data element and the attributes of the element were an inherent part of the application system. Even with the emergence of relational data base technology, proper data management and design is still required if the data base structure is to be flexible enough to meet changing business requirements. Normalization and synchronization (see the section on "Controls") are required to ensure that business needs can be met now and in the future.

Lack of Integrity

Information engineering is an emerging discipline for the design of application systems that meet the long-term information needs of an organization. Information engineering is the application of automated tools and techniques to the development of computer systems. Using the definition of the data that drives the business (as contained in a data repository) it should then be possible to automate the analysis, design and development of computer systems and maintain a high degree of consistency between these three elements of development.

Information engineering gets to the heart of the need for data integrity which is the assurance that the data maintained for the organization contains as few definitional, relational or factual errors as possible. Without data integrity, an organization simply cannot realize the benefits of its information systems potential.

Redundancy

There is an implied inefficiency with maintaining the same data element in more than one place. However, this is not the primary problem with data redundancy. The problem revolves around keeping each of these different representations of the same data element up-to-date. The problem of corporate ownership is also an issue when there is data redundancy.

Where there is more than one version of a data element, inconsistent or conflicting information may be presented to management. For example, if the payroll application system and the human resource application system maintain the same data elements it is possible that each system will show different values for even the most fundamental data elements, such as salary or benefits. This depends on which functional department has the primary responsibility for keeping the data element current; in other words, which functional department "owns" the data element.

As discussed earlier in this chapter, a certain amount of data redundancy may exist from circumstance or from choice. The key is to make sure that instances of redundancy are recognized and that there are plans in place to compensate for the redundancy or to ensure that the redundancy is not of significance to the organization.

Lack of Accessibility

The final objective of data management is to make information available to those who have a right to this information. A great deal of time is spent discussing the prevention of access. However, just as much thought should go into the granting of access and making sure that barriers to access are not built inadvertently. Barriers to access can result from a variety of reasons, including:

- The data is not available within the data base.

- The user has not been granted access to the data elements that produce the required information.

- The data base has been structured incorrectly. For example, allowing users access to information to which they are entitled would mean having to grant access to data to which they are not entitled.

Access to data is controlled by the data security software, the data base management system and application systems. A procedural interface usually exists whereby any or all of these software systems are informed of the level of access to be allowed to each user or group of users. There should be an overall architecture to define these levels of access. This architecture is a combination of procedural and technical rules. From a procedural standpoint, "someone" in the organization has to be given the authority and responsibility to set access levels both conceptually and within the technical structure of the software products mentioned above. The "someone" is usually the data security officer. The procedural and technical rules also should protect the organization from the data security officer. No one in the organization, including the data security officer, should have unlimited access to the system. There should be a monitoring or auditing device in place so that the activity of the data security officer can be monitored at periodic intervals.

CONTROLS

Applicable controls that are intended to prevent, detect and/or correct the causes of exposure just described as relevant to the area of data management are as follows:

- Management commitment.

- Corporate data model.

- Data-driven methodology.

- Normalization.

- Synchronization.

Management Commitment

Management commitment involves taking the time to understand and appreciate the concepts of data management and to factor these concepts into the business planning cycle of the organization. Management should look for ways in which the use of data can provide a return on the investment used to manage the data. This may seem like a circuitous argument — manage the data to realize a return on investment to manage the data. However, the reality of the matter is that many of the aspects of managing data have to be performed whether or not the organization is able to leverage any advantage from these activities. Even in the most traditional approaches to system development, data still must be captured, organized and maintained. These are many of the elements of data management. What is missing is the flexibility to do more with the data than was originally intended. It is the planning and organization that goes into ensuring that this flexibility exists that distinguishes data management from previous efforts at file management.

Management commitment can be expressed in many ways:

- Through the appointment of a chief information officer.

- Through the appointment of a data administrator who is separate from the data base administrator.

- Through investment in data modeling tools.

- Through an investment in training and education for the information systems staff.

Corporate Data Model

It is commonly accepted that the base of data for an organization is relatively stable, assuming that the organization stays within its main line of business. What changes is the type and volume of information required. What an organization strives for over time is to gain knowledge and understanding of how various conditions will affect the business. Data is the raw resource which can be readily converted into information through the application of general business context(s). Information can usually be directly obtained from raw data.

Knowledge requires the additional context of experience in addition to information. Experience is gained over time. After information has been provided over a period of time, trends can be determined — either directly from the sum of available information or by applying other contexts to this information (such as applying the state of the economy to financial information derived from the raw data of sales results).

Understanding is gained through the application of knowledge to the point where it is possible to anticipate, within acceptable margins of error, what the results of this application will be.

In today's world, computer systems provide information. It is left to human intervention to attain the higher levels of knowledge and understanding. Decision support systems and so called "expert" systems (see Chapter 16) are an attempt to reach a "knowledge" level. We are many years away from the level of artificial intelligence that is needed for the computer to acquire true understanding of a particular situation.

The corporate data model (often referred to as the enterprise data model) is a schematic that shows progressive layers of the data that drive the business. Once these data have been identified, the role of the information systems department is to collect, organize and maintain these data and provide tools to the end users which will allow flexible, timely and controlled access to these data items.

Data-Driven Methodology

In a data-driven organization, the information strategy will be derived from the corporate data model. Systems to be developed will provide a level of information or service that was previously not available. In a typical system development project a major part of the effort is spent in acquiring and storing the data which will be used to produce information.

Although data analysis and design is a separate activity within the definition of data resource management, application programs must still be written to collect and validate data items and add them to the appropriate data base. The interaction between the three groups (System Development, Data Administration and Data Base Administration) must be in place if the acquisition of data for the corporate data base is to be effectively handled.

There are certain types of information not usually derived from data bases designed as input to application programs. Table 13.1 illustrates several good examples of external information, such as political and social climate. However, these "textual" types of information are no less important to the corporate data model than the "factual" information which is the natural product of application systems. Therefore, there must be a way to acquire this information in a form that is readily accessible by the users. Electronic mail and the corporate "bulletin board" are methods that many progressive organizations are using to capture and deliver information throughout the organization. Through proper archival procedures, it is possible to preserve this type of information for an indefinite period, thus allowing analysis of trends and regression analyses.

Although a data-driven methodology is described here as a control for effective data management, this does not mean that a process-focused methodology is wrong. Data-driven and process-focused are two sides of the same coin. What is required within the methodology is measured consideration of the data, independent of the application system being developed. What this means in practical terms is that the data administrator and/or data base administrator should be involved in all stages of application system development as an important part of the development team, and not as a technical consultant to the project. The reconciliation between the process view of an application system and the data view is covered in the section on "synchronization."

Normalization

Normalization is the application of a series of rules to ensure that the data base structure is amenable to data maintenance thereby providing the maximum possible flexibility in terms of the data bases ability to support changes in the business requirements for access to data. In an article for Auerbach's System Development Management publication, William Kent indicates that the "... general characteristics of a data base in normal form are summarized as follows:

- Certain, but not all, redundancies are eliminated.

- Certain update problems are eliminated.

- The data base is fragmented into many small records.

- Data retrieval tends to be slower, and more code must be written and executed to maintain consistency within the data base."

There are five levels of normalization, termed the first normal form through to the fifth normal form. Typically, data bases are normalized down to the third normal form. Each level of normalization is a progression from the previous level. For example, a data base in third normal form must, of necessity, be in first and second normal form.

The interest that the auditor has in the normalization process revolves around the entire issue of flexible access to data and the minimization of redundant data. Normalization is required if data redundancy is to be minimized and flexibility maximized. The trade-off for these advantages is typically system and programming overhead.

Synchronization

There has been much discussion in the information systems community about the relative merits of data-driven development versus process-driven development. The reality is that most application development exercises are a combination of both. The system analyst will almost always focus on the process being automated and will view data as an inherent part of the process. The data administrator also should be involved as a full team member during all phases of the application system development exercise.

The synchronization exercise refers to the comparison between the data flow diagrams (the process descriptions) and the entity-relationship model (the data description). A common approach to this synchronization exercise is to use an association matrix, which, as the name suggests, is a matrix approach with the data entities shown on one axis and the files used in each process shown on the other axis. As the design of the system progresses, the level of detail provided on each axis becomes more refined, to the point where it should be possible to tell which data elements are used by which processes. This association matrix is valuable both in terms of ensuring that all entities and processes are matched and in indicating the impact of any change in either a process or a data element. This latter benefit is of considerable value in the maintenance of existing applications systems.

TYPES OF EXPOSURE

Listed below are the types of exposure which can occur as a result of the inadequacy or failure of the system of control to prevent the occurrence of a cause of exposure in the area of data management.

Erroneous Record Keeping

Poor data management practices can lead to erroneous record keeping in the sense that incomplete data may be stored, the attributes for data elements may be improperly specified and misleading relationships between data elements may be established. These types of problems are more difficult to detect than pure logic errors where the problem results from an error in the code of an application system. Conventional testing techniques may not detect data management errors in the same way as they can detect program logic errors. A greater degree of attention to detail has to be taken during the design process. The rules of normalization and the process of synchronization are key controls to prevent, detect and correct erroneous record keeping as a result of poor data management practices.

Erroneous Management Decisions

The point of having flexible access to data is to provide management with information that will allow better decision making. The integrity of the data is crucial if management is to place reliance on the information that emanates from these data and to base important decisions on the information that is provided. This is particularly true given the move to decision support systems and expert systems.

Ensuring consistency of data values through the elimination, or at least minimization, of data redundancy, providing referential integrity and domain checking, and normalizing the data all contribute toward data integrity. Without these integrity checks it is possible for management decisions to be based on outdated versions of data, data which is outside the bounds of reasonableness (from the organization's standpoint) or data which has meaningless values.

Excessive Costs

Excessive costs are a direct result of tightly integrating an application system with the data used by that system. This tight integration is one of the principal reasons why system maintenance consumes such a large percentage of the information systems department's budget. Whereas the business processes change on an ongoing basis, the data that forms the underpinnings of an organization's business remains fairly stable. By separating data from its uses, as determined by individual application systems, an organization should be able to reduce its overall costs of maintenance by only having to change the process component of the logic and not the data structures.

Given that effective data management can reduce the overall cost of maintaining systems, it seems reasonable to expect that poor or non-existent data management practices will result in excessive costs over and above what should be spent.

Loss or Destruction of Assets

Data is now recognized as a major corporate asset. Poor data management practices could very well lead to the loss or destruction of data. As discussed in a previous section of this chapter, data protection is a major component of data management.

Competitive Disadvantage

New forms of application systems (primarily decision support systems and executive information systems) are being built with the principal objective of providing a competitive advantage. These types of systems tend to focus on the requirement for non-structured access to data. If competitive advantage could be gained by the routine use of data, all organizations would be on the bandwagon by now. This is not the case. One of the main reasons is that although most informed people would accept that data is a potential weapon for competitive advantage, very few have any idea what this means in practical terms. Flexible access to data, combined with powerful reporting query languages and a strong desire for experimentation, are needed to start to turn the potential of data as a competitive tool into reality. The principals espoused by data management techniques set the scene for the use of query languages and experimentation.

CONTROL EVALUATION TABLE

The Control Evaluation Table for data management is given in Figure 13.1 The evaluation numbers are subjective and should be adjusted based upon the conditions that exist in individual organizations. Note that, in practice, the completion of the Control Evaluation Table is in two parts:

- During detailed information gathering where, from the review of available documentation and the results of personal interviews, the key to reliance on individual controls and the "overall control rating (design)" are determined.

- During the execution of the audit program where, as a result of various audit tests, the strength of individual controls is fully assessed and the "overall control rating (tested)" is determined.

AUDIT APPROACH

Data management should be the subject of a periodic audit. The objectives of this audit are as follows:

- Ensure that the approach to data management is consistent with the needs and culture of the organization.

- Ensure that the development methodology reflects the organization's selected approach to data management.

- Ensure that the roles and responsibilities of the personnel involved in data management are defined and incorporated into the development, maintenance and operation of the organization's application systems.

- Ensure that the tools and techniques that are appropriate to the selected method of data management are installed and are being used according to defined procedures.

- Ensure that the objectives adopted by the investment in data management techniques are in fact being achieved.

The auditor should address the subject of data management from a top-down perspective starting with an examination of the corporate commitment to the objectives of data management. In technical terms these objectives talk about minimizing redundancy and ensuring data integrity. What the auditor should be concerned about are the objectives of data management from a business perspective. Are the users (including the management of the organization) able to obtain information that is timely, accurate and relevant to their needs and can they continue to receive this type of information as their needs change? Too often, the achievement of the technical definition of data management is considered a success whereas the users still do not consider themselves to have the level of access to information that they desire and require. In other words, the "operation was a success but the patient died" syndrome. The auditor should spend time with the users and discuss with them the success from their point of view of the data management program within the organization. If they do not even know the program exists, there is clearly a major problem with the effectiveness of the program.

The development methodology should be examined for consistency with the data management approach adopted by the organization. Too often, the data management tools and techniques are not incorporated into the methodology. Systems that are developed using these tools and techniques are, therefore, left out of the controlled development environment that the methodology provides. This can only lead to problems with these systems either during development or after implementation. We have seen enough of ad hoc system development to know that it can only lead to excess costs of development and/or maintenance.

During individual application development audits, the auditor should comment on the adherence to the data management tools and techniques in place within the organization. Once again, it is common to pay lip service to new tools and techniques but, in light of impending deadlines, decide to revert to the techniques of old which, as we know, do not provide the flexibility of access to data that modern organizations now require.

Maintenance procedures over the tables which define the data should be examined in the same light as program change control. Changes to data tables should be approved, documented and tested. A report should be made to senior management on the effectiveness of the data management program within the organization.

The Institute of Internal Auditors

Table 13.1 — Types of Information

EXTERNAL	INTERNAL
Economic	Financial
Political	Products and Services
Social	Productivity Analysis
Market Conditions	Precedents
Competition	Inter-departmental Correspondence
Non-competition	Customer
Fiscal	
Technological	

Reprinted from *Data Base Management* (New York: Auerbach Publishers), 1990, Warren Gorham & Lamont Inc. Used with permission.

Figure 13.1 — Control Evaluation Table Data Management

	CAUSES OF EXPOSURE				
CONTROLS	Ignorance	Inflexibility	Lack of integrity	Redundancy	Lack of accessibility
Management Commitment	3	2	1	1	2
Corporate Data Model	2	2	1	2	2
Data Driven Methodology	2	3	2	1	2
Normalization		2	3	3	2
Synchronization	1	2	2	2	2
Overall Control Rating - Design					
Overall Control Rating - Tested					
EXPOSURES					
Erroneous Record Keeping	1	1	2	2	
Unacceptable Accounting					
Business Interruption					
Erroneous Management Decisions	2	1	2	2	2
Fraud and Embezzlement					
Statutory Sanctions					
Excessive Costs	2	2	2	2	2
Loss or Destruction of Assets	1		2		
Competitive Disadvantage	2	2	2	1	2

KEY TO RELIANCE ON CONTROL
3 - High reliance
2 - Moderate reliance
1 - Control has only a peripheral effect on the cause of exposure
Blank - No significant impact

KEY TO OVERALL CONTROL RATING
3 - Strong control
2 - Moderate but adequate control
1 - Inadequate control

KEY TO DEGREE OF CERTAINTY OF OCCURRENCE IN THE EVENT OF AN INADEQUATE CONTROL STRUCTURE
3 - Virtually certain
2 - Probable
1 - Possible
Blank - Very unlikely

14
DATA BASE MANAGEMENT SYSTEM/ DATA DICTIONARY

INTRODUCTION

Chapter 13 deals primarily with the conceptual and logical elements of data management. Once the conceptual/logical data model has been built it is necessary to translate it into a physical data model that can be processed by the computer. The computer is able to process (read, write, update, delete) this physical data model through the use of a software product called a data base management system (DBMS). Therefore, in order to allow this processing to take place, the physical data model must conform to the specifications set by the DBMS in place within the organization. The DBMS will be a proprietary product, the internals of which will be unique to each product. However, there are some basic issues that each DBMS must address. It is these common issues that will be addressed in this chapter.

This chapter also addresses the philosophies behind the use of a data dictionary which is a method for recording and maintaining information on the data and processes used within the organization. As such, the data dictionary has a close relationship with the data base management system.

The first section of this chapter describes the control perspective for including the chapter topic as one of the basic building block elements of information systems. This section also describes the relevance of this subject area to the skill set and knowledge requirements of the Level 1 and Level 2 auditor. Causes of exposure are described, as are the more common types of control that act upon these causes of exposure. The types of exposure which may occur as a result of a deficiency or breakdown in the control structure are then discussed. Finally, the audits to be performed are described in terms of relevant objectives and frequency.

CONTROL PERSPECTIVE

Vendors supply data base management systems to allow multiple users to share common data. These software products are utilized in all sizes of systems from large mainframes to those that are PC-based. The security, control and auditability of the data base is to a large extent dependent on the imbedded control structure supplied with the data base management system. In turn, the reliability of the total control structure is in direct relationship to the quality of the controls administration and the appropriate utilization of the security and control features supplied by the vendor.

Access to data is controlled by the data base management system and associated reporting tools. In order for an application system to obtain data for processing and reporting, a request has to be issued to the data base management system. Where the user wishes to inquire directly into the data base, a request has to be issued to the database management system via some type of query language. Given that the principal, legitimate access path to data is via the data base management system, the auditor has a great deal of interest in ensuring that proper controls are inherent in the software. He or she should also ensure that proper procedural controls have been put in place around the administration of the data base management system.

SCOPE OF DATA BASE MANAGEMENT SYSTEM/DATA DICTIONARY

Data base management system/data dictionary includes the following subtopics in its scope of activities:

- Data base management system (DBMS).

- Structure.

- Usage requirements/characteristics/performance.

- Access control implementation.

- Data dictionary.

Data Base Management System

A data base can be viewed from three different perspectives:

- The conceptual schema (also referred to as the conceptual model) which is the overall model of the data used within the business.

- The external schema (also referred to as the logical data model) which is the view held by the programmer during the development of an application system.

- The internal schema (also referred to as the physical data model) which is the layout of the data as it appears on computer-readable media.

The data base management system is the term given to the software which maintains the internal schema and passes the required data elements to the application systems based upon an interface convention established by the DBMS. Bernard Boar in his article, "Selecting a Mature Data Base Management System,"[1] describes four classes of physical data models, three of which are DBMS based:

- Class 1: Files — in this class of physical data model a DBMS is not used. Data elements are grouped into physical files which are then used by the application systems. Typically these files are designed for the exclusive use of one application system. This type of data model was the only option prior to the introduction of DBMS's.

- Class 2: Application data bases — in this class of physical data model a DBMS is used but the organization of the data is geared to the use of one application system. There is no effort at data sharing between application systems.

---

[1] *System Development Management,* (New York: Auerbach Publishers, 1990): 3, 4.

The Institute of Internal Auditors

- Class 3: Subject data bases — the data bases are created separately from the use of any individual application system. There is a great deal of data sharing between application systems.

- Class 4: User computing — in this class of physical data model, ad hoc information retrieval is balanced against the need for high volume throughput. The data needs of the application system which are typically known and well structured are balanced against the ad hoc data needs of the user which are usually unknown and poorly structured.

Boar argues that the optimum data environment is a ". . . mixture of Class 3 and Class 4 environments. The Class 3 environment supports the production side of the business, and the Class 4 environment provides tools to analyze the business; there is a data pipeline between the two environments."[2]

In addition to the data dictionary which will be described later, the DBMS has two major interfaces to the user of the DBMS:

- Data Definition Language (DDL) which defines the physical layout of the data to the DBMS.

- The Data Manipulation Language (DML) which provides the means of indicating to the DBMS which data elements are required.

The objective of the DBMS is to be able to provide the organization with the promised benefits from an effective data management program. Flexible access to data, minimization of data redundancy and data integrity are only achievable to the extent that the DBMS supports these goals. The next section covers the ways in which a DBMS supports the goals as stated in the data management policy.

---

[2] Ibid, p. 4.

Structure

When DBMSs were first introduced, they were classified as either a hierarchical model (one that organizes data in a hierarchical tree structure) or as a network model (one that interconnects record types into a "network"). However, both of these philosophical models to data base management systems have been replaced in recent years by the relational data base model. This is not to say that the hierarchical or network model is totally inappropriate in certain circumstances. High volume, transaction processing systems may still benefit from either of these approaches. However, the reality is that most organizations now use the relational data base model for their data base management system.

The relational model is based on relational calculus and was invented by E.F. Codd at IBM. Rather than presenting the users of the data base with a view that is based on hierarchies or networks, the relational data base model presents the information in tables, with rows and columns.

As described by Robert W. Taylor in his article, "Trends in Data Base Technology," the ". . . relational model is based on several simple-to-understand principles:

- All data is organized into a series of tables in which each row of the table contains a number of simply structured fields.

- All relationships between tables are represented explicitly by values in the tables — there is never any hidden or machine-dependent structural links.

- A data manipulation language can access and update any data value, and a value-matching JOIN operation can combine multiple tables.

- Most important, the model is a user abstraction in that the system can employ any number of means to enhance the performance of these operations. Because the language used to express these operations does not refer to how they are carried out within the data base software, there can be no built-in

The Institute of Internal Auditors

dependence, as with earlier approaches, and therefore no hidden software maintenance cost. Furthermore, because the structures and operations are simple and machine independent, programmers can develop easy-to-learn languages for expressing data requirements. Thus, programmers can manipulate data in high-level, machine-independent terms."[3]

As was discussed earlier, the concept of data management has three distinct perspectives — the conceptual model, the logical data model and the physical data model. The conceptual model is DBMS independent. The logical model should be prepared according to the conventions demanded by the type of DBMS in place (hierarchical, network or relational). Once the conceptual/logical data model has been prepared, the data base administrator should translate this model into the physical data model.

In the relational data base environment this translation of the conceptual and logical data model into the physical data base is quite straightforward. Once the logical data base has been normalized, it can then be made into tables for the relational data base management system. The access to data in the data base is based on data values which are matched to field values in the tables. There are no predefined access paths to the data. In fact, there may be many different access paths to the data. This means that the relational model can provide a high level of flexibility. As new values and new tables are created the data base designer does not have to make changes in the access paths to existing data elements.

In the case of hierarchical and network data base structures the translation from the conceptual/logical data model to a physical data base requires much more effort. Access paths and index keys must be determined and inserted into the data base records. The application system must also be aware of these access paths and must pre-define to the data management system the route to be taken to a particular data record. Where changes are made to the data base structure it is likely that changes will have to be made to a number of application systems.

---

[3] *Computer Programming Management*, (New York: Auerbach Publishers, 1989): 2, 3.

Usage Requirements/Characteristics/Performance

Having said that the relational data base model most closely resembles the way in which the user looks at data and that this structure offers the highest level of flexibility to meet changing business requirements, it should also be stated that there is a price to pay for these advantages. That price has usually been system performance and DASD usage. The relational model has always been recognized as the best available approach for ad hoc data base enquiries. However, there has always been a concern about the ability of the relational data base model to support high volume application systems. Even with the improvements that have been made in the throughput capabilities of relational data base software, this performance issue still exists. The auditor should ensure that proper benchmark tests are conducted before the commitment is made to go with a relational data base solution.

In the network and hierarchical data base structures, the access paths to data are pre-defined. This means that the system performance can be tuned to meet specific application system requirements. This "fast-path" approach is not available to the same extent in the relational data base model.

Accompanying the relational data base management system is a relational data base language. In the past, relational languages were classified as either algebraic or calculus-based languages with the distinction being based on the level of structure inherent in the language. However, in recent years, Structured Query Language (SQL) has emerged as the standard relational language. Originally developed by IBM, SQL was approved by the American National Standards Institute in 1986.

Access Control Implementation

The data base management system provides the access vehicle for a user to access data. The identity of the user requesting access to the data may be further screened by the fact that the request is made through an application system rather than directly through some form of query system. Complicating the issue of access control is the fact that the data base management system allows data sharing between application systems and between users. Prior to the emergence of data base management systems, data files were most often created for the one application system and, consequently, for one discrete set of users. Although this approach caused other business problems relating to data redundancy and lack of flexibility to support the long-term needs of the business, it did simplify the access control issue. Access controls in a data base management system environment have to be viewed within the bigger picture of all functions (or departments) within the organization that may have access to any part of the data base.

For effective access control implementation, the data base management system must be properly interfaced to the data security software package installed within the organization. Controlling access to data held within the data base is the joint responsibility of the data security software, the application systems and the data base management system. The auditor should be concerned that the cumulative effect of the measures taken in each of these software entities is sufficient to restrict access level of access to data to those who are entitled to such access.

As described in detail in Chapter 5, access control implementation requires planning. The data security officer is usually responsible for establishing the levels of access allowed to each user or group of users. The level of access is determined by the needs of the organization. The presence of a data base management system does not change the requirements for access control as described in Chapter 5 but, in fact, makes their implementation even more important.

Data Dictionary

Data dictionary systems are a mechanism for maintaining data about data (or meta data). The data about which data are stored in the dictionary include data attributes, data sources, data definitions (such as items, elements, groups, forms, screens, and so forth), system documentation, system processes, edit rules and test data. Definitions of data records or tables are incorporated directly from the data dictionary into application system programs.

There are two types of data dictionaries:

- A passive data dictionary which is used only as a documentation aid.

- An active data dictionary which is used as a control vehicle so that, unless the data are defined and described in the data dictionary, they cannot be used in any application system process.

One of the principal intentions of the data dictionary is to have only one definition of each data element in use within the organization and to have all references to that data element use the definition contained within the data dictionary. Cross references to each process using the data element would also be maintained within the data dictionary. In this way, any time a change was made to the data element or to any process that used the data element, it would be a simple matter to determine the impact of this change. This facility would greatly assist in system maintenance and change control.

Most data dictionaries are attached to specific data base management systems. The principal disadvantage of this approach is that of scope; the vendors of these tightly integrated products usually do not accommodate the fact that there may be other vendors' products in use within the organization in question. A tightly integrated data dictionary will rarely support "foreign" products in anything other than the most superficial way. What this means in practical terms is that the data dictionary can only control the definition of data elements managed within the scope of the products supplied by the DBMS vendor.

Another limitation that is common among current data dictionaries is the support of the conceptual and logical data modeling processes. The basic problem is in being able to support the translation of the conceptual and logical model into the physical model. Current data dictionaries are designed only to use the physical model; it is this model which is of interest to the application system programs. However, by not being able to provide a complete end-to-end trail of the design of the data base, it is possible that inconsistencies will be introduced.

The Institute of Internal Auditors

The trend that appears to be shaping the direction of the data dictionary approach is the move to the concept of repository and data services. The repository will contain all of the information that has been discussed in the context of a data dictionary. The repository will itself be based on relational data base technology and will have defined entity relationships. Users will be able to access the repository and determine if the information they are looking for actually exists and, if it does exist, will acquire the navigation tools that are necessary for access. Data services will manage the data elements and provide consistency and transparency across all of the hardware platforms that exist within the organization. The user will not care that a particular data element exists on a workstation or on an external enterprise mainframe. The data services will ensure that the data are provided to the user, if the user is authorized to access these data. Although not currently available to any great extent, the integration of repository and data services appears to be the way of the future.

LEVEL 1 AUDITOR — SKILL AND KNOWLEDGE OBJECTIVES

Overall Objectives

Know the functions of a data base management/data dictionary product, the control issues related to such a product and the general approach to auditing this type of product.

Data Base Management System (DBMS)

Know the underlying principles and features of a data base management system and the impact that this type of technology has on the organization and on the method of building and operating information systems.

Structure

Understand the differences between the various types of DBMS structures and the advantages and disadvantages of each. Be able to relate this knowledge to the situation that exists within the organization.

Usage Requirements/Characteristics/Performance

Know the types of business applications that can be best serviced by particular data base structures and, when conducting an application audit, be able to comment on the appropriateness of the data base structure to the usage characteristics and performance requirements of the application.

Access Control Implementation

Know the facilities offered by the DBMS in terms of access control and be able to execute an audit program to determine how effectively these facilities have been implemented.

Data Dictionary

Know the role of the data dictionary in the development of new systems and its inter-relationship with the DBMS.

LEVEL 2 AUDITOR — SKILL AND KNOWLEDGE OBJECTIVES

Overall Objectives

Be able to design and execute an audit of the data base management/data dictionary product and relate the results of this audit to the other areas within information systems which may be impacted by the findings of the audit.

The Institute of Internal Auditors

Data Base Management System (DBMS)

Understand the impact of the existence of a data base management system on the various audits that need to be conducted in an information systems environment.

Understand the specific features of the DBMS in place within the organization with particular reference to the control features built into the product. Be able to design and execute an audit to determine the adequacy of these features and the level of compliance with the intended control features.

Structure

Understand the structure of the DBMS in place within the organization and be able to design an audit program to ensure that the use of this structure is appropriate to the information system needs of the organization.

Usage Requirements/Characteristics/Performance

Understand that even within particular data base structures there are methods of tuning the performance of the data base to meet specific application needs. Be able to factor this knowledge into an application system or data base audit.

Access Control Implications

Be able to relate the facilities offered by the DBMS in terms of access control to the business risks to be addressed. Be able to structure an audit program that measures the adequacy of the access control implementation.

Data Dictionary

Understand the difference between active and passive data dictionaries and be able to design an audit of the procedures surrounding the control over access and use of the dictionary.

CAUSES OF EXPOSURE

The causes of exposure in the area of data base management systems/data dictionary are as follows:

- Poor performance.

- Loss of data.

- Inflexibility.

- Lack of integrity.

- Incomplete documentation.

Poor Performance

During the design and development of a data base application, the development staff have to know the throughput requirements of the application system being built. The data base management system must be able to support these throughput requirements. There have been some well documented cases of large system developments using relational data base technology which simply could not function in a production environment. Typically these systems were developed rapidly using prototyping techniques supported by a relational data base management system. During the development process, especially for large, mission critical systems, there should be a benchmark exercise completed to ensure that the data base management system can handle the throughput volumes for the application both at current levels and those projected for the next three to five years.

The reader should not assume that high transaction volume systems are not suited to relational technology. A great deal of performance enhancements have gone into recent releases of relational data base management systems. However, performance is still an issue that should be explicitly addressed and not left to chance. Data base tuning in the data base design stages may go a long way to removing any performance issues. Once the system is designed and implemented it is much more difficult (and costly) to take corrective action.

Loss of Data

In a data base management system environment, access to data is controlled by the DBMS. For an application system to obtain data for inquiry or processing purposes, a request must be made to the DBMS. Similarly, if the application system wants to write to the data base, the DBMS manages the update function. It is the DBMS which makes the calls to the operating system software's I/O routines to effect the physical movement of data from the storage device into main memory and vice versa. The DBMS is responsible for formatting the data into the form requested by the application system, whether to pass data back to the application system or to update the data base from data passed from the application system. Where the data is not available or there is any kind of I/O problem, the DBMS is responsible for passing this "status" information back to the requesting application system. The application system is responsible for interrogating the status of the data sent back from the DBMS and taking the appropriate action.

Errors in setting up the physical form of the data base, errors in the request issued from the application program or any combination of the two could result in loss of data. The data may still be physically present on the storage device but not accessible to the application system through the DBMS. Complete testing of the interface between application systems and the DBMS is essential if loss of data is to be avoided. This interface testing should take into account all read, update, create and delete functions.

A failure on the part of the storage device upon which the data base resides or corruption of the data due to a software problem are also considerable risks which can result in loss of data. This risk is greater in a data base environment because of the sharing of data between application systems and, consequently, between user groups. In terms of data corruption, the DBMS should provide a fail-safe environment to protect against corruption of the data base by any application system. The reality of the matter is that this level of safety does not exist. Comprehensive testing continues to be the best way to mitigate the risk of corrupted data as a result of an application failure. In the event of a system software failure, the data base management system should provide roll-back and roll-forward capabilities to allow the data base to be reset in a consistent state which is usually just before the system problem occurred. In the event that there is a global failure of the data base, there must be backup and recovery procedures in place to restore the data base.

There are a number of fault tolerant systems on the market today, such as Tandem, that combine mirroring of the data base (the maintenance of two identical copies of the data base on different physical devices) with sophisticated error detection and recovery routines. The way this works is that the copy of the data base that is having problems can be taken off-line and corrected. Meanwhile the other copy of the data base is used to keep the business functioning. Once the problem has been solved on the problematic version of the data base it is brought back up-to-date automatically from the version that remained problem free. In this type of environment the chance of lost data as a result of hardware failure is considerably reduced.

Inflexibility

The business objective of data management is to have data when required, where required and in a form that is understandable to the user. Although the business objective does not change, the data required to meet the objective will almost certainly change over time. This requires that there be considerable forethought given to the organization of the data base if it is to satisfy changing business requirements. The normalization process that is associated with the preparation of the conceptual and logical data model is intended to ensure that the maximum flexibility is provided. Translation from this conceptual or logical data model to a physical data base must ensure that this flexibility is not lost in the process. Of all the data base management structures available, the relational data base structure provides the closest translation from the conceptual and logical model (such as entity-relationship diagrams) to a physical data base structure (or relational tables).

The other data base management system architectures (hierarchical and network) require considerable intervention by the data base administrator to produce the physical data base from the conceptual or logical data model. Physical addresses have to be built into the data base structure to allow the data base management system to link its way through the data base to find the required data items. When the data base structures are changed (for instance, when relationships change or new items are added), these physical addresses may have to be changed. In addition, the application systems that use these types of data base management systems may also be adversely impacted by changes in the physical data base. This requirement to explicitly state the access path to data is a major weakness in hierarchical and network data base management systems and significantly reduces the flexibility required by organizations to access data.

Lack of Integrity

The data base management system will provide a number of features that protect the integrity of the data. In relational technology, referential integrity checking is a feature that can be specified to the DBMS as being applicable to a particular data column. Where the referential integrity flag is defined for a particular column, the value of the column is automatically checked against the table which has the column as its key. If a row corresponding to the value of the column is not found in this table, the column is flagged as violating the referential integrity rule.

The interaction between an application system and the DBMS consists of a series of parameters that are passed by the application system to the DBMS. One of these parameters is a return code which the DBMS will set according to how successfully the DBMS was able to perform the actions requested by the application system. A referential integrity violation would show up in the return code passed back from the DBMS. As stated earlier in this chapter, it is important that application systems that use a DBMS have a routine that interrogates these return codes and takes whatever action is appropriate based on the return code.

Domain checking by the DBMS ensures that the adherence of the values in a data element to the attributes or value ranges that have been established for that data element. When redundant data must be retained, the DBMS needs some way of being able to cross-reference between these various versions of what is essentially the same data element.

Incomplete Documentation

In today's computer environment, complete automated documentation does not exist. Typically, data dictionaries are tied to specific data base management systems. Data elements not included in the DBMS are excluded from the dictionary except, perhaps, as commented items. In addition, the data dictionary is usually passive as opposed to active and the only way to ensure conformity to the definitions in the data dictionary is through adherence to procedures, which is typically a weak form of control. The emergence of relational data base management systems has exacerbated rather than helped solve the problem. It is usually difficult to combine the relational table definitions with the definitions of other data base management systems in use within the organization (a common occurrence in large organizations; for instance, IMS co-existing with DB/2).

Lastly, today's data dictionaries are focused on the physical data model and do not support the conceptual and logical data models particularly well. Inconsistencies between conceptual/logical data models and the physical data model are common.

The only real solution to this problem is the long-term development of a data repository as described earlier in the chapter and dealt with in more detail in the Controls section.

CONTROLS

Applicable controls that are intended to prevent, detect and/or correct the causes of exposure just described as relevant to the area of data base management systems/data dictionary are as follows:

- Data repository.

- Policies and procedures.

- Data security measures.

- Testing.

Data Repository

Based on relational data base technology, the data repository is a complex series of tables that describe all forms of data within the organization. The organization of the data repository is based on entities and the relationships and attributes of these entities. The entities in the case of the data repository are those data objects about which the organization wishes to know. Therefore, the data repository can be considered to maintain data *about* data.

Before a full data repository is introduced on a commercial basis there are certain technological issues that should be resolved, mostly concerned with the volume of data that will need to be stored. These problems will be solved in time. However, until that time comes, we are left with having to make do with the limitations of data dictionaries as they currently exist.

Policies and Procedures

As mentioned in the section on "Data Repository," the only way to ensure complete documentation of the data elements of importance to an organization is through adherence to policies and procedures. Standard naming conventions, the degree of normalization to be achieved, the mandatory use of the data dictionary and the use of inherent data integrity features should all be part of a policies and procedures manual governing the use of the data base management system. The person responsible for these policies and procedures should be the data base administrator. The role and responsibilities of the data base administrator should be documented and communicated to others involved in the data management process.

The system development methodology is a procedure for the development of application systems. The involvement of the data base administrator should be included throughout the development process and not just as a technical consultant at intermittent stages when an original or amended data design is required.

The use of tools and techniques also falls into the category of policies and procedures. The entire area of data management requires automated tools. The requirement for constant revision of the model is such that manual methods of documentation are unable to facilitate effective data modelling and the consequent translation into a physical data base. There are a number of "workbench" products now on the market that can be used to develop data diagrams. The more sophisticated of these products can then generate data base definitions and even application program code from the data design diagrams. Using this approach means that changes in the design can be easily incorporated into the finished product. Without this degree of "seamless" integration between the system analysis, design and development stages, the impact of a design change at anything other than the earliest stages of an application development project usually has a significant, adverse impact on the schedule and cost of the eventual development.

When the policy of the organization is to use a data management approach to system development, it is practically essential that automated tools and techniques are in place to effect this policy.

Data Security Measures

Data security measures involve a broad spectrum of controls. Chapter 5 covers this topic in detail. Suffice it to say in this chapter that the DBMS must support the goals of a data security program which is to protect, detect and/or correct any unauthorized disclosure, modification or destruction of data, whether accidental or intentional.

The DBMS should be able to interact with the data security software to prevent unauthorized access of any type (read, write, update, delete). Additionally, the DBMS must be able to recover from data failures through some form of "roll-back, roll-forward" mechanism. When performing an update to the data base, before and after images of the data base records should be maintained by the DBMS to facilitate data recovery in the event of failure.

Testing

The DBMS/data dictionary is in place to support the access to data by a user. The request for access will usually come via an application system but may come more directly from the user through the use of a report generator or query language. In the regular course of developing these access requests there should be testing criteria which specifically addresses the validity of the design of the data base to provide the required information. It may be that the design of the data base will preclude the access of certain data to all or a group of users. Therefore, the design of the data base is as much a testing issue as the application system's interface to the DBMS.

Benchmark tests of the data base's ability to handle the required volume of data and the expected volume of activity against the data base should be conducted in the early stages of development. It may be possible to use a prototype for this type of testing. Some form of simulated processing is almost certainly required to attest to the adequacy of the data base management system to handle the expected volume of data and activity. Volume testing should also be conducted as part of the operational acceptance test to confirm that further tuning of the data base is not required to provide the required level of response.

When a new version of the DBMS is received from the vendor, exhaustive testing must take place before it is migrated into the production environment. Not only must all the features of the DBMS be retested but the contents of the existing data bases must be tested to ensure that there are no peculiarities in these data bases that will cause an adverse reaction from the new version of the data base management system. The point was made when discussing system software that new versions of the software tend to be stricter about ensuring adherence to defined protocols when interfacing with application systems and that what used to work may no longer work but produce an error instead. One always hopes that the error will be properly trapped and an appropriate error message returned so that corrective action can be taken and no harm is done. Unfortunately, that is not always the case. Frequently, the new version of the software abends and the technician is left to find out what the real problem is.

What has just been described for system software also applies to data base management system software. There may be structures within the current version of the data base that are not allowed within the new version (and should not have been allowed to happen under the old version, but did anyway). When the new version of the data base management system comes across these data structures, unpredictable errors may occur. For this reason any new versions of the DBMS must be tested (in a test region) with data from existing production data bases.

TYPES OF EXPOSURE

Listed below are the types of exposure that can occur as a result of the inadequacy or failure of the system of control to prevent the occurrence of a cause of exposure in the area of data base management system/data dictionary.

Erroneous Record Keeping

Reliance is on the data base management system to properly store and then retrieve data elements that are of interest to the organization. Whereas the accuracy and completeness of the processing logic for these data elements is the responsibility of the application systems, the completeness and accuracy of the storage of these data elements is the responsibility of the DBMS.

If the DBMS allows a data integrity problem to enter into the data base, erroneous record keeping could result. In testing application systems which use a DBMS it is even more important than in conventional flat file processing that the content of the data base be checked in addition to the input and output produced by the application system. Dumps of the data base contents should be taken. Alternatively, the content of the data base can be interrogated through the use of a query language.

Business Interruption

The DBMS, if used effectively, holds shared data. There are many advantages to this approach of sharing data between applications. However, there is a clear disadvantage. If there is a catastrophic failure of the data base or the DBMS causes unpredictable results, the scope of the resultant problem may be so widespread as to cause some degree of business interruption. Backup and recovery procedures combined with exhaustive testing of new versions of the DBMS prior to its introduction into the production environment are essential to minimize any business interruption as a result of problems with the DBMS.

Erroneous Management Decisions

If the integrity of the data presented by the DBMS to the user is in question or the user cannot retrieve the required information from the data base, erroneous management decisions may result. The data base management system is the software that provides, in actual terms, the data integrity and flexibility which is the cornerstone of effective data management. Even if the conceptual and logical data models appear to provide data integrity and flexibility, it is the DBMS which ultimately defines just how well these objectives are achieved.

Statutory Sanctions

It is conceivable that statutory sanctions could result from an inability of the DBMS to support statutory reporting requirements placed on an organization.

Excessive Costs

The DBMS allows data to be separated from its uses and to provide for flexibility in the changing requirements for information by the organization. Without an effective DBMS, excessive cost will almost certainly occur as the organization has to build new systems and reorganize its data bases in order to produce the required information.

Another area where excessive costs may occur is when a new data base is not adequately tested. Testing is required in terms of suitability for a chosen application (based on a benchmark test) and in terms of the consistency of the data base with any existing data bases (based on a data conversion test).

Loss or Destruction of Assets

Data is now recognized as a major corporate asset. The DBMS is the link between the organization and that asset (or at least a large part of that asset). Problems with the data base management system software or the inability of the software to recover from any type of hardware problem may cause the loss or destruction of an important corporate asset.

Competitive Disadvantage

Decision support systems and executive information systems are being built to try and realize a competitive advantage through the use of information systems technology. These types of systems tend to be unstructured in nature and require access to data in a flexible, relatively unstructured manner. The data base management system used for these types of systems has to be able to exhibit qualities of flexibility and ease of use. For these reasons, the relational data base model is almost always used for these types of systems.

Competitive advantage is not restricted purely to decision support or executive information systems. There have been well documented examples where traditional, transaction-based systems were used creatively to provide an advantage. What is significant about many of these examples is that it was the creative packaging of information that led to the advantage being achieved. If an organization is not the first into the marketplace with a competitive advantage they may want to follow quickly and minimize the competitive disadvantage that has been created. Having a flexible data architecture fully supported by a data base management system is usually essential if the organization is to be in a position to respond quickly to what is happening in the marketplace.

CONTROL EVALUATION TABLE

The Control Evaluation Table for data base management systems/ data dictionary is given in Figure 14.1. The evaluation numbers are subjective and should be adjusted based on the conditions that exist in individual organizations. Note that, in practice, the completion of the Control Evaluation Table is in two parts:

- During detailed information gathering where, from the review of available documentation and the results of personal interviews, the key to reliance on individual controls and the "overall control rating (design)" are determined.

- During the execution of the audit program where, as a result of various audit tests, the strength of individuals controls is fully assessed and the "overall control rating (tested)" is determined.

AUDIT APPROACH

The auditor's objectives in the area of data base management system/ data dictionary are to answer the following questions and to report the answers to senior management:

- Is the DBMS/data dictionary that is in place within the organization suitable to the business needs of the organization?

- Are the inherent controls within the DBMS/data dictionary consistent with the data security objectives of the organization?

- Is the control structure provided by the DBMS/data dictionary being used effectively?

- Is the use of the DBMS/data dictionary properly integrated into the application development methodology used within the organization?

- Are proper change control procedures in place to ensure that new versions of the DBMS/data dictionary are properly authorized and tested before being introduced into production?

- Does the organization have sufficient technical skills to maximize the use of the DBMS/data dictionary and to ensure the software is operating at maximum effectiveness?

The auditor has several opportunities to obtain answers to these questions:

- During a review of the purchase of a new DBMS and/or data dictionary. The auditor should ensure that selection criteria have been determined and weighted and the process of selection follows definite steps to ensure that the best decision for the organization is made and that technical considerations do not supersede business considerations. Bernard Boar's article, "Selecting a Mature Data Base Management System," provides an excellent framework for assessing the selection process.[4]

- During the implementation of a revised version of the DBMS/ data dictionary. The auditor should ensure that proper change control procedures are understood before the new version is moved into the production environment. The principles of change control discussed in Chapter 7 apply equally to new versions of a DBMS/data dictionary.

- During the development of individual application systems. The auditor should ensure that the policies and procedures relating to the use of the DBMS/data dictionary are being followed.

- During the audit of the data center. The auditor is in a position to assess the adequacy of the administrative procedures surrounding the use of the DBMS/data dictionary. Backup and recovery procedures, interactions with the data security proce-

---

[4] *System Development Management*, (New York: Auerbach Publishers, 1990): 3, 4.

dures and the interface to the systems programming function are all areas that warrant observation during the data center audit.

The auditor should understand the DBMS being used and the interaction between application systems and the DBMS. Once this understanding has been achieved, the auditor is in a position to assess how well the DBMS/data dictionary meets the required business needs of the organization. This understanding will also allow the auditor to make use of any report generator/ad hoc query features of the DBMS to perform substantive testing on the content of any of the data bases managed by the DBMS.

It should not be overlooked that the DBMS/data dictionary are complex software products. The services of a Level 3 auditor (a technical specialist) may be required to assess the adequacy of the internal control structure of the software.

Figure 14.1 — Control Evaluation Table
Data Base Management System/Data Dictionary

CAUSES OF EXPOSURE

CONTROLS	Poor Performance	Loss of data	Inflexibility	Lack of Integrity	Incomplete Documentation
Data Repository	2	2	2	2	3
Policies and Procedures	1		2	2	2
Data Security Measures		3	1	3	1
Testing	3	2		2	
Overall Control Rating - Design					
Overall Control Rating - Tested					

KEY TO RELIANCE ON CONTROL
3 - High reliance
2 - Moderate reliance
1 - Control has only a peripheral effect on the cause of exposure
Blank - No significant impact

KEY TO OVERALL CONTROL RATING
3 - Strong control
2 - Moderate but adequate control
1 - Inadequate control

EXPOSURES

	Poor Performance	Loss of data	Inflexibility	Lack of Integrity	Incomplete Documentation
Erroneous Record Keeping		2		2	1
Unacceptable Accounting					
Business Interruption	1	1	1	1	1
Erroneous Management Decisions	2	2	2	2	1
Fraud and Embezzlement					
Statutory Sanctions			1		
Excessive Costs	3	2	2	2	2
Loss or Destruction of Assets		3	2	2	1
Competitive Disadvantage	1	1	2	1	1

KEY TO DEGREE OF CERTAINTY OF OCCURRENCE IN THE EVENT OF AN INADEQUATE CONTROL STRUCTURE
3 - Virtually certain
2 - Probable
1 - Possible
Blank - Very unlikely

15
TELECOMMUNICATIONS NETWORKS

INTRODUCTION

An organization's telecommunications network is a collection of hardware devices, transmission facilities and software supported by a network control group from the computer services department. In the past few years there have been enormous changes in the field of telecommunications with the future rate of change expected to far outstrip anything that has taken place so far.

Access to applications systems and to data is achieved through communication between operator (user) and computer. In a batch environment, this access is restricted to a small group of people and the means of initiating this communication is very limited. However, in an on-line environment, access to applications systems and to data is wherever there is a terminal device. The vast majority of applications systems being built today are on-line systems. With data now being considered a corporate asset, the thinking seems to be that there is no point in having an asset if no one can access and therefore make use of it. The telecommunications network provides the path of access.

The first section of this chapter describes the control perspective for including the telecommunications networks as one of the basic building block elements of information systems. This section also describes the relevance of this subject area to the skill set and knowledge requirements of the Level 1 and Level 2 auditor. Causes of exposure are described, as are the more common types of control that act upon these causes of exposure. The types of exposure that may occur as a result of a deficiency or breakdown in the control structure are then discussed. Finally, the audits to be performed are described in terms of relevant objectives and frequency.

The Institute of Internal Auditors

CONTROL PERSPECTIVE

Telecommunications networking technology has created the ability to use computer data at any location in the organization, whether local to the computer installation or many miles away. The key issues are to ensure that the data are secure from unauthorized viewing, modification, delays, duplication, theft or destruction while within the network. More and more businesses are relying heavily on continuous network availability. For these reasons, network failure prevention and rapid recovery have become key issues in telecommunications network design and operation.

Auditors have always been reluctant to get involved in trying to audit the control adequacy of the telecommunications networks within their organizations. This reluctance is not difficult to understand. Telecommunications networks are a complex interaction of hardware and software with many technical protocols for how these interactions take place. The services of a Level 3 auditor will almost certainly be required to delve into the internal workings of the network control software and to fully understand the intentions and workings of the communication protocols that are supported by the software.

However, given the fundamental importance of the telecommunications network to the workings of most applications systems, Level 1 and Level 2 auditors must understand the basic elements of the networks in place within their organizations.

SCOPE OF TELECOMMUNICATIONS NETWORKS

In this text, telecommunications networks are defined as data networks. Voice is not addressed, although it should be recognized that future developments will increasingly put voice and data into the same context. Telecommunications networks, within the definition of this text, includes the following subtopics in its scope of activities:

- Network components.

- Network structures.

- Network options.

- Major participants, roles and responsibilities.

- Security.

- Change management.

- Planning and design.

- Product acquisition.

- Accounting and chargebacks.

Network Components

Figure 15.1 shows a highly simplified view of a traditional telecommunications network. Although highly simplified, the principal components are readily identifiable. These are:

- Hardware Devices:
  - Terminals.
  - Modems.
  - Controllers (devices that attach a number of terminals to a single line).

- Software Products:
  - Network monitoring software.
  - Encryption/decryption programs.
  - Security packages.

- Communication Lines:
  - Switched or leased.
  - Analog or digital.
  - Satellite and microwave channels.
  - Cellular and fixed channel radio.

Communication lines are classified as switched or leased, digital or analog. Similar to a telephone connection, a switched line is a dial-up facility with more service subscribers than lines. A busy signal is received if no line is available or if someone else has already dialed into the port at the controller attached to the central computer (the port is identified by the dial-in number). A leased line is a dedicated line between the terminal (or terminal controller) and host computer.

The terms digital and analog describe the form of transmission. Terminals receive and send data via digital signals. However, traditional communication lines can only transmit information in an analog form. Therefore, a modem that converts the signal from analog to digital and digital to analog form is required at each end of the communication line. In more recent networks, the trend is toward digital data channels that have various performance advantages over voice grade, analog data channels.

In addition to hardware, communication lines and software products there is an important people component in the management of telecommunications networks. The people involved include:

- Network support analysts.
- Systems programmers.
- User help desk staff.
- Installers.

The mainframe computer typically controls the network by using a programmable front-end communications controller and teleprocessing monitor to:

- Determine when terminals have messages to transmit.

- Verify that the transmission has been received correctly.

- Direct the messages to the proper applications systems.

- Transmit messages back to the terminals.

For a telecommunications network to work effectively, all of these components must be designed to work together with the applications software which provides the users' view into the network.

Network Structures

There are two basic network structures — point to point and multipoint. The structure shown in Figure 15.1 is an example of point to point. Point to point allows one device to communicate with another at any one time. Multipoint structures are more complex and allow multiple devices to communicate over one line. There are a number of structures (or topologies) which can be used in a multipoint environment. The most common topologies for multipoint networks are as follows:

- Star topology.

- Ring topology.

- Bus topology.

Figure 15.2 provides a diagrammatic representation of each of these topologies, including a description of the primary operating characteristics and examples of commercial products that use each topology. This figure is taken from the recently published *Systems Auditability and Control (SAC)* report.

Network Options

The options available in the design of a telecommunications network include:

- Communication channels.

- Communication methods.

- Data communication speed.

In general there are three types of data **communication channels**:

- Simplex channels that transmit data in one direction only (such as the display of airline flight arrival and departure times on monitors).

- Half-duplex channels that allow data to be sent in either direction, though not at the same time. To accomplish this, the sending device must indicate to the receiving device when it has completed transmission and is ready to receive. The receiving machine must then wait for the receipt of a line turnaround character before it can send data.

- Full-duplex channels that allow data to be sent in both directions simultaneously (for example, it is not necessary for a device to wait for the other device to finish sending data before it can begin transmission). The full-duplex data channel is typical of most terminal to mainframe communication today.

Communication methods are a combination of communication codes and methods of transmission. The communication codes most commonly used are EBCDIC for IBM and IBM-compatible networks and ASCII (American Standard Code for Information Interchange) for other manufacturers. The communication codes are binary strings which, through the respective convention, represent the data that are to be communicated. The binary strings representing the data can then be transmitted serially or in parallel fashion, synchronously or asynchronously. Sending the binary string (seven bits for ASCII, 8 for EBCDIC) in parallel means that all of the bits are sent at once. This requires a minimum number of wires in the physical connection corresponding to the number of bits being sent. Parallel communication can therefore support very high data transmission rates. A good example of parallel communication is the interprocessor bus inside a computer's central processing unit. Data are sent in parallel between circuit boards in 8, 16 or 32-bit chunks, which makes transmission rates of millions of bytes per second possible. The major drawback with parallel communication is cost.

Serial communications entails breaking the binary string into its component bits and transmitting one bit at a time over a single wire. The data string is recreated upon receipt by the receiving device. In practice, for electrical reasons, two wires are required to send data serially. Serial communication is considerably less expensive than parallel communication. Most, if not all, terminal-based communication networks use serial communications.

For a serially transmitted data string to be correctly reassembled, the transmitting and receiving devices must be synchronized. This can be accomplished by adding a timing line to the data transmission line, but this method doubles the cost of a communications link. Two other methods of serial communications that do not require an additional clock line are available. Synchronous communication describes a method of transmitting data with special characters used to synchronize transmitting and receiving devices. Blocks of data characters are sent at one time using synchronous communications. The two most common synchronous protocols are the character-oriented Binary Synchronous Communication (Bi-sync) and the bit-oriented Synchronous Data Link Control (SDLC) used in IBM's System Network Architecture.

Asynchronous communication is the term used to describe data transmission without special timing characters. Data characters are sent one at a time when using asynchronous communications.

In synchronous communication, the sending machine issues special sync characters that indicate the start of transmission of a series of data characters. During synchronous communication, the receiving device waits for sync characters to be received. Once received, the receiving device is synchronized in time with the sending device. Both sending and receiving devices rely on an accurate internal or external clock signal to distinguish data characters. In asynchronous communication, data characters are separated by fixed time intervals. The beginning and end of a data character are indicated by start and stop bits of fixed duration. In general, one start bit and two stop bits are used, so one data character usually requires 11 bits.

Synchronous data communication requires a number of sync characters, eight bits each, to delimit the beginning and end of a block of data characters. Clearly, if large numbers of data characters are to be transmitted, the synchronous method would devote less time to the task of synchronization, thus transmitting the entire data stream faster. On the other hand, if relatively few data characters have to be transmitted, the asynchronous method eliminates the need to send entire synchronization characters, decreasing the time required to send small numbers of data characters.

Equipment costs are also an issue in deciding whether synchronous or asynchronous communication is the most appropriate in given situations. Asynchronous communication requires circuitry that is much less sophisticated than the synchronous method. Accurate clocks are required to keep synchronous receivers and transmitters in sync. These are expensive. Asynchronous transmission does not require this type of expensive equipment.

Data communication speed is usually a function of cost. The further data has to be transmitted, the more expensive the line required to maintain the transmission rate. Serial data transmission speed is usually measured in number of bits per second (bps). The rating of the modem attached to the communication line determines the speed of communication. Typical speeds in an office environment start as low as 2400 bps and go up to 56K bps and more. Low frequency users may have modems with speeds as low as 300 bps and up to 2400 bps.

Major Participants, Roles and Responsibilities

There are a number of participants with specific roles and responsibilities from both within and outside the organization. Internal to the organization there should be a network control group responsible for monitoring the performance of the network and responding to anticipated or actual network problems. Within the technical area there should be both data communications hardware and software analyst functions responsible for the installation and maintenance of communications hardware and software, respectively.

The question of reporting relationships arises. The network control group can certainly report to the computer services manager.

The software technical support analyst could report to the technical support (systems programming) function with the hardware support analyst reporting to a user support function within the information systems department (attached to the same reporting structure as the information systems hot-line, user support function).

The importance of telecommunications in many organizations is now such that a separate reporting entity has been created that is responsible for all aspects of communications, including all of the job functions described above. A managerial position is created to coordinate all activities within the telecommunications area. This manager may report directly to the Chief Information Officer (VP, Information Systems) or may report to the person in charge of computer services who, in turn, reports to the CIO. The reporting relationship will depend on the importance of the function to the organization (the more important the function, the higher the direct reporting relationship).

Figure 15.3 shows the job outline for each of these internal positions. This figure is taken from the draft fieldwork report of the new SAC study.

From an external point of view, the hardware and software vendor must be considered to play an important role in the overall effectiveness of the telecommunications network. This role includes the provision of adequate control mechanisms to prevent, detect and indicate any problem conditions within that part of the network being provided by the vendor.

Security

A secure and reliable telecommunications network must ensure that a message (or a string of data characters) is not lost, distorted, duplicated, accelerated or delayed without authorization. There are a number of controls which should be in place to assure adequate security over the telecommunications network. These controls (primarily access controls) will be addressed in a later section of this chapter.

In addition to the security measures that are intrinsic to the network, there also should be applications and data security controls so that even if intruders are able to gain entry to the network, they would be unable to gain advantage from this intrusion.

Change Management

Change management should be applied to hardware, communication line and software changes.

Hardware changes can arise due to a variety of reasons:

- The addition of new equipment in an existing location.

- The replacement or upgrading of existing equipment in an existing location.

- The addition of new equipment in a new location.

The main issue with hardware change management is the coordination of the changes with the users who are to receive the equipment. In the case of new equipment, it is often necessary to rewire the user's area. This can be very disruptive to the regular work flow of the user's department and may have to be scheduled after normal working hours. The wiring discussed here should not be confused with the communication line issues which will be discussed shortly. The wiring associated with hardware change management is required to attach the physical devices (usually terminals and printers) to the communication devices that are connected to the communication lines. This internal departmental wiring is not a trivial issue but is an exercise that is often overlooked in the planning of new equipment. It is then dealt with on a catch-as-catch-can basis around the time of the installation.

In brand new installations space must be found in the user department for the internal wiring to be terminated and the communication devices physically housed. This space should be out of the way of regular traffic within the department. The wiring terminations are usually attached to patch panels with the wires coming out of the patch panel and going into the communication device. Any unintentional physical contact with either the patch panel or the communications device could result in a loss of the connection between the communication line and the end-user device (typically a terminal or printer).

In situations where existing hardware is being expanded or upgraded (or replaced), it must be clear that the existing communication facilities can handle the change. Patch panel capacity, existing wiring diagrams and communication device capacity must be checked before the changes are made. It may be necessary to expand the existing facilities to accommodate the new or upgraded hardware.

Communication line changes can also occur for a variety of reasons:

- Upgrading of existing lines.

- Adding new lines.

- Deleting existing lines.

The coordination activity for changes to communication lines includes both the end users and the telephone company. Tests should be conducted to make sure that the new telecommunications configuration resulting from the changes works as expected.

Software changes include changes to the network control software resident in the host computer and to any software that may reside in the front-end controller to the host computer or the controller at the user (or sending) location. Software changes follow the rules of software maintenance and change control which are fully described in Chapter 7. Basically, changes must be approved, documented, tested and moved into production in a controlled manner.

Documentation is an issue that should be addressed in all aspects of change. There should be a complete set of up-to-date documentation of the network within the organization, including the location and characteristics of all communication lines, communication devices and end-user terminals and printers. This documentation must be kept up-to-date whenever a change is made.

Planning and Design

Planning and designing a telecommunications network is a major undertaking for an organization. As discussed earlier in the chapter, there are numerous options that can be used in the configuration of each component section of the network. There is, however, a process that should be conducted in the planning and design of a network. This process consists of several distinct steps:

- Understand and document the network user requirements. This includes the following:

  - Application systems to be accessed through the network.
  - User locations.
  - Frequency of use.
  - Criticality of use.
  - Peak usage times and requirements.
  - Volume of data by period.
  - Response time requirements.

- Identify and evaluate viable network options, including:

  - Technical feasibility.
  - Maintainability.
  - Conformance with the organization's strategic plan.
  - Cost.
  - Reliability and availability.
  - Ability to meet level of service requirements.

There are a number of automated tools that can assist the network designer to determine the configuration of the network that is best suited, within the constraints identified, to meet the service objectives.

Product Acquisition

The investment in telecommunications equipment in many organizations is considerable and is growing substantially every year. For this reason there must be purchasing standards in place to control the acquisition of new equipment. First of all, the equipment that is purchased should be consistent with the strategy and direction established by the network design. The next issue is the selection of the vendor of choice for the equipment. Vendor evaluation criteria should include:

- Vendor's ability to produce products that meet the technical requirements.

- Vendor's track record for research and development.

- Vendor's support record for installed equipment.

- Availability of qualified, local support.

- Financial strength of vendor.

- Cost of equipment.

The acquisition of telecommunications products should go through the same approval process as the purchase of any other product of significant cost. Typically this process entails the involvement of the purchasing department and the adherence to established purchasing procedures. There may also be a quality control check required before payment is made. Payment for purchased products should go through the regular accounts payable process.

Accounting and Chargebacks

Accounting and chargeback is a matter of corporate philosophy. Some organizations charge all costs to a central cost center (usually in the information systems department). Others charge the costs, whenever possible, to the cost center that will benefit from the incurrence of the costs. There are endless variations between these extremes. The subject of cost accounting is a major topic in its own right.

A large part of the costs incurred in telecommunications networks would be treated as capital costs. However, the communication charges levied by the telephone company would fall into the category of operating costs. Through arrangements with the telephone company these costs can either be charged to the sending location or to the receiving location. The decision of which option to choose is a matter of corporate organization and depends largely on who is responsible for the reconciliation and approval of payment of the bill from the telephone company.

LEVEL 1 AUDITOR — SKILL AND KNOWLEDGE OBJECTIVES

Overall Objective

Know the risks and exposures that are inherent in a telecommunications network as they apply to individual applications systems. Be able to execute an audit program to attest to the adequacy of controls as they pertain to the applications system being audited.

Network Components

Know the constituent elements (or network components) of a telecommunications network. Be able to relate these to the audit of individual applications systems and execute the audit sections dealing with whatever constituent elements are relevant.

Network Structures

Know the elements of network structures and be able to execute an audit program to determine the adequacy of controls exercised over these elements as they apply to an individual application being audited.

Network Options

Know what network options are available to individual applications systems and users of the application. Be able to execute an audit program to verify the proper use of these options within an application being audited.

Major Participants, Roles and Responsibilities

Know the roles and responsibilities of each of the major participants in the management of a telecommunications network. Be able to execute an audit program that is designed to assess the adequacy of compliance with these roles and responsibilities as they relate to an applications system being audited.

Security

Know the security features that are inherent in the telecommunications network. Be able to execute an audit program to determine the adequacy of these security features as they relate to an individual applications system.

Change Management

Know the principles of change management and the components within the network that are subject to change management. Be able to execute an audit program to determine the adequacy of compliance with change management policies and procedures as applied to network components associated with individual applications systems.

Planning and Design

Be able to audit the planning and design of the network component of an individual applications system.

Product Acquisition

Be able to assess the appropriateness of the approach to product acquisition as encountered when dealing with individual applications systems.

Accounting and Chargebacks

Know the principles of accounting and chargebacks for the use of telecommunications network services. Be able to execute an audit program to verify the accuracy of the chargebacks to a particular user or system.

LEVEL 2 AUDITOR — SKILL AND KNOWLEDGE OBJECTIVES

Overall Objectives

Be able to design and execute an audit program to ensure that the global objectives that have been set for the network are being met.

Network Components

Understand the constituent elements of a telecommunications network. Be able to design and execute audit programs that deal with these elements individually but can also arrive at an overall conclusion on the adequacy of control over the network.

Network Structures

Understand the elements of network structures and the controls that should be present in each of the elements. Be able to design an audit program to attest to the adequacy of controls that are, in fact, in place.

Network Options

Understand the network options that are available and the control trade-offs that may have to be made if particular options are selected.

Major Participants, Roles and Responsibilities

Understand the roles and responsibilities that should be performed by the major participants in the management of a telecommunications network. Be able to assess the situation existing within the organization against what should be in place.

Security

Understand the security features that should exist in a telecommunications network and be able to structure audits to provide an overall assessment of the adequacy of the security features built into the organization's network.

Change Management

Be able to structure an audit, or extract information from related audits, to determine the adequacy of the change management procedures as they relate to telecommunications networks, including the degree of compliance with these policies and procedures.

Planning and Design

Be able to audit the planning and design of the entire corporate network.

Product Acquisition

Be able to assess the appropriateness of the approach to product acquisition for the network, including the adequacy of the weighting given to the control structure of the product to be acquired.

Accounting and Chargebacks

Understand the technology used in network accounting and chargebacks and be able to design an audit program to verify the accuracy of the figures produced.

CAUSES OF EXPOSURE

The causes of exposure in the area of telecommunications networks are as follows:

- Network failure.

- Message distortion.

- Unauthorized access.

- Performance degradation.

- Inappropriate design.

Network Failure

Failure in the network may be caused by a malfunction of hardware, software and/or the communication lines. The failure may be complete or partial. The first issue is to be able to identify that a problem has occurred. The cause of the problem must then be determined, the extent of the problem must be assessed and a solution must be identified and applied. In some cases it may be necessary to take interim action to minimize the extent of the damage caused by the problem. For example, rerouting of communication lines may be necessary because of a problem with a switching device within the network.

The network should never be allowed to be completely out of service. However, there may be times when the service level is less than optimal. The failure of a single node or transmission path must not cut off one portion of the network from the rest.

The ideal situation is to be forewarned that a problem may occur and may result in a network failure of some type. The quality of line transmission should be electronically monitored. Hardware devices should have self-diagnostic capabilities with a readout to the operator of potential problems.

When a network failure does occur, recovery procedures should be in place. A network failure may result in lost data. Therefore, it is necessary for on-line applications systems to be designed in concert with the possibility of this type of data loss. The applications system has to be supplied with sufficient information to confirm that communication still exists with the user and that an error has not occurred that could corrupt the business transaction being performed. When an error does occur, the data base must be put back in a consistent state which is usually at the point just before the problem occurred.

Message Distortion

The design of a telecommunications network must guarantee message accountability. In other words, once a message (or a string of data characters) has been accepted into the network, it must be delivered, as accepted, to the proper recipient or receiving device. Messages must not be lost, needlessly delayed, or accelerated. The network system must ensure that every message is safely stored on a permanent device from which it can be returned (when required) to the active system. Multiple copies of messages must be placed in storage to ensure accountability if a device fails. In multiple center environments, copies of all traffic should be retained at each center. Such internal system controls as message numbering systems or other addressing mechanisms permit retrieval of data as required. These controls must include audit trail data that, at a minimum, includes I/O station, line identification, sequential number, delivery time and date, number of copies delivered and message status (for instance, normal or duplicated). On-line applications systems must test for the acceptance or rejection of all messages.

After a failure, the network recovery programs must account for all in-transit messages, restore the active message file and continue service without modifying message priorities. Possible duplicate messages must be identified as such when sent to the retrieving station.

Unauthorized Access

There have been numerous, well-publicized instances of computer hackers who have been able to get into a network and then navigate from the initial entry point to other connected networks. The hackers have been able to access confidential data and to cause general disruption and embarrassment to the organization(s) involved. This type of problem has exploded as a result of the use of microcomputers as terminal access devices. The traditional control to prevent unauthorized access is the use of passwords. In the microcomputer environment, the password control system can be stretched beyond its ability to prevent unauthorized access. The microcomputer can be used to generate a vast number of user IDs and methodically calculate authentication passwords which are then sent to the mainframe until a positive acknowledgement is received that access has been allowed. To counteract the unauthorized access resulting from the use of microcomputers, many organizations have instituted much more rigorous checking of passwords. The section on "Access Controls" covers this topic in detail.

Performance Degradation

One of the principal objectives in network management is consistent response time. Response time is influenced by a number of factors, including:

- Network failure.

- The speed of the communications line.

- The design of the network.

- The throughput capability of the computer.

- The design of the on-line applications system.

Network failure was dealt with in a previous section. The speed of the communication line has a direct bearing on response time. The number of devices attached to the communication line and the traffic to each of these devices also has a direct bearing on response time. The design of the network, particularly in a multi-drop configuration, may cause contention on the communication line as a result of traffic volumes. The throughput capacity of the computer may result in delays between receipt of a request for work to be performed and the result of that request being put back out through the communication line. Job mix within the computer, disk contention for access to data bases and basic capacity problems can all contribute to slow response time back to the end user. Where the design of an on-line applications system is inefficient, response time may be slow as the computer processing time for an on-line transaction takes more time than is acceptable to the end user. Applications system inefficiency is usually the result of a design that cannot support the volume of transactions to be processed (for example, the use of a fourth-generation language that cannot meet the production needs of the organization).

The end user of an on-line applications system is generally unaware (and usually not interested) in which of these problems are causing the slow response time. All that is known is that the system does not respond in an acceptable time frame. However, although the user does not care about the cause of the problem, a solution is a definite requirement. Monitoring of network performance is the responsibility of the network control group. Resultant action may also be the responsibility of the network control group but, in certain cases, and depending on what the problem is, responsibility for resolution may be passed to the network software support group, to the computer operators or to the applications system maintenance group.

The Institute of Internal Auditors

Inappropriate Design

In the section on "Performance Degradation," inappropriate design was mentioned as a contributing factor to slow or inconsistent response time. The design may be inappropriate from an applications system or network point of view. Although serious enough, depending on the size and complexity of the applications system, the inappropriate design of an applications system is a localized problem and can be dealt with as such. When the entire network has been poorly designed, the problems will permeate to every applications system and to every user in the network.

Inappropriate network design may result from under-specifying or over-specifying the requirements. Either situation will result in problems for the organization. In the former case, the users can expect poor response time. In the latter case, network performance will be good but the cost to the organization will be higher than is necessary. Network flexibility is also a consideration. If an organization is going through a period of rapid growth, network requirements will be different than for an organization that is stable in terms of locations and number of employees.

A specific, ongoing exercise should be conducted to ensure that the network is appropriate for the current and future needs of the organization.

CONTROLS

Applicable controls intended to prevent, detect and/or correct the causes of exposure just described as relevant to the area of telecommunications networks are as follows:

- Organizational controls.

- Access controls.

- Integrity controls.

- Adequate documentation.

- Design methodology.

Organizational Controls

The introduction of a telecommunications network necessitates a monitoring and control function, such as the network control group. As a focal point for the resolution of daily problems, the group's specific controls include:

- Explicitly stated responsibilities, including job descriptions for network operators and performance monitoring of the terminals and communication lines (producing statistics that give network components mean time between failures and mean time to fix).

- Management-created measurement criteria, including the minimum percentage of uptime that is acceptable to the organization.

- A group within the network control group that answers user questions concerning the performance of the network.

- In-depth training in the fundamentals of data communications and the specifics of the organization's network and on-line systems.

- An organizational policy that specifies adherence to on-line system controls as well as penalties for policy violations.

Access Controls

Access controls must be established for both physical and operational access. In terms of physical access control, the key to establishing a secure environment is the prevention of unauthorized access to the computer installation or to network components. In reviewing the components of telecommunications networks (see Figure 15.1), physical controls can be placed at the computer center end of the line and at the end-user location where the end-user devices (terminals and printers) attach to the communication line(s). Terminals or workstations may be locked and may be under the protection of whatever physical office security exists.

Physical protection of the communication line is outside the control of the organization. Even in a private, leased network, message transmission paths may partly consist of public lines. When paths enter and leave a public facility, they are susceptible to intrusion. Other methods (protective features designed into each message, encryption of transmissions, and so forth) are required to prevent the unauthorized monitoring of transmitted data.

If physical access to the network is gained, another level of security must prevent operational access to any applications system or to any data. Safety features to be considered in the design of the network include stringent sign-on and sign-off procedures, terminal operator identification and verification, and I/O message control (or sequence numbering). The first line of defense is the use of passwords to identify and then verify that it is an authorized user that is attempting to gain access to the system. Password systems are in two parts: (1) the user first identifies himself to the system using a user ID (either by direct keying or by the use of a magnetically encoded card), (2) the user authenticates this ID by providing something unique about himself to the system. Traditionally, this uniqueness was demonstrated by keying a confidential password into the system. More recent developments in biometric technology (for instance, fingerprint scans, retina scans, signature analysis) show promise as being able to substantially improve the use of confidential passwords that have proven to be a tenuous control at best, particularly since the widespread use of microcomputer workstations as terminal emulators. Where the user fails to provide the correct authenticating password after being allowed a number of retry opportunities, the user ID being used should be automatically suspended and a message routed to the data security officer. The user ID should only be reactivated once the data security officer is satisfied that nothing unusual is going on.

When the telecommunications network allows dial-up connections, the following special controls should be considered:

- Telephone numbers must be changed regularly, kept confidential and removed from modems in the network operations area.

- Each dial-up terminal must identify itself and transmit its unique identification to the front-end communications processor.

- Automatic call receipt and connection should be prohibited. Dialled calls should trigger an automatic call-back and connect sequence. In this way the computer controls the telephone numbers to which it will allow a connection.

Integrity Controls

Integrity controls ensure that only valid and authorized data can be received from, or transmitted to, a terminal and that the transmitted data is identical to that received. Once a terminal operator has gained authorized network access and has logged on to a particular on-line system, any messages that are sent must be validated. In order to ensure correct transmission, the content and form of the message should be standardized and strictly followed. The minimum tests for message validity are as follows:

- Positional edits for correct control characters, address and data fields, and line and format constraints.

- Data validation for routing numbers, addresses, type codes, and user specific, content-oriented information.

- Authorization checks for coded data, test words and other security tests, such as identical currency fields.

The validation process increases the level of system security, ensures that the data required for delivery processing is valid and provides an opportune time in the processing cycle to capture data for message accountability. Once the message has been accepted, a positive message acceptance indication should be returned to the originator.

The Institute of Internal Auditors

Several factors ensure that messages are delivered only to their intended recipients. For example, system security should include the design of facilities for proof of delivery. In addition, message routing must be verified and checked for validity and authentication. The routing verification process should ensure the following:

- The destination is a valid point in the network.

- The destination is authorized to receive the traffic involved.

- A positive connection is made and then validated before and after message transmission.

- Notification, including terminal identification, that a message has been accepted is sent by the terminal on receipt.

- Unbroken, sequential output numbers are transmitted as part of the message.

- A historical log is maintained of all messages transmitted.

- The queuing and routing algorithms ensure the efficient processing of traffic to prevent undue delay of messages in transit.

A network communications environment affords little, if any, protection from the unauthorized monitoring of communication lines. To provide the necessary degree of security, the system must protect the data in the message. The unauthorized modification of messages can be limited by using encryption devices and process or message control words. Multiplexing messages increases the difficulty of unauthorized monitoring.

Adequate Documentation

The design of the network should be fully documented, including the termination points of all lines, the speed of all lines, the devices attached to each of the lines and the protocols used for each line. The documentation should be updated with every change in the network.

When a problem occurs the documentation provides an invaluable tool to assess the possible repercussions of the problem. The network control group should maintain records on the reliability of hardware, communication lines and all other system devices. This information can be used to anticipate and correct problems and show the mean time to fix for any malfunctioning component.

Adequate documentation is also a necessity when contemplating a change in the network. If the documentation is not completely up-to-date, decisions may be made on incomplete information. On-line applications system documentation must also be kept up-to-date in terms of the interface between the system and the network.

The documentation discussed up to this point is for reference purposes. The other type of documentation that should be present relates to the ongoing operation of the network. This type of documentation is referred to as an activity audit trail. An audit trail provides sufficient information for reconstructing the events that occurred within the system. This capability can be used to research exception conditions or as an audit verification tool. On-line applications systems have changed the form of audit trail from paper to electronic media. These systems should not, however, diminish the availability of the audit trail. In fact, with the immediacy of access and update offered by on-line systems, adequate audit trails have increased in importance. The means of gaining access to the audit trail, however, have changed. Audit trails must exist at the network and at the individual applications systems level. At the network level the audit trail must detail statistics relating to volumes and exception conditions in hardware, software, or data communication facilities. Transaction logs detailing all on-line activity (including the originator and time of activity) should be maintained for all on-line applications systems.

As mentioned, the means of obtaining an audit trail has changed. Software must be used to interrogate the appropriate file or data base and produce the required report(s). Given the volume of information typically produced by computer systems, it is advantageous for information to be printed selectively using specified criteria.

Design Methodology

As in the case of the design and development of an applications system, the design and development of a telecommunications network should follow a set pattern. Although a formal methodology may not exist, the network designers should have a formal approach to the design, development and maintenance of the network. Without this formal approach, the network may be developed on a piecemeal basis without any real consideration of the "big picture." This piecemeal approach can only lead to excessive costs to the organization as the network is in a constant state of change to adjust to every new requirement. The section on "Planning and Design" described the principal activities that should be included in the approach to network design.

TYPES OF EXPOSURE

Listed below are the types of exposure that can occur as a result of the inadequacy or failure of the system of control to prevent the occurrence of a cause of exposure in the area of telecommunications networks.

Erroneous Record Keeping

When there is an undetected alteration of a message between a terminal and the host computer, there is a possibility of erroneous record keeping. If there is a failure in the network that is not recognized by an applications system, it is possible that a data base could only be partially updated. If the terminal operator is not made aware of the problem, the appropriate corrective action may not be taken.

Business Interruption

Depending on the level of reliance on the network to support the business of the organization, network failure could certainly cause business interruption. Performance degradation, particularly where the customers of the organization are served by the network (for example, bank tellers serving the bank's customers), could cause a degree of business interruption as the organization finds itself unable to process the business at hand.

Hackers who find their way into an organization's systems through unauthorized access to the network may cause business interruption. The organization would have to take the time to ensure that the damage done by the hackers is corrected and to shore up the system against future intrusions.

Erroneous Management Decisions

When the information provided through the network is distorted and management acts on the information as presented, erroneous management decisions could result.

Fraud

Unauthorized access to the network could result in fraud if the perpetrators are able to gain access to data and convert this access into tangible gains. Being able to distort messages going through the network could also result in fraudulent activity. Gaining access to the system to take advantage of available processing cycles is also a form of fraudulent activity against the perpetrated organization.

Excessive Costs/Deficient Revenues

The inappropriate design of the network or of individual applications systems could result in excessive costs if expenditures over and above what was originally planned must be made to correct the problems.

Network failure, message distortion and unauthorized access will all cause excessive costs to the extent that it costs money and resources to correct these problems.

Where the use of the network is directly related to the source of an organization's revenue (for instance, theater ticket agencies), degraded performance may cause reduced revenues.

Loss or Destruction of Assets

Network components often constitute a large investment for an organization. Physical security measures must be in place to prevent loss or destruction of this investment. Whereas physical security measures are most often thought of in the context of the data center, in the case of telecommunications networks, physical security must also be considered for all of the departmental and branch locations within the organization.

The telecommunications network provides an access path to one of the organization's most important assets — data. Through inadvertent or intentional use of the network, this asset could be placed in jeopardy. Recovery procedures must be put in place to ensure that the asset can be recovered in the event of a problem resulting from the use of the network.

Competitive Disadvantage

The degree of competitive disadvantage that is experienced by an organization resulting from its use of a telecommunications network will depend on the importance of the network to the mainstream business operation of the organization. The more important the role played by the network, the more risk there is of competitive disadvantage should something go wrong within the network.

Where hackers have gained access to a organization's network and created problems of whatever magnitude, the organization has experienced public embarrassment and loss of confidence whenever news of the intrusion has been made public. This explains the reluctance of many organizations to ever admit that they have been the subject of this type of computer crime.

Network failure and performance degradation could certainly cause competitive disadvantage, particular when the events are a common occurrence. Many organizations use their networks to deliver service directly to their customers. When these customers are subjected to slow response time or cannot conduct their business transactions when they want to, they will take their business elsewhere. Customer loyalty is in short supply these days. Certain levels of service are now taken for granted. Where an organization cannot perform at these expected levels, the customers will simply not do business with the organization.

For many organizations such as banks, travel agents and insurance companies, an efficient network providing real-time access to information is part of the service which is now expected as a matter of course.

CONTROL EVALUATION TABLE

The Control Evaluation Table for telecommunications networks is given in Figure 15.4. The evaluation numbers are subjective and should be adjusted based upon the conditions that exist in individual organizations. Note that, in practice, the completion of the Control Evaluation Table is in two parts:

- During detailed information gathering where, from the review of available documentation and the results of personal interviews, the key to reliance on individual controls and the "overall control rating (design)" are determined.

- During the execution of the audit program where, as a result of various audit tests, the strength of individuals controls is fully assessed and the "overall control rating (tested)" is determined.

AUDIT APPROACH

Telecommunications networking is a complex, technical subject. To audit the internals of the various components that comprise the network and to comment on the overall adequacy of control within the network almost certainly requires the services of a Level 3 auditor (i.e., a technical specialist). However, that is not to say that both Level 1 and Level 2 auditors should ignore the presence of a telecommunications network when performing audits in and around the information systems area. The Level 1 auditor should know the risks and exposures inherent in a telecommunications network as they apply to individual applications systems and be able to execute an audit program to attest to the adequacy of controls as they pertain to any applications systems being audited.

The Level 2 auditor should understand the risks and exposures that are inherent in a telecommunications network in a global sense and be able to design and execute an audit program to ensure that the global objectives that have been set for the network are being met.

The audit activities to assess the adequacy of control over the design and operation of the telecommunications network will consist of the following:

- A review of the methodology for network planning and design to ensure that a comprehensive, business approach is taken to decide on the network components to be installed.

- A review of the implementation of the network to ensure that the selected components are consistent with the conclusions of the planning and design exercise.

- As part of the data center audit, ensure that network management is performing in a manner that is consistent with approved policies and procedures. Change control issues over network components should also be part of the data center audit.

- As part of individual applications system development audits, ensure that controls assuring message integrity and data recoverability are factored into the system design.

- As part of the audits of operational applications system audits, attest to the adequacy of performance of the network in meeting the requirements of these applications.

Figure 15.1 — Components of a Data Communications Network

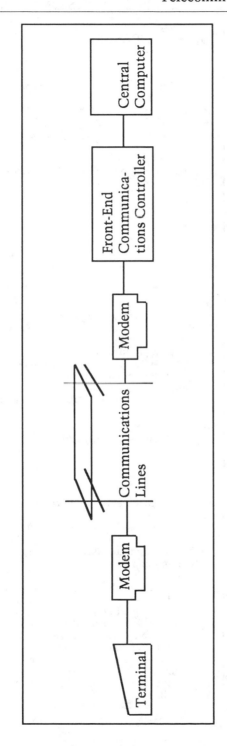

Reprinted from *Data Communications Management* (New York: Auerbach Publishers), 1982, Warren Gorham & Lamont Inc. Used with permission.

Figure 15.2 — Network Topologies

Star Topology

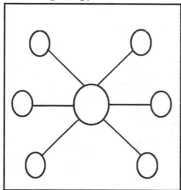

- All network nodes connected to one central site.
- Central site controls the network.
- All nodes communicate through the central site.

Examples: IBM System Network Architecture
Private Branch Exchange (voice and data)

Ring Topology

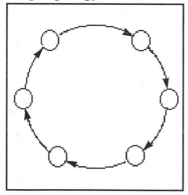

- Each node receives messages from one node and sends messages to the next node.
- All messages are sent around the ring and retransmitted by each node until received by the appropriate node.
- A "token" or special message may be sent around the network as a means of controlling when each node may transmit a message. A node may transmit only while it holds the token.

Example: IBM Token Ring Network

Bus Topology

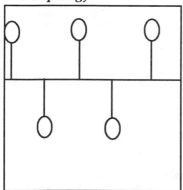

Example: Ethernet

- Each node shares a common communication path.
- When one node transmits, all nodes receive the message simultaneously.
- Two methods are used to regulate access to the common transmission path.

   - Token: Similar to that described on the Ring Topology, a special message is sent notifying all nodes of which node is authorized to transmit. When that node is done transmitting, it must release the token back to another network node.
   - Multiple Accesss: Each station may transmit at any time. If two stations transmit simultaneously, a collision occurs. This collision is detected by both transmitting stations, which then retransmit their messages.

Figure 15.3 — Job Descriptions

Position	Responsibilities
MANAGER	• Strategic planning. • Budget control. • Capacity planning. • Network design. • Vendor management. • Staff management. • Network management. • Training coordination. • Consultant management. • Work-order tracking.
DATA COMMUNICATIONS HARDWARE ANALYST	• Problem determination. • Hardware configuration. • Hardware installation. • Hardware evaluation. • Interface to vendor's technical support. • Work-order completion.
DATA COMMUNICATIONS SOFTWARE ANALYST	• System generation. • Software engineering. • Problem determination. • Custom development. • Software evaluation. • Interface to vendors' technical support.
NETWORK CONTROL OPERATOR	• Inventory maintenance. • Performance monitoring. • User contact. • Network activation. • Problem determination. • Network backup and recovery operations.

Figure 15.4 — Control Evaluation Table Telecommunications Networks

CAUSES OF EXPOSURE

CONTROLS	Network Failure	Message Distortion	Unauthorized Access	Performance Degradation	Inappropriate Design
Organizational Controls	2		2	2	1
Access Controls	1	3	3	2	1
Integrity Controls	1	3	2	1	2
Adequate Documentation	2	1	1	2	2
Design Methodology	2	2	1	2	3
Overall Control Rating - Design					
Overall Control Rating - Tested					

EXPOSURES

EXPOSURES	Network Failure	Message Distortion	Unauthorized Access	Performance Degradation	Inappropriate Design
Erroneous Record Keeping	1	2	2		1
Unacceptable Accounting					
Business Interruption	3	1	1	1	
Erroneous Management Decisions		2	1	1	1
Fraud and Embezzlement	1	1	1		
Statutory Sanctions					
Excessive Costs	3	1	1	1	2
Loss or Destruction of Assets	1	1	1	3	
Competitive Disadvantage	3	1	2	1	1

KEY TO RELIANCE ON CONTROL
3 - High reliance
2 - Moderate reliance
1 - Control has only a peripheral effect on the cause of exposure
Blank - No significant impact

KEY TO OVERALL CONTROL RATING
3 - Strong control
2 - Moderate but adequate control
1 - Inadequate control

KEY TO DEGREE OF CERTAINTY OF OCCURRENCE IN THE EVENT OF AN INADEQUATE CONTROL STRUCTURE
3 - Virtually certain
2 - Probable
1 - Possible
Blank - Very unlikely

16
ARTIFICIAL INTELLIGENCE/ EXPERT SYSTEMS

INTRODUCTION

Expert systems are also known as knowledge-based systems. Knowledge-based systems are one facet of artificial intelligence, based on the discipline referred to as knowledge engineering. Information is frequently referred to as "data in context." To translate information into knowledge requires experience and the ability to apply information to the situation at hand. The same information may mean different things in different situations. Knowledge is the ability to interpret the meaning of information.

The essence of an expert system is to be able to take the collective knowledge of an expert in a particular field and automate so that it can be made available to others who are in need of the expertise but who are not, themselves, experts.

The first section of this chapter describes the control perspective for including artificial intelligence/expert systems as one of the basic building block elements of information systems. This section also describes the relevance of this subject area to the skill set and knowledge requirements of the Level 1 and Level 2 auditor. Causes of exposure are described, as are the more common types of control that act upon these causes of exposure. The types of exposure that may occur as a result of a deficiency or breakdown in the control structure are then discussed. Finally, the audits to be performed are described in terms of relevant objectives and frequency.

CONTROL PERSPECTIVE

To provide more efficient and consistent decision making, many organizations are installing a new generation of systems that simulate the human thought processes as defined through examination and analysis of a group of subject experts. Management and monitoring of this new generation of systems takes on an added dimension of complexity given that these types of systems have no fixed logic and, therefore, no right or wrong answer. The challenge is to build validation/testing methods that confine the system results to certain limits. This ensures that unreasonable results will be precluded from propagation through the organization.

SCOPE OF ARTIFICIAL INTELLIGENCE/ EXPERT SYSTEMS

Artificial intelligence/expert systems includes the following subtopics in its scope of activities:

- Expert systems definitions and terminology.

- Knowledge engineering methods.

- Expert system shells.

Expert Systems Definitions and Terminology

Artificial intelligence/expert systems are also frequently referred to as "fifth generation systems." Likewise, the development languages associated with artificial intelligence/expert systems are referred to as fifth generation programming languages. The concept of a fifth generation of computer technology comes from the Japanese and the project that they have initiated to make the processing of information and the use of knowledge into a worldwide commodity that can be packaged and sold. Making the fifth generation a reality will ultimately require a completely new design of hardware and software. Rather than the Von Neumann architecture that is in place in today's computers (a central processing unit controlled by complex operating system software which interlaces I/O processing with CPU processing), the new generation of computers will be parallel processors able to process many instructions simultaneously, rather than one at a time, which is the principle underlying the Von Neumann model.

Specialized data base machines will replace the current architecture of the data base being controlled through the operating system running on the mainframe.

The intent of an expert system is to replicate the knowledge which is currently the domain of a limited number of expert individuals within an organization. Conventional methods of system development do not lend themselves to solving problems that rely on heuristics (or rules of thumb) and first principles for their solution. Knowledge-based systems, which includes expert systems, have the capacity to deal with these types of unstructured problems.

A knowledge-based system has a knowledge base combined with an inference engine. The knowledge base contains data about a particular subject and, as such, is similar to a conventional data base. However, the knowledge base also contains rules and assertions about these data. Knowledge engineering has provided the means of defining these rules and assertions so that inferences can be drawn based on additional input from a user or from another electronic source. The inference engine is the logic processor that can interrogate the knowledge base and infer conclusions based upon the input received. The inference engine is combined with a dialogue manager to elicit the required input for analysis. A key requirement of the inference engine is the ability to clearly define why a certain conclusion has been inferred.

Knowledge-based systems rely on a declarative structure rather than a procedural structure. A declarative structure describes the nature of the problem by presenting facts and relationships about data elements that are essentially true. From these facts and relationships new conclusions can be inferred and presented for confirmation. The procedural structure presents a rigidly defined way of solving problems and is the structure used to develop most conventional systems.

By relying on a declarative rather than a procedural structure, knowledge-based systems are able to tackle problems that do not have a clear structure for the determination of a solution. Unstructured problems with inexact or uncertain relationships between the constituent elements of the problem do not lend themselves to procedural-based solutions. These types of problems are, however, fertile ground for knowledge-based systems.

The name "expert" systems comes from the idea that an expert has knowledge which allows that individual to solve problems that others cannot solve. The idea of the expert system is to embody that knowledge into a computer-based series of rules that can then be used by a non-expert to do the job that could previously only be done by the human expert.

Perhaps the best known expert system is MYCIN which is a medical diagnostic system. MYCIN is typical of rule-based expert systems in that it comprises a series of rules that are then combined with the input from the user of the system to produce a supported conclusion.

The role of the expert is to provide the rules that make up the system. The role of the knowledge engineer is to formulate these rules into the knowledge base so that they can be used by the inference engine to replicate the conclusions of the expert, given a certain set of facts.

A further refinement of the concept of an expert system is that of an expert assistant. The expert assistant approach recognizes that many expert systems do not have sufficient intelligence to be allowed to make important decisions entirely on their own. However, in combination with someone who is conversant with the domain within which the problem lies (although perhaps not the ultimate expert), the expert assistant allows better and more timely decisions to be made. This teaming of computer technology and human common sense is able to apply intuitive reasonableness tests that may be overlooked in a purely automated solution.

Knowledge Engineering Methods

The knowledge engineer performs three basic functions:

- Populates the knowledge base through representation of the rules that underlie the expert behavior being studied.

- Defines the procedures to infer conclusions based on existing facts and relationships combined with input relating to the problem to be solved.

- Ensures that the reasoning process is well defined and documented.

The first step in the development of a knowledge system is to decide on the problem to be solved. Problems that lend themselves to knowledge-based system solutions are characterized by imprecise definitions of the relationships between the elements of information that are needed to arrive at a solution. The scope of the problem area should, however, be well defined and should be the domain of recognized experts who are able to bring their experience, knowledge and intuition to arrive at solutions to potential instances within the problem area. Lastly, the problem must lend itself to iterative development. The knowledge engineer must be able to grow the system as more data are input to the knowledge base and the number of rules and inferences grows.

The next step in the knowledge engineering approach is to identify the knowledge engineer and the expert(s) who will work on the development. A question that is often raised is whether the knowledge engineer is really required. The role of the knowledge engineer is to elicit and codify the rules that govern the ability to solve problems within the domain of the expert system. Many experts have a great deal of difficulty articulating the reasons why they are able to arrive at a solution when others cannot. There is also the situation where experts disagree among themselves over what are valid facts and rules. By proper analytical techniques, a trained knowledge engineer should be able to elicit these rules from the expert(s).

Once the expert has been teamed with the knowledge engineer, the painstaking process of codifying the rules that lead to solving a given problem begins. It is through this process that the knowledge base is created.

Testing is the next step in the process. Clearly, many typical problem cases must be put through the expert system and the conclusions arrived at by the system compared to the conclusions of the human experts. Refinements to the knowledge base need to be made as discrepancies occur. Explanatory text in support of the system conclusion provides an excellent diagnostic tool as well as being an important feature during the live running of the system.

After the system has been tested and proven to be as accurate as the human expert, it should be made available to non-experts who have a need to access the knowledge base of the experts. A key consideration is to ensure that the users of an expert system have realistic expectations of what the system can do for them. As mentioned earlier in the chapter, most expert systems are really expert assistants and still require human intervention to ensure that the solution space is within the bounds of reality.

Expert systems tend to evolve over time as the body of knowledge about the subject matter grows. At a minimum, the system should be maintained in step with this increasing body of knowledge. Some expert systems have added machine-learning to their range of functionality. Machine-learning is the automatic updating of the knowledge base by the system when a new scenario is encountered. Typically, an existing rule is enhanced as a result of further input during a problem solving session using the expert system.

Expert System Shells

The language for writing expert systems is called a shell. In essence the shell is a development tool that helps mask the complexity of building and then accessing the knowledge base to arrive at solutions to given problems. In terms of the access to the knowledge base, the expert system shell acts as a query manager. In some shells there are two interfaces provided to the knowledge base — one for the system developers (or the knowledge engineers) and one for the eventual users of the system. In his article, "Strategies for Developing Commercial Expert Systems," published in the 1989 Auerbach series on Computer Programming Management, Richard Morgan provides a checklist for evaluating expert system shells. The main criteria are to ensure ease of use in the presentation of the facts and rules that govern the determination of solutions to given problems (for example, to build the knowledge base), the ability of the shell to infer solutions from the knowledge base given certain information from the user, and the control provided by the shell in terms of its ability to navigate its way through the knowledge base. As in the case of any software purchase there are also the concerns of compatibility with existing hardware, integration with other systems, cost and the viability and track record of the vendor that need to be considered.

LEVEL 1 AUDITOR — SKILL AND KNOWLEDGE OBJECTIVES

Expert Systems Definitions and Terminology

Know the nature of artificial intelligence/expert system based systems and the control implications of these types of systems.

Knowledge Engineering Methods

Have a basic understanding of the roles of knowledge engineers and topic experts in the design of systems.

Expert System Shells

Understand the use of expert system shells and the various chaining methods.

LEVEL 2 AUDITOR — SKILL AND KNOWLEDGE OBJECTIVES

Expert Systems Definitions and Terminology

Be able to apply the principles of artificial intelligence/expert systems to computer-assisted auditing.

Knowledge Engineering Methods

Understand the roles of the experts in the design of systems and be able to evaluate expert input to the systems design.

Expert System Shells

Be able to establish audit scope and objectives for critical expert systems used by the organization.

CAUSES OF EXPOSURE

The causes of exposure in the area of artificial intelligence/expert systems are as follows:

- Erroneous results.

- Misapplied expectations.

- Inappropriate development.

- Inappropriate software.

Erroneous Results

There is a common understanding among users that the results produced from computer systems are correct. This understanding is based on the belief that systems are fully tested and consistently produced the "correct" results while being tested. Given that conventional systems usually have a "right" answer to the problems that are presented to them, this understanding is an acceptable position for the users to take. The same position cannot be taken when dealing with expert systems. The very nature of expert systems is to deal with problems that either do not have a completely right answer or have several answers that may be equally correct. The user must be aware of this situation and not get into the position of assuming that the expert system is always correct. In fact, new inferences are an inherent feature of expert systems. Almost by definition, new inferences have not been previously tested. It is the ability to make correct inferences which has been previously tested, not the new inferences themselves.

The reason many expert systems have been redefined as expert assistants is to convey to the users that the element of human questioning and intuition must still be applied before accepting the results of the system as being correct. The nature of expert systems is to provide expert advice that one would expect to be acted upon. This expectation would certainly exist if it were the human expert giving the advice directly. However, when using an expert system the user should always be alert to the possibility of error. The ability to question the rationale behind the conclusions being drawn by the system is a key control in this area.

Misapplied Expectations

This cause of exposure is somewhat related to the previous issue of erroneous results. The expectations of the users must be properly established when an expert system is first installed. The users should be made aware of the goals for the system as set by the developers. It is conceivable that the users of an expert system can see ways in which the system's use could be extended. If this extension in functionality is not fully supported in the knowledge base the integrity of the response from the expert system in these expanded areas may be very much in doubt. Ongoing interaction with the knowledge engineer and with the subject expert is key to any expansion in the use of an expert system beyond the domain for which it was developed.

Distinctions between expert systems and expert assistants should also be clearly in the mind of the user with a solid understanding of the type of system that is being supplied. The user should also be clearly aware of the maturity of the system being delivered. The user will have more confidence and certainty for systems that have been used successfully by other users over time than for a newly developed system.

Inappropriate Development

Not all problem areas lend themselves to solutions through expert systems. Most problem areas are defined clearly enough to be dealt with using conventional development techniques and tools. Other areas are just too complex from an intuitive logic standpoint to be solved with the current state of expert system technology. When deciding whether or not to build an expert system to address a particular problem it is useful to look at what has been successfully built at other organizations. Clearly, diagnostic systems are very likely candidates for expert systems. The medical field has made excellent use of expert systems. Similarly, computer hardware manufacturers are turning to expert systems to run and interpret continuous diagnostics that are built into the hardware. When assessing the appropriateness of an expert system development the question of comparable systems at other organizations should be brought up. The experience gained by these other organizations can perhaps be used. Most organizations are more than willing to discuss their experiences in the use of new technology (particularly if used successfully), unless a distinct competitive advantage has been achieved.

Inappropriate Software

In the past, developing expert systems has proved to be a daunting task. The languages able to develop these types of systems have been esoteric (principally LISP and PROLOG), costly and inefficient. This situation has changed somewhat over the years with the introduction of expert system shells that are able to run efficiently on mainstream hardware platforms. When choosing the expert system shell to be used, the developer should understand the nature of the problem to be solved and choose the shell accordingly. Criteria for selection and additional reference readings were provided earlier in the chapter.

CONTROLS

Applicable controls that are intended to prevent, detect and/or correct the causes of exposure just described as relevant to the area of artificial intelligence/expert systems are as follows:

- Testing.

- Solution explanations.

- Training.

- Development methodology.

- Software purchase methodology.

Testing

The important aspect to be noted about testing expert systems is that it is an iterative process. It is unlike a conventional system, where the code is written and then tested with the expectation that the code is correct. With an expert system, the results from the test may cause changes to the knowledge base. These changes should then be made and the test retried.

Of particular note in expert systems is the fact that the system may not be correct all of the time; in fact, the system will almost certainly be wrong some of the time. This is in keeping with the nature of the expert advice that is being provided by the system and the inexact nature of the problems typically being addressed. The real issue remains: "Is the expert system as reliable as the human expert," given that human experts also make mistakes?

For expert systems that are of significant importance to the organization it may be necessary to exhaustively compare the performance of the system to that of human experts before allowing the system to be introduced into a live setting in the organization.

For any expert system there should a series of examples prepared and input to the system. The human expert should document the expected results from the system. Discrepancies between the conclusions reached by the system and those of the human expert should be reviewed in detail.

Solution Explanation

An important part of any expert system is its ability to reproduce in clear terms the logic used to arrive at a stated conclusion and to be able to state the probability that the solution is correct (in the "mind" of the expert system). This feature is particularly useful when the solution does not "seem" right.

Training

The users of the system must be properly trained in its use. The role of the expert system, its relative maturity and reliability must all be explained to the users. Help facilities must be made available to the user, perhaps including direct contact with the human expert and/or knowledge engineer on the occasions that demand that type of assistance. The ability to interrogate the logic process used by the system to arrive at a stated conclusion must be clearly defined.

Development Methodology

Within the development methodology used within the organization there should probably be a point at which the use of an expert system is considered. However, the reality is that expert systems are still fairly new. The decision to build an expert system will probably be the result of initiative on someone's part rather than happening in the regular course of system design for mainstream systems. Once the decision has been made to investigate the development of an expert system, there are some aspects of the traditional methodology approach that should continue to be observed. Expert systems can be very complex and require tremendous amounts of resources (money, people and computer cycles) to develop and operate. A proper feasibility study should be conducted once it has been determined that an expert system approach is desirable and viable. Initial research and development may be carried out without a formal business case, assuming that there is a budget and tacit approval for this type of activity. However, beyond this viability analysis, proper management approval should be obtained to proceed at each major stage of development. The issues of user involvement, proper testing and training must all be addressed in much the same way as conventional system development.

Software Purchase Methodology

When looking to develop expert systems there is a requirement to acquire a development shell. A formal process of software selection should be gone through to ensure that the most appropriate product is selected for the organization and for the particular application being considered for development.

There is also the situation where an entire expert system is to be purchased. Given the relative newness of expert systems technology there have not, until recently, been many opportunities to buy expert system software packages off the shelf. This situation can be expected to change over the coming years as the state of the technology becomes more mature. Once again, a formal process of software evaluation and selection should be in place. Evaluation criteria should be predetermined and the selected candidate packages measured against these criteria. The track record of the vendor should also be considered when deciding on which software package to buy.

TYPES OF EXPOSURE

Listed below are the types of exposure that can occur as a result of the inadequacy or failure of the system of control to prevent the occurrence of a cause of exposure in the area of artificial intelligence/expert systems.

Business Interruption

In the area of hardware diagnostics, expert systems are playing an increasingly important role. In order to have "lights out" operations, expert systems are used to substitute for the computer operator. Diagnostic messages are trapped and interrogated by the resident expert system. Appropriate action is then initiated by the expert system. Where the expert system fails to recognize a problem or does not take the appropriate action, a serious hardware failure could result in some degree of business interruption. The degree of interruption will depend on the extent of dependency the organization has on its computer processing capabilities.

Erroneous Management Decisions

An expert system provides answers to problems. Actions would typically be taken based upon the answer given. If the answer is wrong, the action taken may also be wrong. Expert systems can, therefore, certainly lead to erroneous management decisions. It should also be recognized that an expert system is unlikely to be right on every occasion. For this reason, the user of the system must continue to exercise judgement over the use of results produced by an expert system.

Fraud

The human experts on a particular topic are usually in short supply in any organization. The reason for the interest in expert systems is to be able to make this expertise more broadly accessible. However, there is a risk in this strategy. If the expert is operating in an area where there is a possibility of benefiting materially from an unauthorized use of this expert knowledge (such as to commit fraud), the organization is in a strong position of being able to institute whatever controls are required to prevent or detect such an occurrence, given that the number of people to be controlled is so small. Once this expertise is more broadly based through the dissemination of the expert system, the relevant controls will need to be reexamined in light of a broad distribution of this expert knowledge to ensure that they still meet the needs of the organization. It is likely that the controls will have to be modified or supplemented by additional controls.

Excessive Costs

Expert systems have typically been very expensive to build because of the technology that is available. This situation has improved somewhat over the last few years and will continue to do so in the future. However, it is still important to give a great deal of thought to the applications that will be developed using expert system philosophies and technologies. Most systems do not need to be developed as expert systems. There is a danger of expert systems being viewed as a solution looking for a problem. Other systems are simply too complex to be automated given the current state of technology. Systems that require the application of common sense is a classic example. Although common sense may seem intuitively obvious, the reality is that common sense is based on a large and complex series of understandings about how the world works. The required knowledge base is simply too large to be automated, at least using today's technology.

In order to avoid excessive costs, care has to be taken over the selection of which expert systems to build. A clearly defined and contained scope has to be established for the system.

Loss or Destruction of Assets

Expert systems may be put in place to watch over corporate assets. There are a number of expert systems in the financial industry that control the use of assets. Failure of these systems to act as expected will almost certainly result in loss of assets. There are numerous similar examples in other industries.

Competitive Disadvantage

Expert systems have the potential to provide competitive advantage. If the system does not work as expected or is inappropriately used, the organization could end up with a competitive disadvantage. The degree of competitive disadvantage suffered will depend very much on how important the expert system is to the organization's position in the marketplace, how badly the system failed and to what extent this failure comes to the attention of the organization's customers and/or competitors.

CONTROL EVALUATION TABLE

The Control Evaluation Table for artificial intelligence/expert systems is given in Figure 16.1. The evaluation numbers are subjective and need to be adjusted based upon the conditions that exist in individual organizations. Note that, in practice, the completion of the Control Evaluation Table is in two parts:

- During detailed information gathering where, from the review of available documentation and the results of personal interviews, the key to reliance on individual controls and the "overall control rating (design)" are determined.

- During the execution of the audit program where, as a result of various audit tests, the strength of individuals controls is fully assessed and the "overall control rating (tested)" is determined.

AUDIT APPROACH

The expertise exhibited by the experienced auditor is one area that seems to lend itself well to expert systems. Expert system philosophies, combined with a continuous auditing approach, hold promise for being able to adequately address the audit issues in large, complex computer systems where it is simply not feasible to perform an effective manual audit. The approach used would be to have an audit subsystem running at all times performing sampling of the transactions being processed through the main system. Records in the master file would also be interrogated and analyzed for conditions that fall beyond the bounds of what is expected. An expert auditor would be required to specify the conditions to be looked for. The input from this human expert would then be developed into the audit subsystem.

Stand-alone audit expert systems could also be developed using the data bases from various applications systems as additional input to the dialogue from the audit user of the system.

In terms of reviewing other expert systems being built within the auditor's organization, the approach is similar to the involvement for conventional application system development. The auditor should be sure that the application being developed as an expert system warrants this type of treatment. An acceptable litmus test is to ask whether the expert system approach has been used previously for this type of application. Few organizations want to be on the leading edge of expert system development. If the organization does not already have an expert system shell available to it and must buy one to support an intended development, the auditor should attest to the adequacy of the approach used to evaluate and select the expert system shell. Once development begins, the auditor should be concerned with ensuring that management approval is given to proceed from phase to phase and that the system is properly tested before being handed over to the user as a production system. The auditor also should be sure that the user fully understands the nature of the system being provided and the scope of its intended use.

Suggested Reading

David King and Richard Morgan, *Knowledge-based Systems: An Overview*, Auerbach Series on System Development Management, New York, 1988.

Richard Morgan, *Strategies for Developing Commercial Expert Systems*, Auerbach Series on Computer Programming Management, New York, 1989.

Jay Liebowitz and Daniel A. De Salvo (Editors), *Structuring Expert Systems*, Yourdon Press Computing Series, Englewood Cliffs, New Jersey, 1989.

John Debenham, *Knowledge Systems Design*, Prentice Hall, Australia, 1989.

Terry Goble, *Structured Systems Analysis Through PROLOG*, Prentice Hall, Hertfordshire, England, 1989.

James Martin, *An Information Systems Manifesto*, Prentice Hall, Englewood Cliffs, New Jersey, 1984.

Figure 16.1 — Control Evaluation Table
Artificial Intelligence/Expert Systems

CAUSES OF EXPOSURE

CONTROLS	Erroneous Results	Misapplied Expectations	Inappropriate Development	Inappropriate Software
Testing	3	2		1
Solution Explanations	3	2		2
Training	2	3	1	1
Development Methodology	2	2	3	2
Software Purchase Methodology			2	3
Overall Control Rating - Design				
Overall Control Rating - Tested				

EXPOSURES

	Erroneous Results	Misapplied Expectations	Inappropriate Development	Inappropriate Software
Erroneous Record Keeping				
Unacceptable Accounting				
Business Interruption	1	1		
Erroneous Management Decisions	2	2	1	1
Fraud and Embezzlement		1	1	
Statutory Sanctions				
Excessive Costs	1	1	2	2
Loss or Destruction of Assets	1	1		
Competitive Disadvantage	1		1	1

KEY TO RELIANCE ON CONTROL

3 - High reliance
2 - Moderate reliance
1 - Control has only a peripheral effect on the cause of exposure
Blank - No significant impact

KEY TO OVERALL CONTROL RATING

3 - Strong control
2 - Moderate but adequate control
1 - Inadequate control

KEY TO DEGREE OF CERTAINTY OF OCCURRENCE IN THE EVENT OF AN INADEQUATE CONTROL STRUCTURE

3 - Virtually certain
2 - Probable
1 - Possible
Blank - Very unlikely

17
MAKING AN OVERALL ASSESSMENT OF THE INFORMATION SYSTEMS FUNCTION

INTRODUCTION

In Chapter 3, several methods of building an audit plan for the information systems function are presented. In Chapters four through 16, each of the 13 building block segments of information systems, as defined by The IIA's model curriculum, are described in detail, including an audit approach to determining the adequacy of internal control in each particular area. Assuming that an audit plan has been prepared and executed to deal individually with each of these areas, the task of analyzing the results of each audit to determine an overall assessment of the adequacy of internal control within the information systems function remains.

Arriving at an overall rating is not a trivial task. Of the audits conducted throughout the year there will undoubtedly be good and bad results; control objectives that are being met and those that are not. There will be instances when the control structure is sound but the controls are not being adhered to. Conversely, although certainly less frequently, there will be situations when the control structure, as defined, is weak but the actual level of control is adequate due to some form of compensating control(s).

This chapter provides some guidelines to arriving at an overall conclusion on the adequacy of internal control within an organization's information systems department. Many audit departments avoid taking this final step in the audit calendar for the simple reason that any conclusion drawn on an overall basis is a direct assessment on the performance of the management of the information systems department. Many auditors feel unqualified to make this assessment and would prefer the safer ground of letting senior management draw its own conclusions based on cumulative impressions drawn from reviewing the audit reports circulated during the year. The reality, of course, is that senior management feels even less qualified to make any kind of qualitative judgement on the information systems function based on audit reviews which, in many cases, seem to address some fairly esoteric areas.

However, it is also true that many executives have an uneasy feeling about the value being derived from their information systems function and would welcome a considered opinion from an independent and qualified group that has spent considerable time in the review of the entire function. The audit department is in an ideal position to fill this executive management requirement.

THE PRIMARY RESPONSIBILITIES OF INFORMATION SYSTEMS

Although 13 segments are presented as the building blocks of information systems, these are not the criteria by which the performance of the information systems function should be measured. These building blocks are simply a means to an end, and that end is service to the organization. In fact, many organizations are now renaming their information systems function to information *services* to recognize the required emphasis on service, which has the connotation of being business oriented, rather than systems, which has the connotation of being technically focused.

Service, from an information systems perspective, has several factors:

- The timely delivery of complete, accurate and relevant information to the end user, either through an on-line network or through the provision of batch reports. The delivery of information can either be formalized through the use of application systems or can be on an ad hoc basis through the provision of query tools to the end users.

- The timely development of computer systems that are capable of producing the required information for delivery to the end users.

- The timely maintenance of previously developed computer systems to ensure that they continue to be capable of producing the required information for delivery to the end users.

- The effective custody over all forms of data (business, system and administrative) so that they are protected from unauthorized disclosure, modification or destruction, whether accidental or intentional.

Each of the 13 building blocks as defined in the model curriculum contributes in some way to meeting one or more of these service objectives. Figure 17.1 provides a matrix view of how each of the building blocks relates to the four service areas. The extent of the relationship between building block and service area will vary from organization to organization but the matrix should be helpful in pulling together the results from the audits conducted in each of the building block areas.

From the findings in each of the building block audits, the auditor should be able to assess the level of service provided in each of the four areas defined. The next step is to translate four individual conclusions into one overall conclusion. Once again, this is not a trivial task. Each organization may place a different emphasis on each of the four service areas. A mature organization may place greater emphasis on ongoing operations and system maintenance than on new system development. A relatively new organization may place added emphasis on the new development area. One might assume that the common denominator among all organizations would be data security. However, the reality is that data security means more to certain types of organizations than to others (for instance, as a broad generalization, data security means more to a financial institution than to a manufacturing organization).

A weighting factor may be applied to each of these areas on a purely subjective basis. Alternatively, analytical hierarchy process (AHP) described in Chapter 3 can be used to do a comparison of each of the service areas and arrive at an evaluation of the relative merits of each area, as it applies to that particular organization.

AUDIT FINDINGS

In order to determine the ratings that should be applied to each of the service areas and ultimately to arrive at an overall rating, the various audits conducted throughout the year should be reviewed in light of what the audit findings mean to the four levels of service being assessed.

Operational Service

Operational service is defined as the timely delivery of complete, accurate and relevant information to the end user, either through an on-line network or through the provision of batch reports

Perhaps the most far reaching of all the audits conducted throughout the year is the data center audit (refer to Chapters 5 and 10). Typically conducted once per year, the data center audit is essentially a compliance audit based on the policies, practices and procedures of the data center. The objectives of the data center audit include ensuring that:

- Adequate separation of duties exists within the organizational structure of the data center.

- Custodial responsibilities for the protection of data are being properly carried out.

- Change control procedures are in effect to ensure separation of the production environment from the test environment(s) and that the migration procedures between the environments conforms to standards established for this purpose.

- Physical security measures are adequate and properly utilized to ensure continuity of processing.

- The controls over the receipt, processing and dispatch of work provide for secure processing and handling of data.

- Management is provided with sufficient information to manage the data center effectively.

From the above objectives it is clear that the results from the data center audit should provide a comprehensive assessment of the operational service level. The findings from the data center audit can be supplemented by the findings from audits conducted in the areas of System Maintenance and Change Control (refer to Chapter 7), Information Processing Problem Management (refer to Chapter 8), Information Systems Contingency Planning (refer to Chapter 9), Application Systems (refer to Chapter 11), Systems Software /Environmental Control Programs (refer to Chapter 12) and Telecommunications Networks (refer to Chapter 15).

Many of the supplemental areas mentioned above also rely on the data center audit as their primary audit vehicle.   However, for whatever reason, there may have been other audits that took place in one or more of these areas throughout the year.   The scope and objectives of these audits (if any) should be examined to determine if service levels to the end users were included for review. As appropriate, the audit findings should be reviewed with the purpose of identifying any that do apply to the area of operational service. The absence of any findings should also be pursued as this may indicate that an adequate high level of service was in existence at the time of the audit.

System Development

The service level for system development is defined as the timely development of computer systems that are capable of producing the necessary information for delivery to the end users.

The first consideration is the adequacy of the methodology for building systems (refer to Chapter 6).   It is very possible that the methodology has not been the subject of a formal review for several years, possibly since the selection and implementation of the methodology. However, with the rate of change that has taken place in terms of system development tools, techniques and practices (such as CASE and purchased systems), it is worthwhile to attempt to assess how well the methodology is being used for different types of development. If the methodology has not been audited recently, an assessment of the adequacy of the methodology will have to be made based on its use in system development.

Adherence to the methodology is the next issue to be dealt with (refer to Chapter 11). If the methodology is not being followed, one of two conclusions can be drawn: the methodology is no longer appropriate to the circumstances, or the system developers are not adhering to the standards of the organization. Either situation is unacceptable in the long run as each will definitely have an impact on the long-term productivity of the system development function and, therefore, on the system development service level provided.

Another key issue is the adherence of the systems being developed to the long-term information strategy (refer to Chapter 4). The systems under development that were audited during the year should be matched against the information strategy. Inconsistencies between the strategy and the systems being developed should be cause for comment. The types of systems being built (such as expert systems - refer to Chapter 16) should also be examined in light of the strategic direction of the organization.

The findings of any audits related to data management (refer to Chapters 13 and 14) as it relates to a method of system development (the data driven approach to system development) should also be reviewed.

Maintenance Management

Maintenance management is defined as the timely maintenance of previously developed computer systems to ensure that they continue to be capable of producing the required information for delivery to the end users. Audits relating to system maintenance and change control (refer to Chapter 7) provide the findings that are necessary to arrive at an overall assessment of the adequacy of the service in this area. With approximately 80 percent of the information systems development budget going to correcting and enhancing existing systems, the entire area of maintenance management is of major concern to senior management.

The audit review of existing system maintenance and change control procedures is a key input to the overall assessment of maintenance management. The method of initiating, documenting, approving, prioritizing, tracking, making, testing and migrating changes should all be clearly thought out, documented and practiced.

Application audits, to the extent that the quality of the software from a maintenance point of view is assessed (usually in a post implementation review), also provide valuable input to the conclusion on maintenance management (refer to Chapter 11).

The data center audit provides valuable input as to how well the migration procedures are being adhered to.

Data Security

A major corporate service provided by the information systems department is data security. Acting in a custodial capacity, the information systems department is responsible for maintaining custody over all forms of data (business, system and administrative) so that they are protected from unauthorized disclosure, modification or destruction, whether accidental or intentional. Without effective custodial arrangements in place, the ability to offer information to the end users that is complete, accurate and timely is severely handicapped.

The audits of interest in this area are the data security audit and the data center audit (refer to Chapter 5). Audits related to data base management systems/data dictionary (refer to Chapter 14) are relevant as are audits of the on-line access paths to data (such as telecommunications network audits - refer to Chapter 15).

Audits related to system maintenance and change control (refer to Chapter 7), to the extent that they deal with the security of system data, provide useful input into an overall assessment of the adequacy of data security. Contingency planning (refer to Chapter 9) has major implications to data integrity and security as does information processing operations (refer to Chapter 10) to the extent that the data is handled within the data center. The ability of the systems programming function to access data is a significant control issue that is addressed in Chapter 12, System Software/Environmental Control Program.

THE REPORT TO MANAGEMENT

The report to management on the overall adequacy of the information systems function should be made on a yearly basis. The most appropriate time would usually be at the end of the fiscal year and would conclude the annual plan of audit activity in the information systems area. The report should comment on the adequacy of service in each of the four service areas and then provide an overall conclusion on the effectiveness of the entire function.

Each set of conclusions should be supported by salient facts. The conclusions drawn from the findings in individual audits can be supplemented by comparisons with industry averages for each of the four service areas. There are numerous sources of statistics on average performance in the information systems field, both in general across all industries and specifically within individual industries. Investment in technology, the ratio of maintenance to new development, the number of professional staff hired, turnover statistics, and so forth are all available for comparison to what is happening within the organization under review.

In the overall assessment of the effectiveness of the information systems function within the organization, the organization and administration of the function requires special consideration (refer to Chapter 4). Without a clear vision of purpose and direction from top information systems management, it is difficult to imagine that the performance of the information systems function will be entirely adequate for the needs of the organization.

However, it is not just the commitment of the information systems management team that should be evaluated. The commitment of the other executives within the organization to the use of computer technology should also be evaluated and commented upon. There are many instances of an enthusiastic and committed information systems management being unable to effect change because of the uncompromising views of the executives from the other line departments. One way to assess this commitment by non-information systems executives is to look at their involvement in the preparation of the information strategy (refer to Chapter 4) and in the operation of the computer steering committee (refer to Chapter 6). Active involvement of these executives in the development of systems within their own areas is also indicative of a high level of commitment to information systems.

The final section of the audit report should lay out a series of recommendations for improving the effectiveness of the information systems function. These recommendations need not be restricted to action that has to be taken by the information systems function. It may be that other areas in the organization have to make changes in order to benefit from the potential of information systems technology.

As with all audit opinions, the conclusions drawn should first be discussed with the auditee before release of the report to its intended audience which, in this case, is likely to be the corporate management group. The principal auditee is, of course, the head of the information systems function within the organization. This individual's direct reports are also likely to be involved in the presentation of the audit opinion. Any differences of opinion can be resolved during this meeting. As required, further material can be presented in the report to substantiate the findings or the findings can be amended to reflect changes agreed upon at the meeting.

Where the findings and/or recommendations affect other departments in the organization, they should be discussed with the department manager(s) of the appropriate area(s) in the same way as with the head of the information systems function.

Figure 17.1

	Operational Service	System Development	Maintenance Management	Data Security
Information Systems Organization and Administration	X	X	X	X
Information System Security	X			X
System Development		X	X	
System Maintenance and Change	X		X	X
Information Processing Problem Management	X			
Information Systems Contingency Planning	X			X
Information Processing Operations	X			X
Application Systems	X	X	X	X
Systems Software/Environmental Control Programs	X			
Data Management		X	X	
Data Base Management/Data Dictionary		X	X	X
Telecommunication Networks	X	X		X
Artificial Intelligence/Expert Systems		X		

Appendix 1
Systems Acceptance Testing

PAYOFF IDEA. An inadequate computer system can cause severe processing delays, create dissatisfaction among users, and reflect poorly on the entire information systems department. These difficulties can be minimized through acceptance testing, which helps determine a system's completeness and readiness for implementation. This appendix describes the objectives of acceptance testing and each of the stages involved — from planning the test to evaluating its results.

PROBLEMS ADDRESSED

Inadequate acceptance testing is a major cause of the failure of information systems to meet business objectives. Because effective acceptance testing treats the new system as both a computer system and a business process, the test plan must not only verify the accuracy and completeness of all computer programs but also ensure that user procedures and training and operational considerations have been adequately addressed.

Selection of the best individuals to assume responsibility for acceptance testing may prove difficult, however, and could lead to inadequate testing or no testing at all.

Although systems developers are concerned primarily with computer components, they must not overlook nontechnical considerations. If the user department is unable to use a computer system, that system will fail, regardless of its technical sophistication. A system that cannot deliver timely results is likewise doomed.

A low-quality computer system can destroy carefully created production schedules, degrade on-line response time, and prevent the data center from attaining its service-level objectives. In addition, poor implementation can weaken morale in the operations department; employees become frustrated by the overtime needed to make the system work. When implementation problems are controlled, processing delays are minimized, which benefits the entire organization as well as the user department and information systems operations.

The Institute of Internal Auditors

Ongoing systems maintenance can also be directly affected by the quality of acceptance testing. Poor acceptance testing results in the implementation of systems that require an inordinate amount of maintenance effort immediately after implementation into the production environment. This instability in the system often leads to an endless series of problems. Time does not permit adequate testing procedures to be developed; consequently, fixes applied to the system introduce problems of their own. In many cases, systems never recover from the lack of adequate acceptance testing before their initial implementation into production. As a result, the organization has a system that is inordinately expensive to maintain over its lifetime.

If acceptance test procedures have been followed, test data has been created, and the results have been documented, the organization is in the position of using regression testing techniques when installing new releases of the system. Regression testing entails running the previously created test data against the new version of the system to ensure that the changes made to the system have not gone beyond what was expected to take place. Whenever the system is changed, the original acceptance test can be rerun and the two sets of system output compared (i.e., the output before and after the change was made). Any unexpected discrepancies can then be examined by the individual conducting the test.

The purpose of acceptance testing is to verify a system's completeness and readiness for implementation. Systems acceptance testing comprises two areas — user acceptance testing and operations acceptance testing. End users (both primary and secondary) own the application system and, therefore, are responsible for ensuring that the system functions according to their expectations and not just to those of the application developers. For this reason, users should prepare their own test data and run their own tests before signing off on the application.

So far, this appendix has focused on conventional systems development, in which the information systems department develops systems for end users. End users, however, are increasingly developing their own systems on microcomputer workstations or on mainframes through the facilities offered by some type of information center. It is important to understand that the guidelines for systems acceptance testing apply equally in an end-user environment.

THE OBJECTIVES OF ACCEPTANCE TESTING

The objectives of acceptance testing can be stated in relatively straightforward terms. First, the system must attain the business objectives that were established for it when the system was approved for development. In practical terms, this means that the functional capability of the system to be tested must match the specifications contained in the requirements definition document prepared at an early stage of systems development. Second, the system must be operable within the production environment for which it was designed. If the systems development process anticipated a change in the production environment to accommodate the new system, it is important to ensure that these changes have been successfully installed. In other cases, the system has been developed assuming that it will operate in the existing production environment; acceptance testing must determine whether this assumption is valid.

Most information systems departments have implemented a formal systems development methodology dictating several user approval steps. These are primarily performed at the end of the system requirements definition and the system functional specifications design. A frequently overlooked task in these methodologies is user approval of acceptance test criteria. These standards frequently help define the service level a user expects. Whether a data center uses service-level agreements or another methodology, user expectations of the new system must be controlled. Therefore, the user, the data center manager, and the systems development team should develop a rigorous test plan for systems acceptance.

The following paragraphs review acceptance testing objectives.

Meeting Design Specifications. After acceptance criteria have been established, it must be determined whether the new system operates according to its design specifications, which in turn must meet the acceptance criteria. If design specifications do not meet those criteria, either the business needs have changed during development or the methodology used is deficient. Given the current movement toward the use of CASE technology and the transition from design specification directly into generated code, the verification of the design specification at systems acceptance is particularly crucial.

The Institute of Internal Auditors

Achieving Optimal Performance of On-line Systems. A major objective of any acceptance test is to verify the ability of the computer operations staff to use the new system. Disruptions can result if the operations staff cannot run the new system, and erroneous output caused by faulty operations can create havoc among users.

In the case of on-line systems, this objective is critical because any error typically becomes immediately apparent to the end user. In addition, disruptions of the end user's business process can result in staggering costs. For example, an idle assembly line can cost thousands of dollars per minute, and an incorrect product run can cost hundreds of thousands of dollars in both lost revenues and wastage.

To achieve optimal performance in on-line systems, response time as well as proper classification of transaction classes must be verified. Equally important is verification that the new system will not overload the current computer configuration. If the system is just below the critical point on the response curve, even a minor increase in the work load can be too much.

To ensure that the system will provide adequate response time at peak volumes, a volume test should be included in systems acceptance testing. Volume testing involves simulating the expected maximum transaction volume and terminal access attempts for the system at its busiest period. This type of testing also has the effect of putting the systems architecture under stress to ensure that the system itself can adequately handle high-volume throughput. In addition to volume testing, stress testing in an on-line environment should also be performed. Stress testing measures the system's response to a failure at any point in its architecture (e.g., terminal failure, line failure, data base integrity error, disk problems). Each failure should be simulated and the system's actual response should be measured and compared with its anticipated or designated response.

Preventing Batch System Scheduling Problems. For batch systems, actual computer run times must be verified before full production begins. In certain rare cases, the daily processing time of new systems can exceed 24 hours. More commonly, the addition of a new system overloads the existing configuration.

The critical elements of the operating schedule must be compatible and represent realistic expectations. For example, if a computer run must be completed by 8 AM daily and requires 10 hours to process, delivery of the input at midnight presents an insolvable scheduling problem. Another example is the inclusion of a 15-minute balancing operation in the critical path of the schedule. Although it may be possible to perform the balancing operation in 15 minutes, balancing problems will most likely delay processing on a regular basis. The detection and elimination of scheduling problems before implementation can remove a major cause of friction among personnel in the various departments participating in system operation.

Verifying User Readiness. As mentioned, one of the most important objectives of the acceptance test is to verify the user's ability to use the new system. An improperly trained user staff can negate the benefits of a well designed and implemented system. Problems arise when, for example, an improperly equipped or staffed user department must run the new system in extended parallel operation with the old system. Parallel operation often requires double work by the computer operations and user departments. Users often inaccurately estimate the effect of such operations on their departments. In addition, staffing and equipment deficiencies may occur when a system is converted from batch to on-line operation. Planners often underestimate the additional effort required of the user department to operate on-line terminals.

Prototyping and Acceptance Testing

The user of prototyping as a development approach requires special mention at this point. In a prototyping mode, the user and systems developer work together in designing the system. Successive iterations of the system are developed until the user is satisfied with the end results. The danger in this approach is that proper acceptance testing is overlooked in the haste to attain a system that looks right. If prototyping is being used to arrive at a production system, the elements of planning and executing the acceptance test are equally as critical as when a conventional approach to systems development is being used.

PLANNING THE ACCEPTANCE TEST

Planning the acceptance test is central to the eventual success of the system. A test plan is best constructed during the early phases of systems development, when sufficient time can be devoted to it. Its design can begin after the conceptual design has been completed. When the detail design phase has been finalized, the acceptance test plan should be near completion.

Before planning can begin, the individual responsible for creating the plan must be familiar with the proposed system. This individual should study all design documentation and interview the system designers and users.

Acceptance test planning comprises the following steps:
- Identifying the tasks required to accomplish the acceptance task.
- Estimating the employee hours required to complete each task.
- Assigning an individual the responsibility for completing each task.
- Scheduling start and completion dates for each task and distributing copies of the test schedule to those involved in the acceptance test.
- Obtaining formal user approval of the acceptance criteria and test plan.

System planners can identify tasks by dividing the acceptance test into subsystems and determining the tasks for each subsystem. (Exhibit 1 provides a list of representative subsystem components.) The selection of subsystem components is accomplished by dividing the entire system into functionally independent sections. The division used by the systems development staff can be helpful in this activity. After the major components of the system have been determined, the tasks required to test each component can be selected. (Exhibit 2 presents a list of typical testing tasks.) Each task should have a specific product that can be reviewed in order to measure the completeness of the task. The individual in charge of acceptance testing should regularly review task progress.

Exhibit 1 — Typical Acceptance Testing Subsystem Components

Subsystem	Component
Computer System	Master File Conversion or Creation
	Edit or Update
	Transaction Processing
	Reporting
	Backup or Restore
	Audit Trail
	Computer Resource Requirements
Operations Department	Operating Procedures
	Operating Schedule
	Balancing
	File Retention
	Conversion and Transition Procedures
User Department	Operating Procedures
	Balancing
	Error Handling
	Document Retention
	Conversion and Transition Procedures

Exhibit 2 — Typical Acceptance Testing Tasks

Review documentation	Interview user personnel
Review procedures	Analyze user personnel
Review schedules	readiness
Review training	Analyze documentation
Create test data	Analyze procedures
Review test data	Determine schedule feasibility
Document test data	Estimate input volume
Determine test data results	Estimate input preparation time
Evaluate test run results	Estimate file sizes
Present plan and criteria to	Estimate run time
users and developers	Obtain formal approval of
	acceptance criteria and plan

Estimation of the time required to finish each task is one of the most difficult activities in the planning process. Testing tasks are particularly difficult to estimate because of the relatively infrequent use of the acceptance test in systems development cycles. Many activities (e.g., preparing test data) are mechanical in nature, however, and can be estimated reliably. The smaller the task, the easier it is to estimate. In general, the more detailed the task list, the better the overall estimate. Traditionally, information systems-related estimates have been consistently low. As task size diminishes, however, the total estimate rises. Based on both observations, it follows that as the task size approaches zero (in terms of employee-hour effort), the total project estimate approaches the true value.

Responsibility for specific task completion should be assigned to individuals to properly control the acceptance testing project. If tasks are assigned to departments rather than to individuals, the tasks are usually neglected. Individuals often have more incentive to complete a task on time if their names appear on a planning document or if the completed plan and subsequent progress reports are sent to supervisors.

The level of effort required to schedule start and completion dates for each task relates to the size of the system being tested. A small acceptance test can be scheduled simply with the aid of a calendar and a vacation schedule. A large system may require the aid of a sophisticated PERT/CPM analysis. One frequent mistake is to base a plan on a 40-hour week. Such interruptions as routine tasks and illness reduce the true work week to approximately 30 to 32 hours. The project's priority also affects available staff time.

Acceptance test planning results should be documented and sent to all interested individuals. Exhibit 3 represents a sample document that could be used for developing an acceptance test plan as well as for monitoring and reporting the test's progress.

Like all plans, an acceptance test plan is subject to frequent change. For maximum value, it must be updated regularly. If an outdated plan is discarded rather than updated, the benefits of the acceptance test may be substantially reduced. Consequently, a major responsibility of the test leader is to keep the plan current and to announce schedule and activity changes.

Example 3 — Sample Acceptance Test Documentation Form

Acceptance Test Plan

Prepared by: _____   Date: _____

Revised by: _____   Date: _____

Activity	Assigned to	Estimated Hours	Actual Hours	Start Scheduled	Start Actual	Complete Scheduled	Complete Actual

PREPARING TEST DATA

Much of the effort required to conduct an acceptance test lies in the preparation of test data, which is designed primarily to demonstrate the proper functioning of a computer system. The development of effective test data is a complex process. Several available products are designed specifically to generate test data. Effective system test data should be used during the acceptance test and then preserved for use in testing future system modifications.

The program type, complexity, and unique system requirements and constraints must all be considered in test data development. A system cannot be tested adequately with a single run. A series of runs must be designed to verify that month-end, quarter-end, and year-end options are operating properly. The test data should also be designed to check the adequacy of system controls and system error and exception reports. The following sections present guidelines for preparing test data for several types of programs.

Edit Programs. A range of transactions should be prepared for each data element that can be processed by the edit function. The transactions should cover such situations as:
- Numeric fields containing all nines, all zeros, all blanks, and alphabetic data.
- Numeric values greater than valid upper limits and less than valid lower limits.
- Numeric values equal to valid upper and lower limits.
- Numeric values with both positive and negative signs.
- Valid and erroneous combinations of values in related data fields.

Update Programs. Various combinations of file maintenance transactions should be prepared to test the functioning of update programs in the system. Attempts to do the following should be tested:
- Create a master record with a zero value key.
- Create a master record with a key containing all nines.
- Create a master record with a key containing all blanks.
- Create a master record with all possible data combinations.

The Institute of Internal Auditors

- Create a master record with a key equal to a record that already exists on the file.
- Change data in a nonexistent record.
- Change data in the first and last record on the file.
- Add a record with a key lower than the lowest existing record and greater than the largest existing record.
- Create and change a record in the same run.
- Delete a nonexistent record.
- Create and delete a record in the same run.
- Change and delete a record in the same run.

Calculation Programs. Although calculations may occur in different types of programs, each calculation function must be treated separately. The following are typical tests that should be applied to each system calculation:
- Cause a condition for multiplication and division by zero.
- Cause an arithmetic overflow to occur.
- Cause results with high, low, and average values to occur.
- Attempt to create out-of-balance conditions.

Report Programs. Report programs are tested with data that creates various conditions. Situations should be created to test report programs, including:
- Create report values that are negative.
- Create report values that are all nines.
- Create report values that are all zeros.
- Attempt to create an out-of-balance condition.

Sources of Test Data
Test data generators are available to create and submit test data for acceptance testing purposes. The advantages of using a test data generator (rather than manually preparing test data) are speed, accuracy, and completeness. In the case of an on-line system, test scripts must be prepared for the on-line user to follow when submitting transactions. The results from each transaction can be recorded on the script.

A parallel operation can be used to augment or replace the preparation of acceptance test data. In general, although a parallel operation is a poor substitute for carefully designed test data, the use of a parallel operation to augment synthetic data can be a valuable addition to the acceptance test. The parallel operation permits evaluation of the system in a real-life context.

Parallel operation should be carefully evaluated in the context of each situation before it is selected as part of the acceptance testing procedure.

Insufficient user department personnel or equipment often makes it impossible to conduct a valid parallel operation.

During the preparation of acceptance test data, an acceptable result for each piece of data must be predicted. Although time-consuming, this task is critical to the successful completion of an acceptance test. In addition, the minimum level of performance should be established to determine whether the system has passed the acceptance test. After the data has been gathered, it can be retained for future use in regression testing of subsequent versions of the system.

RUNNING THE ACCEPTANCE TEST

How the acceptance test is run can affect its outcome. The user and operations departments should run the system exactly as they would in a production environment. This tests not only the programs but also the user manual and the operator's run book.

Personnel associated with system operation should perform their usual functions. All input should be formatted exactly as in the user documentation or procedures. The development team should not be involved in running the test except under abnormal conditions (e.g., system failure or inadequate documentation).

Every program used in the test should be complied from the most recent version of the source program to help ensure that the current source program exists and that patched object modules are not being used. Master files used for the acceptance test should be created during the acceptance test and should not be provided by the systems development team. Software change control procedures are critical at this stage to ensure that any corrections or other changes are retested before they are incorporated into the production copy.

The individual supervising the acceptance test must carefully monitor the test run. Because acceptance testing occurs late in the development cycle (when deadlines are most critical), personnel will often be urged to implement the system quickly. The acceptance test supervisor must refuse to curtail the acceptance test in favor of implementation, despite pressure from others to do so. It may be necessary at the eleventh hour to reemphasize the advantages of the acceptance test to complete the test successfully.

Users and the data center manager must plan to minimize the adverse impact of these pressures on the validity of the acceptance test. Realistic schedules, use of independent personnel (e.g., personnel other than the original program developers) to conduct the test, and integration of the review process into the actual testing help maintain the test's validity.

EVALUATING TEST RESULTS

The value of developing acceptance criteria early on becomes evident when test results are evaluated. Without previous agreement on acceptance criteria, it would be difficult to convince management to abort an implementation for reasons other than catastrophic system failure during the acceptance test. The prevailing mood during implementation usually favors deemphasizing problems and proceeding with the system. To counteract false optimism, it is necessary to ensure that acceptance criteria are documented and used in evaluating acceptance test results.

RECOMMENDED COURSE OF ACTION

The following are important considerations for ensuring effective acceptance testing:

- The ultimate criterion for accepting a system into production is whether it accomplishes the end user's business objectives.
- An acceptance test must exercise more than just the programs and transactions. It must validate the documentation and business procedures that the end user will use.
- Acceptance testing should be conducted by the operations and end-user staffs that will actually use the production version and should be conducted in the environment in which the production version will be used.

- A standard should be established so that the acceptance test plan will be part of the original external design specifications. This minimizes wasted programming effort and often crystallizes vague user requirements.
- Specific acceptance criteria must always be included in a test plan and must be approved before any testing is started.

Appendix 2
Conducting an Impact
Analysis

PAYOFF IDEA. The introduction of a new system may have a significant impact on an organization quite beyond what was anticipated in the analysis phase of the systems development life cycle. Unless the impact of an implementation is identified and planned for, the effects may extend throughout the organization and be difficult to control because the underlying causes is not understood. An impact analysis, which is conducted after the system is built, assesses how the system will affect the organization after it is implemented. This appendix offers guidelines on how and when to conduct an impact analysis, who should conduct the study, and its role in the systems development life cycle.

PROBLEMS ADDRESSED

The analysis and design phases of the systems development life cycle (SDLC) concern the identification of a business problem and the development of a solution. All to often, however, rather than finding a solution, the problem is merely shifted around in the organization or is reshaped so that it appears in a different form. For example, shortly after one on-line, real-time system was developed and successfully implemented, several problems began to appear. Not only was the system falling short of its expected savings, but the overall cost of operating the business unit increased.

An analysis of the situation revealed several unforeseen problems. First, the system contained extremely sophisticated functional capabilities and could combine several activities that previously seemed quite distinct steps in the process. To use this new functional capability properly, the operators needed a thorough understanding of the entire business process. Previously, the operators were accustomed to working at a clerical level and, as a consequence, could not regularly meet the demands of the new system. There was a great deal of confusion because the operators did not know what commands the

The Institute of Internal Auditors

system expected, which resulted in a high error rate, frustrated employees, and a throughput rate that was well below expectations.

Second, the system was designed to address the needs of the organization's principal business. Shortly after the system was implemented, however, the organization expanded some of its traditionally less important lines of business and assumed that the system could accommodate this expansion. This seemed like a logical assumption, given that the original analysis and design indicated the system performed satisfactorily when these lines of business were in a low-volume state. In reality, the system was hopelessly inadequate in dealing with the expanded volume of business. There was, however, no option but to use the system. Users became adept at finding ways of tricking the system into responding as if the system requirements had been met (note that it was the system's — not the users'— requirements that were being met). This strategy produced all kinds of anomalies in other areas which had to be investigated, some proving costly to remedy.

Third, the system was expected over time to change the work flow within the principal user departments and, consequently, the structure of these departments. This expectation was not reevaluated at the point of implementation, and a hybrid situation arose whereby when the work flow changed, the departmental structure did not and, conversely, when the structure changed, the work flow remained the same.

It may be argued that this was merely an example of bad development work. In fact, however, many organizations experience the same situation; the system simply does not meet the requirements for which it was built and even seems to have introduced a whole new set of problems. Other arguments that could be made are that these problems could have been anticipated at the detailed analysis and design phases of the SDLC or that the problems might have been foreseen if a prototype had been developed.

The reality is that detailed analysis and design focus on examining a problem as it exists at a particular time. Although some thought is given to the future implications of whatever solution is selected, the human brain simply cannot foresee every eventuality — particularly in such situations as a change in corporate strategy or a mix in the lines of business. Very often, hindsight is the only way in which these previously unforeseen eventualities can be identified and understood. By conducting an impact analysis, however, the systems development manager can help minimize surprises that occur after a system has been implemented.

WHEN TO CONDUCT AN IMPACT ANALYSIS

Computer systems involve the interaction of people and technology and are designed to solve a defined business problem. Changes in the nature of any of these interacting components (i.e., the system itself, people, technology, or the business problem) create the need for an impact analysis study.

An impact analysis should be conducted when the following situations arise:

- A new system is to be implemented — Whether it is an in-house system or an external system that will be used extensively by the organization.
- Major enhancements are about to be made to either an internal or an external system.
- The organization or department undergoes a significant change in technology related to either an internal or an external system — The change in technology may be related to the system itself (e.g., the use of a relational data base architecture) or to the method by which the system is built (e.g., the use of computer-aided software engineering technology).
- There has been a significant change in business lines or corporate strategy.
- There has been a significant change in organizational structure.
- A significant change is expected in the type of system being developed (e.g., decision support systems, expert systems, end-user computing).

The common denominator throughout all of these scenarios is that the system has already been built. An impact analysis is not concerned with problem definition or the identification of a solution — these steps have already been taken. Impact analysis concerns how the problem and its solution, which have already been identified, will affect the entire organization after the system is implemented.

WHY CONDUCT AN IMPACT ANALYSIS?

As mentioned previously, many systems fail to meet their objectives after they are implemented. There are many reasons why this is true, but one principal reason in a lack of understanding about how the new system will affect the interaction between the manual and automated systems that constitute the internal operation of an organization. By fully understanding this impact, the systems development manager will substantially increase the chances of successful implementation of a new system.

Some of the work that goes into an impact analysis can and should be conducted while the system solution is being designed and built. However, all aspects of the system will not be clearly understood until the system has been implemented, and it is likely that the system will have changed greatly from how it was originally conceived as a solution to a particular business problem. In addition, the user departments probably will undergo various changes in their methods of operation since the system solution was first designed. If these levels of change are not analyzed and understood, the system will probably experience considerable difficulty when first implemented.

THE ROLE OF IMPACT ANALYSIS IN THE SDLC

As mentioned throughout this appendix, impact analysis should be conducted as close to actual implementation as possible to allow the systems development manager to identify and control the maximum inherent variables. During the implementation phase, the number of unknown factors should be minimal.

The objective of the implementation phase is to ensure that the new system meets the operational requirements for which it was designed and integrates smoothly into the production environment. Often, the implementation phase involves acceptance testing at both the user and computer operations levels as well as training the user in the use of the system. Because conversion from an old system to a new one is also part of the implementation phase, an impact study can be considered a formal extension of the activities that already take place during the implementation phase.

It is possible, however, that the results of the impact study will have more far-reaching effects than the development work done to date. This is because the impact study is not concerned with the details of the system — that is for the acceptance testing team to handle. Rather, impact analysis is concerned with such broad issues as how well this new system will integrate with the organization, how it will affect other areas or systems, and whether the organization is properly prepared for this implementation.

Relationship to Risk Management
Because there is an increasing emphasis on the need for effective risk management throughout the entire development cycle of a new system, it is important for the systems development manager to understand how risk management relates to impact analysis. Risk management is concerned with:

- Understanding the risk the system being developed brings to an organization.
- Communicating the risk factor to senior management.
- Establishing the necessary checks and balances to limit risk exposure to acceptable levels.

The factors that influence the degree of risk in the development of any system are:

- Project size.
- Whether new technology will be used.
- The degree to which the user departments understand the desired end results.
- The importance of the system relative to the entire organization.

When the feasibility study for the system was being prepared, a risk rating should have been attributed to the project. For development projects that are classified as high risk, the systems development manager should certainly assign an individual or team to conduct an impact study before implementation.

Risk assessment is not the same as impact analysis, though both activities are certainly related. In risk assessment, the intention is to quantify the difficulty and risk exposure that the organization will be subject to when selecting to build or purchase a particular system to solve a defined business problem. The focus of risk management is the system itself and the damage the organization may sustain if the system is not installed.

Impact analysis, however, assumes that the system will be installed. The focus of the impact analysis is the organization and the damage that may be done to the organization if problems occur now that the system is about to be installed or if it is poorly installed.

Relationship to Post-implementation Review

The post-implementation review is probably most similar to the concept of an impact study and may in fact be the ultimate impact study. The post-implementation review is typically conducted about six months after a system has gone into full production. It should assess how well the system satisfies the preestablished requirements. These requirements include the business and economic justifications for initially having built or purchased the system, as specified in the feasibility study. As an additional objective and benefit, the post-implementation review determines what went right and wrong during the development process. This insight can prove invaluable for future systems development efforts.

The scope of the post-implementation review should be directed toward the entire organization and should cover every facet of the system, particularly when it is apparent that certain parts of the system are not working as expected or that unexpected repercussions are taking place either in the user areas or in other parts of the organization. The fact that actual experience and data are available makes the post-implementation review an invaluable tool for recognizing and correcting any deficiencies in individual systems or in the process of developing these systems.

The primary strength of the post-implementation review (i.e., the after-the-fact nature of the process) is the primary reason why it cannot replace impact analysis. The objective of the impact analysis is to identify the problem areas before production. However, even when impact analysis is used, a post-implementation review is still necessary because an impact analysis will not identify every potential problem inherent in a new system. In addition, the level of experience and expertise of the personnel conducting the initial impact analysis is low. The findings from the post-implementation review will help hone the skills required to conduct effective impact analyses in the future.

WHO SHOULD CONDUCT THE STUDY?

The person or team selected to conduct the impact analysis must have strong analytical skills and be fully conversant with the organization and with the functional capabilities of the system being reviewed. A historical view of how the system arrived at its current situation is also helpful. This historical perspective often helps clarify issues and situations that at first seem to make no sense whatsoever. To act on this first impression without understanding the underlying reasons or rationale, however, may lead the systems development department to draw erroneous conclusions.

From these observations, it would seem that only someone from the organization who has been closely involved in the development of the system is qualified to conduct the impact analysis. This is not true, however, for two reasons. First, impact analysis is a full-time commitment. Therefore, given the stage of development at which the impact analysis is to take place (i.e., during the implementation phase), someone from the organization who has been involved throughout the development process will probably be needed to assist in the traditional tasks associated with this phase of development (i.e., acceptance testing, user training, and system conversion).

Second, impact analysis requires complete impartiality. An individual who has been closely involved with the development may have great difficulty identifying the smaller problems or might not be able to see anything negative in what has been done to date. Conversely, the individual may have an adversarial relationship with the development team and may not be able to see anything positive in the system or in the development process. In either case, there is too much vested interest for a person in this position to be impartial.

If someone from the project team cannot conduct the impact analysis, the systems development manager must decide who will. There are a number of choices, as outlined in the following sections.

Internal Audit Department. The internal audit department could assign someone to conduct the impact analysis. The question of impartiality should not be an issue where internal audit is concerned, given its independent nature. In addition, auditors should possess knowledge of the system because they have been involved in the development process from its initiation. The only drawback to having internal auditors conduct the impact analysis may be their reluctance to prescribe solutions to noted deficiencies for fear that they might be seen as part of the solution rather than as purely independent reviewers.

The issue of independence is one of degree. If internal audit managers can reconcile the objectives of conducting an impact analysis with those of performing the department's role as independent reviewers, the internal audit department is an excellent candidate for conducting an impact analysis.

Quality Assurance Group. Some organizations have a quality assurance group, which could conduct impact analyses. Similar to internal auditing, the quality assurance group should be closely involved in the development of all major systems. In addition, the quality assurance group's mandate of ensuring that all systems meet a consistently high standard before being installed is entirely consistent with the purpose of impact analysis.

Systems Management Group. Some organizations separate their systems development function from the systems maintenance function, often forming a systems management group to handle all maintenance and enhancements after the system has been successfully installed. Because this group will ultimately have to maintain and support the system, the knowledge and experience it gains while conducting an impact analysis should prove invaluable.

Systems Consultants. The final alternative is to hire a systems consultant to perform the impact analysis. The main advantage of this alternative is that consultants are independent and can be devoted full-time to completing the assignment. The problem with using internal personnel is that they will almost certainly be distracted with other work. In addition, in establishing the selection criteria for consultants, the organization can emphasize the need for extensive experience in conducting impact analyses.

The disadvantage of using consultants is their lack of knowledge of both the system and the organization. The organization can overcome this limitation in several ways. The systems development manager can choose a consultant who has worked extensively for the organization. Similarly, the organization can choose a consultant who has experience in the type of system being installed. Whenever using external consultants, however, it is important to properly specify the requirements of the assignment and take sufficient time to select someone who is fully qualified to do the job.

THE IMPACT ANALYSIS APPROACH

An impact analysis consists of the following steps:

- Determining the scope and objectives of the study. This step includes some basic information gathering about the system under review.
- Gathering detailed information covering the entire scope of the system, as determined in the previous step.
- Organizing, sorting, and reviewing the information gathered with the purpose of satisfying the objectives established for the study.
- Formulating conclusions and recommendations and presenting them to the party that commissioned the study.

These steps are discussed in detail in the following sections.

Determining Scope and Objectives

At this point, it is important to discuss who would normally commission an impact study because the scope and objectives may vary significantly depending on who will be presented with the conclusions and recommendations. The following sections outline individuals or groups most likely to commission an impact analysis.

Corporate Computer Steering Committee. This group typically comprises senior executives from the major line functions and must oversee the use of computer development resources within the organization. This group usually has the final sign-off authority to permit new systems to go into production. When certain systems have been identified as being of high risk to the organization, the steering committee would be prudent to commission an independent review of the system before sign-off.

If the computer steering committee commissions the impact study, the scope is likely to be very broad, given that the span of responsibility covered by this group is corporate-wide in nature rather than restricted to any one function or department.

Executive Sponsor. The executive sponsor for the development project may commission the impact analysis. The executive sponsor typically has overall line responsibility for the principal user departments affected by the system. The job performance of an executive sponsor should, at least in part, be measured by the success or failure of the system's implementation. It is likely that in the case of large or complex systems or systems that have experienced problems throughout the development cycle, the executive sponsor is uncomfortable about the success of the planned implementation. A properly conducted impact analysis can greatly alleviate or confirm any such discomfort. (If it is confirmed, action can be taken to remedy the problem.)

If results will be presented to the executive sponsor, analysis may be restricted to the impact on the primary user areas. However, any such restriction in the scope to accommodate the principal concerns of the study sponsor should be carefully considered. A thorough analysis may justify limitation of the scope in some way.

User or MIS Departments. The user or MIS departments may commission the study because of some particular or general intuitive or explicit concern about the system. The study tends to have a fairly parochial scope when it is initiated to address the concerns of one of the groups involved in the development structure. In this situation, it is also important to use caution in restricting the scope of the analysis.

The objectives of the impact analysis vary somewhat according to the situation. The identity and concerns of the group commissioning the study will influence the objectives to the same degree that they affect the scope. To customize the objectives to the needs of the organization, the systems development department will likely need to gather some basic information about the system.

Despite this variance, several generic objectives should be addressed in an impact analysis. The impact analysis should ensure that:

- Users were adequately involved in the development process and are fully aware of their responsibilities throughout the implementation phase.
- The users have exercised or will exercise due diligence over their responsibility to sign off on the system and have not abdicated this responsibility to the development group.
- Adequate user procedures and training programs are in place and users are scheduled to use such facilities.
- The new system will integrate properly with the existing manual or automated systems within the user departments.
- The new system adequately handles any interfaces to the manual or automated systems operated by other user groups that should not be directly affected by the system.
- All aspects of the new system (i.e., hardware, software, telecommunications, and all manual procedures) have been adequately tested and that the entire system is stable.
- The overall system of internal control is not adversely affected by the new system.
- Proper documentation is in place to allow the system to migrate from a development mode to a maintenance mode.
- Proper estimates and verifications have been conducted to ensure that the new system can be introduced into the computer operations production environment without adversely disrupting other existing systems.

Gathering Detailed Information

Several sources must be examined when gathering detailed information. A historical review of the system, from its initiation to its current status, is needed. This can probably be achieved best through a review of the documentation emanating from each phase of development. The feasibility study, general design, detailed design, and implementation strategy as well as all documentation relating to the system (which is contained in the project management system) should be reviewed.

This historical review will clarify what the system was originally supposed to do and achieve, and this can then be compared to the actual system.

After reviewing the historical documentation, the impact analysis should conduct interviews with all interested parties, such as:

- The user departments. These interviews can be conducted with the principal user liaison and the department manager or executive.
- The systems development group.
- The systems maintenance group, if it is distinct from the systems development group.
- Computer services, including production control, network operations, and computer operations.
- The quality assurance group, if one exists.
- The internal audit department.
- The computer steering committee.
- The executive sponsor.

Each interview should be conducted with the use of a questionnaire that has been prepared in advance and designed to elicit the information necessary to meet the objectives of the impact analysis.

Organizing and Analyzing the Data

After the detailed information-gathering phase is completed, the information must be organized so that conclusions can be drawn, which will help formulate appropriate recommendations. The establishment of explicit objectives and preparation of detailed questionnaires will greatly assist the impact analyst in organizing the information in a logical fashion.

The straightforward part of this analysis is determining whether the automated portion of the system meets users' needs and has been adequately tested. It is much more difficult to assess how well the new system can be integrated with the other systems currently operating in the user departments and how the new system will affect the structure of the user departments as well as the current overall system of internal control within these departments and within the entire organization.

Some systems are designed to have a profound effect on the whole organization, either procedurally or culturally. For example, the underlying premise of one system's design was to eliminate the need for central batching and the input of orders. Through the use of a new on-line, real-time system, the salespeople would enter their own orders and would be able to keep track of these orders through on-line inquiry and consequently deal directly with their customers when an inquiry arose. The impact of this system on productivity and customer service was obvious. However, with regard to the functional and cultural impact on the organization, this system required a great deal of management involvement to ensure that the system was properly accepted and implemented in the intended manner. The impact study focused mainly on assessing the attitudes of both the individuals who would now enter the orders and those who previously entered the orders (i.e., the sales support staff). The new system envisioned new roles and responsibilities for the sales support staff. It was important that these dramatic changes in the operation of the organization were understood and accepted by those most affected. The impact study covered these issues at length.

Perhaps the most important area to be analyzed is the interface that the new system will have with any external entities. The organization might supply information to an external agency that in turn provides the organization with a value-added service using the information supplied by the new system. Or the system might supply a new service to the organization's customers. In this case, the impact analysis should focus on how well the liaison between the systems implementation team and the affected customers has prepared the customers for the introduction of the new service.

The timing of the implementation from the customers' viewpoint is a critical issue. For example, one new system was introduced very close to the year-end period of many of the customers who were to use the service this new system offered. The system had problems during implementation, which permeated the customers' own systems. If these problems had arisen at any other time of the year, they would have been considered only a nuisance. Because the problems affected the customers' accounting records, however, the year-end closing of the books became a major problem. This resulted in major customer dissatisfaction and the expenditure of a great deal of resources, time, and money to fix the problems. If an impact analysis had been conducted, it is likely that the implementation would have been postponed until after the year-end period.

Formulating Conclusions and Recommendations

In the ideal situation, the impact analysis will conclude that everything is on track and that implementation should proceed as planned. From a practical standpoint, however, it is likely that the impact analysis will conclude that certain areas of the implementation plan require additional work. For example, the system may lack certain functional capabilities or may not have been properly tested in all aspects, the user may not have been properly prepared for the implementation, the impact on the organization may not have been properly assessed, or the interfaces to external entities may not have been adequately addressed.

It is difficult to generalize on what the conclusions will be because they will undoubtedly vary among each system and each organization. The objectives established for the impact analysis should serve as a map of the critical areas that must be addressed and where conclusions must be drawn. The recommendations will automatically follow from the conclusions that are drawn. Additional testing or development work may be required, or the business analysis function may need to spend more time on the procedural flow of the system and its impact on the organization.

Given the critical stage at which the impact analysis is conducted (i.e., the implementation phase of development), any recommendations that are made will likely delay implementation or, at the very least, place the current schedule in jeopardy. Therefore, the impact analysis should indicate the risk associated with each recommendation. The impact analysis should address whether the recommended action can be delayed until after implementation or whether it must be executed concurrently with or before implementation.

An impact analysis report should be written and presented to the individual or group that commissioned the analysis. The scope and objectives of the analysis, the work that has been completed, the conclusions, and the recommendations should be clearly defined within the report.

RECOMMENDED COURSE OF ACTION

It is recommended that at the implementation phase of the development of a new system, an impact study be conducted to assess how well the system can be integrated into the overall architecture of the systems that comprise the organization.

The Institute of Internal Auditors

The impact study is conducted after the business problem to be solved has been defined and a solution to the problem has been developed. The impact analysis approach recognizes, however, that there are many changes from the time the original feasibility study was conducted to the current situation in which the system is about to enter production. The system may have evolved a little differently than was first envisioned because of the learning evolution that occurred along the development cycle, or the business may have changed in the areas affected by the new system. In either case, it is worthwhile to take the time to analyze the impact the system will have now that it is about to be implemented.

An impact study may be sponsored by several different groups. It is important that the scope of the study is broad enough to encompass all relevant areas and is not restricted to only the areas of immediate interest to the sponsor of the study. The objectives to be achieved by the impact study should be formally established and the information-gathering exercise should be designed to address all the issues inherent in meeting these objectives.

When drawing conclusions, the individual or team conducting the impact analysis should incorporate a broad view of the system and should not be restricted to the automated portion. The biggest problems are often found when assessing the adequacy of the manual procedures that interface with the automated portion of the system. Similarly, reconciliation and control issues should be examined globally to assess how well the new system can be integrated into the overall system of internal control within the organization.

The proposed recommendation should take into account which phase the system is presently in — the implementation phase — and should recognize that following any recommendations can delay the implementation of the system. Therefore, it is important that the risk factors inherent in each of the recommendations be clearly defined.

The Institute of Internal Auditors

APPENDIX 3
CONTROLLING END-
USER COMPUTING

INTRODUCTION

End-user computing can be defined as "computer processing that takes place outside of the realm of responsibility traditionally associated with information systems." This definition can be expanded as follows: "and outside of the framework of controls put in place by information systems over the last decade or so." With the emergence of the computer as a major force within many organizations, the issues of auditability, security and control have received a great deal of attention by corporate management. Audit involvement in the area of computer processing as practiced by information systems has reached a high degree of sophistication. In addition, corporate management is generally well informed on where they stand on the auditability, security and control issues related to traditional data processing within their organization, especially when a data processing operation has been in place for a number of years.

There is no doubt that a great deal of progress has been made by many information systems departments in addressing the issues of auditability, security and control. Certainly, more work needs to be done in this area, especially as systems become more complex, sophisticated and pervasive. However, a reasonable start has been made. The same cannot be said for end-user computing.

When end-user computing was first introduced, it was on a stand-alone basis for fairly non-critical applications. This situation has changed dramatically:

1.   Microcomputers are in widespread use throughout many, if not most, organizations.

2.   Access to the mainframe computer is becoming a necessity.

3. The ability to share resources between microcomputers is increasingly essential.

In short, end-user computing is reaching a state of maturity and, as such, its impact on the system of internal control can no longer be ignored.

THE CONTROL ISSUES

When dealing with end-user computing the control issues are similar to those that had to be addressed during the maturation period for traditional data processing:

Management Controls — deal with the most effective use of resources in the attainment of corporate goals and objectives.

Data Security Controls — concerns the standards and procedures that are designed to protect corporate data against unauthorized disclosure, modification or destruction, whether accidental or intentional.

Processing Controls — these ensure that the organization receives timely, complete and accurate processing of data from the systems that run in an end-user environment.

MANAGEMENT CONTROL

The first issue to be addressed under management control is the separation of duties. The conclusions drawn for an end-user computing environment can be described as follows:

- End-user computing can have an insidious effect on a user department. It would not be the first time that users have been enthralled by the prospect of developing their own computer system(s) only to find that they are spending so much time analyzing, designing, programming, and debugging their system that their day-to-day function is not being performed adequately. This is particularly serious when the user is a senior member of the department whose regular function may be part of the internal control system within the organization (such as a senior member of the accounting department).

- Management must ensure that responsibilities for end-user computing are clearly defined. The end users should not have to design and develop their own computing environment from scratch. The users should have an end-user computing "environment" that already has the tools, techniques and access to data necessary to produce the levels of productivity that has become associated with end-user computing. This is where the concepts of the information center and the microcomputing consulting groups come into play.

- In an end-user computing environment, the user is frequently given the authority to buy hardware. The justification for this action is that the per unit cost of a microcomputer is not very high. However, there are several problems associated with this approach, especially in larger organizations: many microcomputers are purchased; there is little consistency or compatibility between individual units; single unit prices arc paid when substantial volume discounts are probably available; inventory records are not properly maintained. The problem with the lack of consistency and compatibility between individual units can be serious when trying to tie these units together into some form of networking. In addition to these problems, there is also the question of hardware maintenance. When the unit breaks down, the user is frequently confused about what the problem is and how to get it fixed.

The bottom line is that end-user computing should be centrally controlled by information systems. The reaction to this statement by many people will be one of complete horror. After all, end-user computing exists in large part to get away from the constraints of having to rely on information systems for computing services. This reaction is certainly justified.

The Institute of Internal Auditors

There is no doubt that information systems must structure the interface to end-user computing in such a way as to promote efficiency and productivity. The structure and mandate of the information center and the microcomputer consulting group is to provide this type of productive environment. When this is the case, the user can continue to reap the productivity advantages of end-user computing (including the services of professional support staff) while the organization is assured of consistency between departments, economies of scale through volume purchases and the introduction of consistent standards covering the elements of end-user computing (such as data management, communication protocols, documentation and software packages).

If the premise of centrally controlling end-user computing through some form of information center concept is accepted, there are certain management issues that must then be addressed. Putting data processing capabilities in the hands of the user community undoubtedly causes a rapid proliferation of small systems. Initially, the information center concept was used to provide "inquiry only" capabilities to the user. However, the concept has fired the imagination of the user to the point where many "update" systems are being developed. Many of the fourth generation programming languages have proved to be sufficiently "user friendly" that the user is, in fact, developing entire systems with little or no interaction with information systems. Users have also begun to rely on the information produced by these update systems when making day-to-day business decisions.

Management must have a means of determining the systems that are being developed in an end-user environment and assessing whether or not these systems require special control considerations. The criteria to be used in deciding which end-user developments require special monitoring includes whether or not the eventual system will perform update functions and to what extent the information produced by the system will influence the operation of the user. This leads back to the issue of risk management and understanding where the exposures lie. The subjects covered under data security controls and processing control will further highlight the need for management to understand what is going on in the area of end-user computing and ensure that proper controls are in place.

The last subject to be addressed under the topic of management controls is the use of the internal audit function in the control of end-user computing. The audit community deserves a great deal of credit for the advances in auditability, security and control at the traditional levels of data processing as practiced by information systems. Management should promote the audit function as a positive contributing force and ensure that the auditor has a proper mandate with respect to end-user computing. The auditor is a control specialist and should therefore be able to bring a well-defined control perspective to bear upon end-user computing.

DATA SECURITY CONTROLS

Data security can be defined as the standards and procedures designed to protect data against unauthorized disclosure, modification or destruction, whether accidental or intentional. An effective data security program must be balanced between the various aspects of controls as categorized below:

Physical Security
With respect to data security, physical security is concerned with safeguarding the hardware used during the processing of data and the media on which the data resides.

Employee Education
Employees must be aware of the importance of data security and privacy. This is perhaps the strongest control against many causes of exposure. Employees must also be aware of the disciplinary action that will be taken against anyone who violates corporate guidelines in this area.

Logical Security
Logical security refers to the software or hardware-wired controls built into the system to prevent and/or detect unauthorized access to data.

Physical Security

Physical security in a typical end-user environment ranges from weak to non-existent. The microcomputers that are standard in this type of environment are not afforded any more consideration than other pieces of office furniture used in the same area. Environmental controls that deal with damage from fire, water and smoke are not usually considered. Data files are maintained on diskettes or on a hard disk that can be read by anyone who has access to them. Diskettes are not normally afforded any special security procedures and are usually retained in special purpose "diskette holders" that sit on the user's desk. Files retained on hard disks are even more readily available to perusal and alteration as they are always readily available to the microcomputer user.

The previous paragraph describes a typical end-user computing environment. From a purely control-oriented point of view it is a nightmare. From a productivity standpoint, the informality and easy access to all resources provides an optimum environment; this is assuming, of course, that nothing ever goes wrong. When end-user computing first came into existence, the data being held and processed and the work being performed was generally not overly critical to the organization. If data or the ability to process were lost for some time, it was not the end of the world. This may still be the case in some organizations. However, in a great many organizations, the situation has changed dramatically over the last few years. The following points illustrate what has been happening in many organizations:

1. Important business decisions are commonly made as a result of end-user computing.

2. Individual departments have come to rely on "their" computer systems for effective day-to-day operations.

3. The systems developed for the department belong to the department and not to the individual who happened to develop them in the first place. If the individual happens to leave the department (for whatever reason), the department must still be able to continue using the systems that were developed.

Physical security measures must, therefore, be sufficient to counter any and all of the four levels of loss of computer processing capabilities which can occur, including:

1. Temporary and partial loss, such as the loss of a disk drive through mechanical failure.

2. Temporary but total loss, such as the loss of the systems unit through mechanical failure.

3. Permanent but partial loss, such as the accidental or intentional destruction of a data file.

4. Permanent and total loss, such as the accidental or intentional destruction of a hard disk.

Each of these categories must be assessed in light of each organization's individual circumstances. However, it is clear that certain areas must be specifically addressed:

- Physical access to certain microcomputer units may need to be restricted. An example would be the file server unit on a Local Area Network. A "systems administrator" will usually be assigned to control the use of the LAN. There should be some method of preventing unauthorized access to this unit. Software controlled logical security is one approach that will be discussed later. From a physical security perspective, some microcomputers now come with physical locking devices. Having sensitive microcomputers stored in a secured area is another alternative to providing physical control.

- There should be a contingency plan in place to counter any malfunction at the microcomputer level. With the level of reliance on the use of microcomputers that now exists in many end-user departments, it is not acceptable to have to wait a week to have the unit repaired. With the degree of use to which all microcomputers are put in this type of environment, it is usually inconvenient to have to rely on someone else's machine while the broken one is being repaired. What is required is a method of quickly restoring computer facilities back to the user of the broken unit. One alternative is to arrange on-site maintenance contracts for all microcomputers. With this type of arrangement, the maintenance supplier guarantees to have someone on-site to repair the unit within a certain number of hours after hearing about the problem. If the problem cannot be fixed on-site, it is usual for a replacement unit to be provided until the problem unit is properly repaired. This type of maintenance agreement is expensive and may only be appropriate in the major centers where the maintenance supplier has facilities. This type of arrangement does, however, have a place in organizations that place a high degree of reliance on the availability of their microcomputers.

Another alternative is to retain a central inventory of equipment that can be used to swap out malfunctioning units. This alternative only works well when there is a high degree of standardization in the equipment used throughout the organization. The equipment inventory can be either passive or active. A passive inventory means that the equipment in the inventory is not used until it is required to repair a malfunctioning system. This type of inventory ties up a substantial dollar investment. An active inventory involves using the inventory equipment in the inventory location until it is required to repair a malfunctioning system. One approach to maintaining an active inventory system is to establish an "overflow center" within the organization. The "overflow center" consists of several full microcomputer systems and is available for use by anyone in the organization who does not have a system of their own but who has a periodic need for one. The equipment in the overflow center is the active inventory. When there is a hardware problem with an end-user system the appropriate component is taken from one of the overflow center systems and used to substitute for the malfunctioning component. When this component is repaired, it is returned to the overflow center. The availability of equipment in the overflow center does, therefore, fluctuate according to the number of concurrent problems being experienced with the end user's systems.

However, experience tells us that the overflow center concept allows an organization to provide an efficient maintenance program while providing extra end-user computer capacity for those users who cannot justify a dedicated computer system.

- Having just discussed the management of inventory for the purpose of maintenance raises the question of tracking inventory in an end-user computing environment. There should be an inventory system maintained that details who has what and where. Given the number of accessories that are available for the microcomputer, this is not a trivial undertaking. Not only must the inventory system keep track of all systems and components as they are purchased, but it must also keep track of them as they are moved about through the organization and out to maintenance. It has been said that this level of inventory control is unnecessary for microcomputers. Organizations do not keep track of pencils, pens or paper clips, so why should they worry about a substitute tool called the microcomputer? For those readers who have not heard this argument and who wonder about comparing low-cost items to one of relative significance, I can assure you that the argument has been made many times and by people with the experience and professionalism to know better. There are some very practical reasons for needing an inventory management system for equipment used in end-user computing:

  — Many organizations are going through a period of having to rationalize their microcomputer equipment. Resource sharing through the use of a LAN is a common example of the type of rationalization being discussed. It is not possible to rationalize what you don't know exists.

  — When an organization has many branches, there is often a need to distribute software to these branches. Software is frequently configuration dependent (it requires a certain amount of memory, requires graphics capabilities, can only print to certain types of printers, and so forth). It is necessary to know the configuration of each system before any type of global distribution can be made.

The Institute of Internal Auditors

— If an organization is managing its own maintenance program, there is clearly a need to know the configuration of all units in order to ascertain the validity and possible cause of reported problems and to be able to send a compatible component to substitute for the one that is causing the problem.

• Backup and recovery standards and procedures for data files held in an end-user computing environment should be developed, implemented and enforced. Standards for data retention, including the use of off-site storage facilities, should be included in these backup and recovery standards and procedures. With the volume and importance of the data being maintained at the end-user level, combined with the increasing use of hard disks, the informality of backup and recovery that has characterized end-user computing to date can no longer be tolerated. The hard disk scenario provides a new level of complexity to the backup and recovery problem. It is simply not practical to back up a hard disk on diskettes, especially as we now have in excess of 100 megabyte disks readily available and economically priced. The use of tape backup systems either built in to the hard disk or as separate components are a necessity. They are also relatively expensive. There has to be a conscious decision made on the volume and importance of data that can be held at the microcomputer level. From this decision springs the tools that need to be provided to ensure adequate backup and recovery.

Employee Education

It has been a frequent observation that our cultural value system makes most people uncomfortable if they have to search through someone's desk drawers in that person's absence. This cultural value system has not yet come to grips with the morality issues introduced by the microcomputer. In general, people do not have any reservations about browsing through someone else's diskette or hard disk files looking for information. There may, in fact, be nothing wrong with this action just as there is usually nothing wrong with searching through someone's desk drawer. What is really at issue is the amount of reflex thought that is given before the action is taken. In other words, does the person's conscience react to the action being taken? One of the biggest problems to be faced in the prevention of "hacking" is overcoming the idea that the hacker is doing nothing morally wrong in trying to access (not tamper with or destroy) other people's data files.

To preserve effective data security in an end-user computing environment there has to be employee awareness as to the need for security and control. This implies that the end user's conscience must react in situations that involve the access and use of other people's (or the organization's) data. Therefore, there is a need for a user education program on security and control. This program should instruct the users of the computing facilities on the organization's policies and procedures with respect to data security. This includes the reasons why the procedures are necessary, the risks they are designed to protect against and how they are to be employed. The purpose of this program is to heighten the user's awareness of the need for security and control and to describe the user's involvement and responsibility in this area, including the disciplinary action that will be taken against anyone who violates any of the corporate policies and procedures surrounding data security.

Logical Security

With regard to data held at the main data center, data security and, in particular, access to data have probably been the subjects of in-depth analysis for most organizations. The level of access control to data files ranges from a full-blown access control software package (such as ACF2 or RACF) to no control at all. Surprisingly enough, the latter situation is not uncommon even within installations with the most sophisticated hardware and software. The basic problem with controlling access to data files appears to be defining which data should be protected, what level of access should be allowed and to whom. The classification of data files and the establishment of the data security administration function to control the software supporting this classification is considered essential if an organization is to have efficient and effective access control to data files.

In an end-user computing environment, logical security is in its infancy. There have certainly been "locked" disks on the market for some time that are designed to protect data (generally vendor software) from being copied. The software used to manage local area networks is also beginning to include logical security checking before allowing a user access to particular files. There is still, however, a vast amount of unprotected data (from a logical perspective) resident on diskettes and hard disks. Implementation of the controls described under physical controls and employee education will go a long way toward ensuring the integrity of the data on these media. What is of particular concern in the area of logical security for data is the issue of the micro-to-mainframe connection.

CONTROLLING THE MICRO-TO-MAIN-FRAME CONNECTION

The use of microcomputers to access the organization's mainframe is for two principal reasons:

1. As a terminal on the network.

2. To transfer data from the mainframe to the microcomputer and vice versa.

The first issue to be addressed in both instances is controlling access to the mainframe. The first line of defense at the mainframe level is typically the use of passwords. The principle behind password control is that the user first identifies himself to the mainframe system. This is usually through keying in a user ID at the terminal, but it may also be through the use of other, more sophisticated methods (such as the insertion of a magnetically encoded card through a reader attached to the system).

The second stage of password control is where the operator must prove (or authenticate) that he is who he says he is. This authentication is crucial to the security of the system. Whereas the user identification may be considered as non-secure, the authentication password should be unique to each user and should be changed at regular intervals or whenever an operator feels that his password may have been compromised. This awareness of the importance of the authentication password should be stressed as part of the organization's education program on the needs and facilities for security and control. There should also be clearly defined procedures regarding how, when and by whom passwords may be changed, added or deleted from the system's password data set.

Password control has been, for many years, the minimum standard for controlling access to the mainframe system. The problem in a microcomputer environment is that the microcomputer can be used to stretch the password control system beyond its ability to prevent unauthorized access. Numerous cases have been documented where the power of the microcomputer was used to generate vast numbers of user IDs and methodically calculated authentication passwords that were then sent in a consecutive stream to the mainframe until a positive acknowledgement was received that access had been allowed.

To counteract this possibility many organizations have instituted more rigorous checking of passwords. A typical approach is to allow three attempts at specifying the correct authentication password. If the correct password is not specified, the user's ID is suspended from use and the corporate security officer is informed. The user's ID is not reactivated until the security officer is satisfied that nothing unusual has happened. Another approach has been to insert special codes into the BIOS ROM of the microcomputers that are authorized to access the mainframe. This special code is incorporated into an automated log-on procedure that is supplied to each authorized user. The mainframe checks each request for access to ensure that the special code is present. If not, access is denied. This latter check has the added advantage of ensuring that only authorized microcomputers as well as authorized users are allowed access to the mainframe system.

There seems to be a concerted effort on the part of many organizations to provide the microcomputer user with an automated log-on procedure to the mainframe. The mechanics of the log-on procedure are therefore transparent to the user. Organizations simply do not want their microcomputer users experimenting with the connection to the mainframe. "The less the user knows about the actual mechanics of connecting to the mainframe the better" seems to be the attitude of these organizations. Please refer to the section on control-

The Institute of Internal Auditors

ling on-line systems in Chapter 15 for information on the other controls to be used when a microcomputer is used as a terminal on the network.

When operating in a file transfer mode, the microcomputer user should be required to go through the types of access controls just described. Beyond the initial point of access, the control system must limit access to those data files that the user is authorized to read (for example, in the case of data transference to the microcomputer) or write (such as in the case of data transference from the microcomputer to the mainframe). This implies the need for a formal data security program that has the ability to restrict user access to data based upon established "need to know" criteria. Given that end-user computing can only be truly effective when it is able to access a comprehensive data base, it is apparent that the ability to combine ready access to authorized users with strict exclusion of non-authorized users is a mandatory requirement.

The need for the comprehensive treatment of data security (for traditional and end-user computing users alike) has led to the introduction of several Access Control Software packages (such as RACF and ACF2) that are designed to protect data from unauthorized disclosure, modification or destruction, whether accidental or "intentional" and to permit access to each user on a strict "authorized to access" basis. Before access control software can be introduced, the organization must complete a great deal of pre-planning, including the classification of users according to what they have access to, the type of access (read, write, delete) and the classification of data according to its relative need for security.

PROCESSING CONTROLS

Processing controls are concerned with ensuring that the organization receives timely, complete and accurate data. In an end-user computing environment this means ensuring that the software works and that the output reports can be produced regardless of who happens to be at work that day or, more appropriately, regardless of who is *not* at work that day.

There is little doubt that end-user computing offers the users immediate relief from many of the inefficiencies of the information systems department. The first few systems that are tackled will be developed quickly and with a minimum of fuss. However, as more systems are developed, various interrelationships between the systems will be identified. This will exponentially increase the complexity of these systems. The individuals who originally developed the systems will leave the organization without leaving any documentation. Each system will be constructed differently depending on who did the original development work.

Meanwhile, the departments for which the systems were developed will have placed a high degree of dependency on the accuracy and timeliness of the output information. All this should sound very familiar. It is exactly the situation experienced during the growth of the information systems department. There should be a degree of the same standards and procedures applied to end-user computing as have been progressively applied by the information systems department. It may not be necessary to rigidly apply the same rules but the principle of control must be present. There are three areas that require special attention if there is to be an adequate level of control at the processing level:

1. Program change control.

2. Data integrity.

3. Documentation.

Program Change Control

An effective system of change control is essential if an organization is to have a stable and reliable processing environment. Change control procedures are intended to ensure that only authorized changes are made to production systems. Many users view end-user computing as an end run around the inefficiencies of the information systems department. A major part of these inefficiencies is the endless amount of time it takes to make program changes. The user has control over program changes in an end-user computing environment. Management must ensure that the subject of controlling changes is not ignored by the end user. Again, the level of control that is necessary will depend upon the uses of the systems developed through end-user computing.

The Institute of Internal Auditors

Data Integrity

When a system performs an update function, management must be concerned about data integrity. Generally speaking, systems developed by a user are not tested as thoroughly as those developed by the information systems department. The user assumes that he or she knows what results to expect and is content to rely on the systems after a few "clean" runs. It is possible, therefore, that erroneous data could be passed from update to update without the user realizing that a problem exists. This situation most commonly occurs with data that is carried on the master file but is not printed regularly. The user's testing procedures generally revolve around the review of printed reports. Dumping output data files to ensure that the data is being correctly carried forward tends to be overlooked. Management must ensure that proper testing procedures are in place and are being followed.

Documentation

The last subject to be discussed in this section concerns the need for documentation of the systems that are run in an end-user computing environment. The documentation should be at two levels:

1. **System Documentation** — covering the input data to the system, the processing logic, assumptions, and calculations used in turning this input data into output information. This documentation is necessary so that someone other than the original developer can understand the intent of the system and can maintain the system if the need arises. Even in the situation where general purpose software is being used (such as Lotus 1,2,3), it is still advisable to document each system. In the case of a Lotus spreadsheet, there should be documentation that describes the format of the spreadsheet, what assumptions were made in the preparation of the spreadsheet and descriptions of any complex formula or macros that were used.

2. **Operating Documentation** — that describes how the system is to be run. This documentation will describe the flow of the system, the user's interaction with the system, the files being used and the meaning of any error messages generated by the

system. The purpose of this documentation is to ensure that the system can be run in the absence of the original developer or regular operator.

Without minimum standards for documentation in an end-user environment there is a real danger of being left "high and dry" when the person who developed a critical system decides to leave the organization. It would not be the first time in the information systems area that an organization has had to agree to terms that it found less than palatable with an individual who appeared to have exclusive knowledge of a particularly critical system. Without adequate documentation, the same thing will happen in an end-user computing environment.

CONCLUSION

End-user computing can be controlled. The trick is to be able to institute an adequate level of control without killing the productivity that makes end-user computing so attractive in the first place. Management should assess the exposures that are present in their organization's end-user environment. Only then can the proper controls be put in place. Certainly, the employee education program is a "must" as is the tightening of controls at the mainframe level to accommodate the micro-to-mainframe interface. Finally, there is a need to depersonalize the systems that are developed by individual end users. These systems should be shared among the individual developer's co-workers. Only in this way can the organization guarantee continuity of the system should the developer no longer be available, for whatever reason. Adequate documentation is the key to the sharing of end-user systems.

The material in this appendix has previously appeared in EDPACS and is reprinted here with permission of the publisher.

The Institute of Internal Auditors

Index

A

Acceptance testing, 144, 145, 169, 170-173, 175, 182-183, 185, 186, 268, 277, 443-457
Access control procedures, 58, 85-87, 102, 104-105, 143, 239, 275, 302, 304, 313, 315, 329, 335-338, 344-345, 354-358, 360, 387, 401-404
See also User identification and authentication
Access control software, 82-83, 88, 94, 105, 110, 352
Access levels, 84, 87-88, 94, 105, 358
Accountants (external auditors), 21-22, 25-27, 35
ACF2 data protection software, 86
Activity diagrams, 121
Ad hoc reporting, 269-270, 357
Administrative data, 79, 83-84, 93, 163, 222
Albrecht, A., 64
Alternate processing sites, 216, 219-221
American Hospital Supplies, 15, 51
American National Standards Institute, 357
Analytical hierarchy process (AHP), 29-30, 35, 435
Application development group, 145, 240, 315
Application systems audit, 190, 191, 210, 264-270, 275, 276, 278, 293-296, 410, 437, 439
Application systems programs, 79, 85, 93, 95, 102, 105, 144, 161, 163, 203, 204, 237, 243, 250, 255, 263-297, 329, 331, 341, 357-359
critical, 213-220, 227, 291, 363
testing of, 278-279, 289-290, 364, 443-457
Archival storage, 93, 341
Artificial intelligence, 6, 340, 415-432
Association matrix, 343
Asynchronous communication, 385-386
Audit department, 21-27, 30, 35
See also Level 1, Level 2, Level 3 auditors
Audit prioritization matrix, 28-29, 36-37

I

M

N

O

P

The Institute of Internal Auditors